D1453270

THE SOUTH AFRICAN ECONOMY

ITS GROWTH AND CHANGE

THE SOUTH AFRICAN ECONOMY

ITS GROWTH AND CHANGE

JILL NATTRASS

1981
OXFORD UNIVERSITY PRESS
CAPE TOWN

Oxford University Press

OXFORD LONDON GLASGOW
NEW YORK TORONTO MELBOURNE WELLINGTON
NAIROBI DAR ES SALAAM CAPE TOWN
KUALA LUMPUR SINGAPORE HONG KONG TOKYO
DELHI BOMBAY CALCUTTA MADRAS KARACHI

ISBN 0 19 570194 1

Copyright © 1981 Oxford University Press

All rights reserved. No part of this publication may be reproduced, stored in a retrieval system, or transmitted, in any form, or by any means, electronic, mechanical, photocopying, recording, or otherwise, without the prior written permission of Oxford University Press, Southern Africa

The author gratefully acknowledges the HSRC for the grant towards the research that has gone into this book.

Printed and bound by Citadel Press, Lansdowne, Cape
Published by Oxford University Press, Harrington House,
Barrack Street, Cape Town 8001, South Africa

Contents

Figures

Chapter Seven

Chapter Eight

Chapter Nine

Chapter Ten

Chapter Eleven

Glossary

As a result of historical circumstance, a great deal of confusion exists concerning the names that are applied to the different population groups in South Africa, and the use of the word 'black' can be particularly misleading.

In this book the terms have been used in the following manner:

African   – denotes all those population groups which are Bantu speaking.

Asian   – refers to the various sub-groups who are classified as Asian in terms of the population register and will include those of Indian and Chinese descent.

Coloured   – refers to the sub-groups who are classified as so-called 'Coloured' in terms of the population register and includes the descendants of the Khoi Khoi, the San, the Malay Slaves and a large number of inter-racial marriages.

White   – refers to those classified as White.

Black   – has been used as a synonym for African.

black   – refers to all those South Africans who are not White and includes the African, Asian and Coloured groups.

Acknowledgements

For permission to use material previously published, the author wishes to acknowledge the following:

BENSO, Pretoria, for material from Development Studies, Southern Africa; The Economics Society of South Africa, Braamfontein, for material from The South African Journal of Economics; The Institute for Industrial Education, Durban, for material from the The South African Labour Bulletin; and the South African Foundation, Johannesburg, for material from South Africa International.

Preface

South Africa has the somewhat unhappy reputation of being one of the most unequal societies in the world, yet one that has, over the past sixty years, enjoyed one of the fastest rates of economic growth. This combination of inequality and rapid growth has led to a great deal of speculation as to the relationship between these two variables. This book tries to deal with this relationship and is an attempt to explain the present inequalities, in terms of the patterns of economic growth, that have occurred since the founding of the modern South African economy.

This book is written as a first year university text, avoiding wherever possible the use of economic terminology, so as to make it accessible to those studying geography, sociology, history and political science, as well as to students of economics. As it is written by an economist, it takes an 'economic' line and is used in places as a vehicle to introduce economic concepts to students.

The research that lies behind this book has taken place over the past fourteen years and I have incurred a vast debt of gratitude over this period – so vast that I have virtually neither any hope of repaying it, nor of successfully acknowledging all those who have helped me. I would, however, like to give particular mention to a number of my colleagues at the University of Natal, to whom I owe a particular debt of gratitude: Lawrence Schlemmer, whose views have helped to shape my own; Michael McGrath, Charles Meth and Trevor Jones, with whom I have had a number of theoretical discussions; and George Trotter, who has been helpful and understanding. I obviously owe a great deal to the people whose names appear in the bibliography and I would like to express my thanks to all of them, particularly to the staff of the Department of Statistics over the past fifty years, whose work provided the major proportion of the source material used in this book.

I owe especial thanks to John Parsons of the Chamber of Mines, who read, with great care, the chapter on mining and made a number of valuable comments which were subsequently incorporated. I would also like to thank Jimmy Gordon and John Syropolou, who read and commented on Chapters Seven, Eight and Nine; the delegates of the 1st Economic History Conference, who commented on Chapter Eight; and the members of the Platform 80 Seminar, who commented on Chapter Eleven. Their help was gratefully received, as indeed was that of successive years of students in the Department of Economics at this University, who suffered through parts of the earlier drafts of this book.

I would like to thank Neil Muller, Graham Perlman, Nicoli Nattrass and Beverley Allen, for the research assistance that they gave me over a number of years, which contributed significantly to the data presented in this book; Brenda Williams-Wynn for compiling the index; Lyn Kirkwood, Margaret Knee and Pam Kilpin for assistance with the typing of the manuscript; and the editors and staff of the Oxford Press who have made valuable contributions to the final presentation.

I would also like to acknowledge, with gratitude, the financial help that I have received from the Human Sciences Research Council, who provided me with funds for research assistance and enabled me to have six months' leave from my lecturing duties. In thanking them for their help I would like to point out that the Council is in no way responsible for the views expressed in the book, which are very much my own. Naturally any errors that remain are also my responsibility.

Finally, I would like to thank my husband, Lee, and my children, Nikki, Roger, Richard and Lucinda, who have had the unenviable task of living with me through the completion of this manuscript and who have remained loving and understanding throughout.

JILL NATTRASS

University of Natal
DURBAN
1981

ONE

South Africa –
The Land and the People

THE LAND

The Republic of South Africa is located on the southernmost tip of the African continent. The country stretches from the shores of the Limpopo River in the north to Cape Agulhas in the south and shares common boundaries with Mozambique, Swaziland, Zimbabwe, Botswana and Namibia, whilst the independent Kingdom of Lesotho lies wholly contained within South African territory.

South Africa has a surface area of 1 221 042 square kilometres, which is larger than the combined areas of West Germany, France, Italy, Belgium and the Netherlands, but smaller than the states of New South Wales or Texas.

South Africa is bounded on the east by the Indian Ocean and on the west by the Atlantic. She has an exceptionally long coastline for her surface area and it extends for a total of 2 955 kilometres. There are, however, few natural harbours on this coastline. Whilst probably the best of these harbours is Saldanha Bay, the most famous is certainly the Cape Town harbour of Table Bay.

The long coastline with its attendant sea currents affects the climate in many areas of South Africa. There are two major currents, the warm Agulhas current, which flows southwards down the eastern seaboard and the cold Benguela current, which flows northwards from the Antarctic, up the western coast of South Africa. Both currents affect the climatic conditions in the coastal areas as well as the nature of the marine life found in the coastal waters.

The Climate

South Africa enjoys a warm climate and is on average a rather dry country. The national average rainfall, however, is a somewhat misleading statistic, as there is a marked increase in the average levels

1

of rainfall as one moves from west to east. The west coast has on average less than 200 mm a year, whilst the eastern coastal areas enjoy yearly average precipitation levels of over 1 000 mm. The major proportion of the country receives most of its rainfall in the summer months, with the exceptions of the western coastal areas, which are winter rainfall regions and the southern coast, which receives rain throughout the year.

It has been estimated that the daily run-off from South African rivers is approximately 140 175 million litres. Unfortunately the water resources, following the rainfall patterns, are also not evenly spread from a geographic viewpoint, and approximately 86 per cent of the water run-off comes from 36 per cent of the land, the major portion of which is situated in the eastern seaboard region and the southern coastal strip (U.G. 34/1970)

The variations in the climate, together with the uneven spread of easily available water supplies, have exercised quite a significant influence on both the patterns of population distribution and of agricultural activity. The dry desert areas of the western coastal regions are sparsely populated, whilst the eastern seaboard areas contain more than one third of the total population.

Rainfall levels not only vary as one moves from west to east, but also change from one year to the next; in general the lower the mean rainfall in an area, the more erratic its incidence. As a result droughts are a relatively common occurrence in South Africa.

The warm climate and the marked seasonal variations in rainfall levels generate significant variations in the volume of water in South African rivers over the year. These variations, coupled with the fact that the continent is slightly tilted, being higher on the eastern side than the western side, have encouraged the rivers flowing into the Indian Ocean to cut downwards and have produced a number of deep ravines in many instances, making irrigation difficult. Due to the poor rainfall and the difficulty of access to many rivers, approximately one-ninth of the domestic yearly water consumption is obtained directly from underground sources through the use of boreholes. The depth of the river channels and the vast seasonal differences in the flow rates also means that South Africa has no navigable waterways.

Mineral Resources

South Africa is extremely well endowed in terms of mineral deposits and is a major world producer of gold, diamonds, chrome, platinum, uranium, coal, iron ore, manganese, asbestos, antimony, vermiculite and vanadium. In addition to these ores a number of other minerals are also found in South Africa in significant quantities such as andalucite, barytes, beryllium, copper, corundum, feldspar, fluorspar, graphite, lead, marble, nickel, tin, titanium, tungsten, zinc and zirconium.

South Africa's mineral deposits are not evenly distributed through her geographic space, but tend to be concentrated in the north-western areas. Map 1 shows the areas in which the major known mineral deposits are to be found.

At this stage South Africa has no known deposits of oil, although prospecting continues and there have been some finds of natural gas on the continental shelf in both the south and the western areas of the country. The sequel to the lack of natural oil has been the

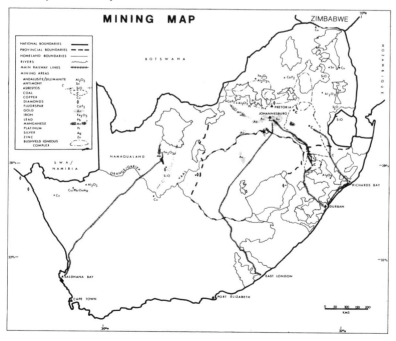

development of a process which extracts oil from coal and allows South Africa to make the optimum use of her massive deposits of coal, which have been estimated to exceed 60 000 million tonnes.

The Agricultural Potential of the Land

Until recently it had become almost a tradition amongst South African agriculturalists to regard South Africa as a land which had a relatively low agricultural potential. A Government Commission reporting in 1940 went so far as to state:

> South Africa must be regarded as a poor crop raising country and this in its turn imposes limitations on animal husbandry for which conditions are, however, better suited. (U.G. 40/1941, p. 7)

Nowadays, however, opinions have changed and it has been recognized that South African agriculture can in fact be made extremely productive, providing farming methods are utilized which are compatible with the physical environment.

The Land Use Patterns

Arable land is in relatively short supply in South Africa, largely because much of the land that would be suitable for growing crops from the rainfall viewpoint, is unusable due to its extremely rugged terrain. The table below shows the approximate land use pattern.

Table 1.1
LAND USE IN SOUTH AFRICA

	Number in 1 000 hectares	Percentage of total
Agriculture and Forestry	106 000	87
Urban Areas	2 000	2
Nature Reserves	3 000	2
Other	11 000	9
	122 000	100

SOURCE: 1980 *Abstract of Agricultural Statistics,* Division of Agricultural Economics and Marketing, Pretoria, 1980.

The agricultural land can be subdivided, not only in terms of the use to which it is put, but also in terms of whether it is farmed on the basis of individual tenure or on the basis of tribal organization. Table 1.2 below shows the allocation of land and its use, in terms of those areas controlled by Whites and those by Blacks. Although this division will not correspond exactly to that between the two types of organization, it is a reasonably good indicator of their relative significance.

Table 1.2

AGRICULTURAL LAND USE PATTERNS

	Land Usage In					
	1 000 Hectares		Percentage of			
			Group Land		Total	
	White	Black	White	Black	White	Black
Cultivated Land	10 028	2 143	12,0	14,0	10,0	2,0
Permanent Crops	821	41	1,0	–	1,0	–
Artificial Pasture	897	35	1,0	–	1,0	–
Natural Pasture	71 342	11 920	81,0	79,0	69,0	12,0
Forest Land	1 071	419	1,0	3,0	1,0	–
Other	3 636	518	4,0	4,0	3,0	1,0
	87 795	15 076	100,0	100,0	100,0	

SOURCE: *1980 Abstract of Agricultural Statistics,* Division of Agricultural Economics and Marketing, Pretoria, 1980.

The nature of the farming and of the crops grown changes with the variations in the climate and the terrain. The major farming areas are illustrated in map 2. In general terms, the eastern seaboard areas are the major regions growing sugar cane and tropical fruit. The northern regions are the main cereal areas, whilst the Mediterranean fruits, such as peaches, grapes and apples are largely grown in the southern regions of the Cape Province. As one would expect, sheep farming dominates in the dryer and more rugged areas. Despite the apparent regional specializations, a good deal of mixed farming is carried on throughout South Africa and in the tribally organized agricultural areas virtually all the activity is directed towards subsistence agriculture.

South Africa has been almost self-sufficient in the production of foodstuffs since the formation of the Union. Over the period 1919/20–1933/34 only 6,2 per cent of the food consumed in South Africa was imported and by 1963/64, this percentage had declined to 2,7 per cent. (R.P. 34/1970). At present, South Africa has the distinction of being the only nation in Africa that is both self-sufficient in food production and a major exporter of certain foodstuffs, notably fruit, maize and sugar.

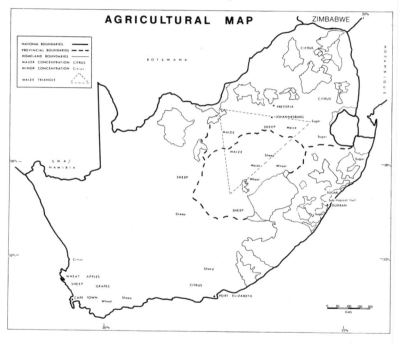

THE PEOPLE OF SOUTH AFRICA

The Total Population

There are four main population groups in South Africa. By far the largest numerically is the group that is officially designated as 'Black' and comprises those people speaking the Bantu languages, who migrated into South Africa over a period of time, which it now appears from archeological discoveries may have extended over more than a thousand years. The second largest group is that designated as 'White', which consists mainly of people of European descent. The third largest group is that known as 'Coloureds', which is an amalgam which includes the descendants of remnants of the original inhabitants of the Cape, the Khoi and the San, those of the Malay slaves imported in the early days of the Cape Colony, and the descendants of mixed marriages. The final group is the one known as Asian, the majority of whom are the descendants of indentured Indian labour brought into the country in the late nineteenth century to work on the sugar cane plantations in Natal.

Because the legal, social and economic positions of the four major racial groups differ significantly from one another, it is useful to analyse certain aspects of the South African economy in racial, rather than class or income terms. Consequently, in this chapter we will look at the relative importance of the major race groups and their demographic characteristics, in order to lay a firm foundation for other future analysis. Racialism has been a way of life in South Africa for at least two centuries and indeed still is. As a consequence, any attempt to analyse South Africa in non-racial terms would be extremely misleading.

In 1979 an estimated 28 million people lived in South Africa. The South African population is culturally and racially heterogeneous. Table 1.3 contains details of the population components for the years 1970 and 1979.

Table 1.3

THE SOUTH AFRICAN POPULATION

	1970 Census		1979 Mid-year Estimate	
	Number	Percentage	Number	Percentage
African	15 918	71	20 004	72
Asian	642	3	802	3
Coloured	2 074	9	2 554	9
White	3 831	17	4 525	16
	22 465	100	27 885	100

SOURCE: 1970 data. *South African Statistics 1978,* Department of Statistics, Pretoria 1978.

Although South Africa's population is generally discussed in terms of these four major racial groups, the groups are themselves not homogeneous. These differences have been fostered by government policies in many instances, some of which date back to the period before the formation of the Union of South Africa and which in general were aimed at separating the races and at protecting the economic position and identity of the White group. These are discussed more fully in Chapter Four. The major classifications serve to delineate the boundaries that separate race groups in terms of certain overriding demographic, social, economic and even institutional characteristics.

The Black Group

Anthropologists categorize South African Blacks into four sub-groups, in terms of the nature of their descent from the major waves of Black migrants who entered South Africa from the north, over a period starting as early as AD 300. (Inskeep: 1969)

The usually accepted subdivisions are, firstly, the group that is descended from the wave of immigrants who spoke the Nguni language and who appear to have been settled in the eastern seaboard regions of South Africa for a considerable period of time. Although the exact dates are still subject to dispute, some archaeologists place the first Nguni settlements as early as the period between AD 300 and AD 500. The second group are the descendants of the Sotho speaking immigrants, who are largely settled in the eastern midland areas which includes the independent Kingdom of Lesotho itself. The other major sub-groups in South Africa, the Venda and the Shangaan, settled in the western and northern inland areas.

These four main sub-groups can be further divided; in terms of the way their languages evolved since the original migration, in terms of the cultural differences that have developed, and in terms of their legal standing. This legal standing results either from the imposition upon them of laws aimed at implementing the policy of 'separate development', or it represents the outcome of negotiations between the British Government, the Blacks themselves, and the different White settler groups, in the days before the formation of the Union of South Africa.

The Nguni group is now subdivided into the Xhosa speaking

people (themselves legally divided into those who live in the area known as Transkei and those who live in the Ciskei), the Zulu speaking people, the Ndebele and the Swazi. These groups, notwithstanding their common heritage, now speak languages which differ quite significantly and have developed their own distinctive tribal traditions. Together, the modern day descendants of the Nguni immigrants form nearly two thirds of the Black population of South Africa. The Sotho speaking descendants within South Africa itself, can be similarly subdivided into the Tswana, the Pedi and the South Sotho peoples.

The evolutionary differences were emphasized and encouraged by the policies of the early administrations and have now been institutionalized. This process of legal entrenchment, which ultimately developed into the vision of the present South African government, (which sees as viable each race group and sub-group in South Africa determining its own destiny), started at the turn of the century with the creation of the areas now known as Botswana, Lesotho and Swaziland as separate states. Ultimately, this policy envisages the creation of ten independent Black states in addition to the former protectorates, in Southern Africa, although there are variants which argue the case for the creation of a Southern African Federation. The policy is not without its critics and indeed seems to be totally unacceptable to the majority of South African Blacks in its present form and consequently seems unlikely to be successfully implemented. This question is discussed in more detail in Chapter Nine, which is concerned with the economic characteristics of these Black areas.

A major division cutting across both the language and tradition variations found in the Black group, is the growing difference in the lifestyles of Blacks living in the towns and those who have remained in the tribally organized rural areas. These are extremely wide and range from the lifestyles of the simple tribesmen, who spend their lives engaged in subsistence farming activities and whose lives are organized almost entirely by tribal customs; through the 'half life' of the rural urban migrant, who lives as a single individual in the town separated from his family and home in the rural area, to the lifestyle of the Black town dweller, who is in general highly sophisticated and is frequently a second or third generation townsman. This growing difference in lifestyles is not adequately catered for in the present policy of separate development and is one of the major sources of Black opposition.

The White Group

The White group too is not homogeneous although the differences are probably less marked than those amongst the Black groups. There are two major language groups – those speaking Afrikaans (roughly 60 per cent) and those speaking English. There are, however, also significant numbers of people who are of German or Portuguese descent.

The origins of the White group date back to the Dutch settlement at the Cape that was started in 1652. The majority of Whites, however, have more recently developed South African roots, as the discovery and exploitation of minerals brought large numbers of settlers to the country. Between the period 1860 and 1920, immigration was almost as important a source of White population increase as the natural rate of growth; and the total number of Whites in the region now known as South Africa, rose from an estimated quarter of a million people in 1860 to over one and a half million people in 1920.

Immigration continued to be an important force determining the size and growth rate of the White group and over the period 1925–77 nearly one million Whites entered as immigrants, their net contribution to the permanent population amounting to approximately 25 per cent over this period alone.

The Coloured Group

The Coloured community is the most diversified of all South Africa's population groups. As was said before, they number amongst them the descendents of the original inhabitants of Southern Africa, (the Khoi and the San) the descendants of the Malay slaves imported into the Cape to alleviate the shortage of labour in the early days of the Colony and those of the many inter-racial marriages that have taken place over the country's history. The group is predominantly Afrikaans speaking and shares many cultural ties with the White Afrikaner community. Although members of the group are found in most parts of South Africa, the major proportion of the community live in the southern and south western areas of the Cape Province.

The Asian Group

South African Asians are the descendents of the members of two major immigrations from India. The first comprised indentured workers, who were imported into Natal in the late 19th century to work on the sugar plantations in the area, whilst the second group consisted mainly of traders who followed in the labourers' path. Although the majority of the Asians initially entered South Africa to work in the agricultural sector, by 1970 they had totally changed this aspect of their economic profile and had become the most urbanized of all the population groups, with only 13 per cent of the group still resident in areas outside the towns. However, the majority of this group is still resident in Natal.

THE DEMOGRAPHIC CHARACTERISTICS OF THE RACE GROUPS

There are major differences in the demographic characteristics of the race groups which are linked to the differences in their average lifestyles. A South African demographer commented on this inter-relationship:

> The differences in respect of the phase of the demographic cycle reached by the four ethnic groups have their counterpart in the economic sphere . . . again this is not a chance relationship. Demographic factors are both the cause and effect, even while not the only factors involved. (Sadie: 1971, p. 207)

There are two components that determine the natural rate of increase in a population, the birth rate and the mortality or death rate and both are affected by changes in the socio-economic conditions faced by a population. In general terms, as average living standards are increased from low levels, the standards of health care in the community improve and these often have a dramatic effect on the death rate and a concomitant impact on the rate of population increase.

Whilst mortality rates appear to react strongly to economic factors, it is changes in the social and cultural factors that seem to affect birth rates. One study that was undertaken on data from a number of countries suggested that population growth rates were positively correlated with income levels, and negatively related to levels of education, the degree of urbanization amongst the population and the level of industrialization. (Adelman: 1963)

Table 1.4 contains data relating to the major demographic characteristics of the four race groups, together with some socio-economic information.

Table 1.4

THE LIFESTYLES AND DEMOGRAPHIC CHARACTERISTICS OF THE RACE GROUPS

Race Group	Average Income Per Head 1970	Percentage of the Group Urban 1970	Demographic Characteristics			
			Rate of Population Growth	Birth Rate 1970 (per 1000)	Death Rate 1970	Life Expectancy (Men) 1965/1970
African	106	33,1	2,7	–	–	51,2
Asian	312	86,7	2,6	33,3	6,9	59,6
Coloured	265	74,1	3,0	36,3	14,1	49,6
White	1 594	86,8	2,1	23,5	9,1	64,5

SOURCE: M. D. McGrath (1977), Sadie (1971), *South African Statistics, 1978*

A population group that is experiencing a high birth rate, is also one that is becoming younger on average. Consequently, the differences in the birthrates shown in Table 1.4 are reflected again in the relative distribution of the population between the different age groups. These are shown in Table 1.5.

Table 1.5

THE AGE DISTRIBUTION OF THE RACE GROUPS IN 1970

Race Group	Percentage of the Population Aged		
	Under 15 years	15–65	Over 65
African	43,4	53,0	3,6
Asian	41,2	57,0	1,8
Coloured	46,2	50,7	3,1
White	31,3	62,1	6,6

SOURCE: *South African Statistics, 1978*

Table 1.4 shows very clearly how high birthrates reduce the percentage of the population that is in the more productive years and increase the percentage of children. The impact of the longer life expectancy is also interesting. Both the White and the Asian communities have a high life expectancy. The White population has a high proportion of people who are over 65 years of age. It is, however, interesting to note that despite the low death rates and the high life expectancy of the Asian group, only a small proportion of this population group was aged over 65 in 1970. This is due to the fact that the decrease in both the birth and death rates for this group have been relatively recent and have not yet had time to affect the age distribution to any significant extent.

The Process of Urbanization

Urbanization or the growth in the relative importance of the towns, is usually closely related to industrialization and both appear to affect the major demographic variables. In 1970, 47,8 per cent of the Republic's population lived in the towns. Further, as the level of economic activity rises in a region so, it seems, does the importance of the urban areas. In the ten districts of the country that had the largest output per head of their resident population in 1970, the urbanization rate was 79 per cent. (Nattrass: 1980a)

The laws relating to the freedom of population movements, such as the influx control laws affecting Africans and the Group Areas Act that affects all population groups, may effectively limit the access of certain groups to the urban areas and by so doing, in some instances, may also limit their access to the areas of growing wealth. However, it seems that the Group Areas Act has not affected the rate of urbanization amongst Coloureds and Asians to any great extent, as these groups have tended to move into the towns in much the same way as have the Whites, who, although they are also nominally affected by the Group Areas Act, are seldom actually limited by it. Influx controls on the Black population do, however, seem to have been extremely effective, since as late as 1970, less than one third of South Africa's Black population lived in the towns.

The Black contribution to the urban sector labour force is, however, very much greater than would seem likely from the level of urbanization. This is because a massive system of oscillating rural-urban migration has built up amongst the Black group. How important this stream is, in terms of the urban sector Black workforce, can be seen from the data in Table 1.6, which contains estimates of the components and origins of the Black labour supply in South Africa for 1970.

Table 1.6

ESTIMATE OF THE ORIGIN AND COMPONENTS OF THE AFRICAN WORK-FORCE, 1970

Area of Origin			Labour Supply Components		
White Areas			*White Areas*		
Urban Section 10a and b			*Urban*		
Men			Men		
Men	889 000		Settled	889 000	
Women	635 000	1 524 000	Migrant	1 490 000	
			Commuter	156 000	2 535 000
Rural			Women		
Men	512 000		Settled	635 000	
Women	573 000	1 085 000	Migrant	260 000	
			Commuter	98 000	993 000
			Rural		
Black States			Men	445 000	
Urban			Women	460 000	905 000
Men	156 000				
Women	98 000	254 000	*Black States*		
Rural			Men	827 000	
Men	1 857 000		Women	659 000	1 486 000
Women	806 000	2 663 000			
Foreign States					
Men		393 000			
		5 919 000			5 919 000

SOURCE: *Report 02.05.07, Population Census 1970,* Department of Statistics, Pretoria, 1976.

Migrant Workers taken from J. Nattrass, *Migrant Labour and South African Economic Development, 1936–1970,* unpublished Ph.D.Thesis, University of Natal, 1976.

Urban settled workforce from the above source, Table A.11.

(Nattrass: 1979b, p. 79)

Reprinted, with permission of the editors, from *South African Labour Bulletin.*

Despite the apparently low rates of urbanization amongst South African Blacks, 60 per cent of the total Black workforce in 1970 was employed in the urban areas of whom only 43 per cent were permanent urban residents.

The Spatial Distribution of the Population

The spatial distribution of South Africa's population is also very uneven, partly as a result of the climatic variations and partly due to the pull exerted by the areas that have developed economically, which are themselves unevenly distributed. In general terms, the eastern side of South Africa is more densely populated than the western regions, but there are also heavy concentrations of people in the major economic areas like the Witwatersrand region in the Transvaal, the Cape metropolitan area and the Durban-Pinetown-Pietermaritzburg region.

The relative distribution of population by province has changed as the economy has developed, again reflecting the very strong pull of the economic centre that is located in the Johannesburg-Pretoria-Vereeniging region (referred to as the P.W.V. Area). The following Table shows how the spatial distribution of the population has altered as the modern economy has developed.

Table 1.7

CHANGING SPATIAL DISTRIBUTION OF THE POPULATION 1911–1970

	Percentage of Groups Situated in			
	Cape Province[1]	Orange Free State[1]	Transvaal[1]	Natal[1]
1911 Black	37,8	8,1	30,4	23,7
White	45,6	13,7	33,0	7,7
Coloured	86,6	5,1	6,6	1,7
1936 Black	31,0	8,4	37,0	23,6
White	39,5	10,0	41,0	9,5
Coloured	88,6	2,3	6,6	2,5
Asian	5,0	–	11,4	83,6
1970 Black	25,5	9,2	43,9	21,4
White	29,7	8,0	50,6	11,7
Coloured	87,2	1,8	7,6	3,4
Asian	3,3	–	13,0	83,7

1. Including the Black homelands situated in the Province.

SOURCE: Estimated from data in *South African Statistics 1978*.

The Administrative Aspects of South Africa

From the administrative viewpoint, South Africa is basically controlled by a central government that operates within a 'Westminster' framework. The constituent members of the central government are elected solely by members of the White population group. There is, however, a good deal of decentralization and devolution of authority.

South Africa is subdivided into four provinces that are controlled by Whites – the Cape Province, the Orange Free State, the Transvaal and Natal – and into a number of other areas, which although in many instances they are situated within the boundaries of the White provinces, are under the control of the other population groups. The major examples are the ten African homeland regions or Black States as they are officially known; Transkei, KwaZulu, Ciskei, Bophuthatswana, Venda, Lebowa, Qwa Qwa, KaNgwane, Gazankulu and the Nedebele State. Three of these – Transkei, Bophuthatswana and Venda, are considered to be politically independent of South Africa by the South African government, but are not generally recognized as such internationally. The other Black States are now all self-governing. In this book, for completeness in the economic sense, in general, all the Black areas have been treated as if they are an integral part of South Africa, although their special characteristics are discussed separately in Chapter Nine. Map 3 shows the major administration areas within South Africa.

In addition to the Black States, there are other areas of South Africa that are under the partial control of the non-white population groups, through such institutions as the Black Urban Councils, the Coloured Persons Representative Council and the South African Indian Council.

In general, the attempts made by the central government to set up political institutions to enable South Africa's other population groups to control their own affairs have been unsuccessful, mainly because they have not been the product of genuine negotiation. In 1979 the central government appointed a Commission (the Schlebush Commission) to look into ways and means of achieving a more satisfactory dispensation. It seems that the present government hopes to find a solution through the process of consultation with those Black leaders that are acceptable to them. The true solution, however, will be unlikely to be found until negotiation takes place; negotiation between all parties that will be affected by the outcome regardless of whether or not they or their leaders are currently considered to be 'acceptable' to the White government.

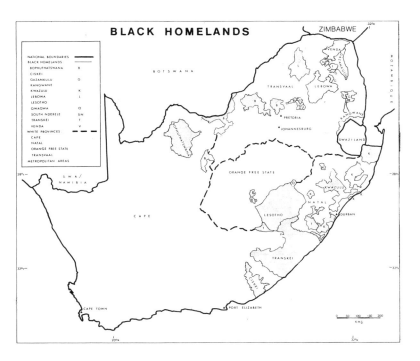

TWO

An Introduction to
the South African Economy

INTRODUCTION

All economic systems, no matter how diverse they appear to be, in fact face the same problem, that of reconciling man's virtually unlimited and expanding desires with the limited availability of goods and services and the shrinking supply of natural resources. There are three aspects involved in the decision-making relevant to this reconciliation, namely:

1. The need to decide what goods and services should be produced with the limited resources available and what the particular output mix should be.
2. The need to determine by what methods and where these goods and services should be produced.
3. The need to decide the share of the output going to individuals in the community.

The first two classes of decisions are essentially concerned with the production process, whilst the third deals with the question of the distribution of the goods and services produced.

Although all economies have to come to grips with these three problem areas, the way they approach them and the nature of the solutions that finally emerge differ, and are a function of the level of economic sophistication present and of the social, political and economic institutions of the society at that particular time.

In a capitalist or mixed market economy such as the South African economy, the basic institution on which the system rests is the right to individual ownership of property and it is the market mechanism that performs the role of linking the production and distribution aspects of the economic problem. People in their capacity as workers, landowners, capitalists or managers enter the market to sell the productive services that they own to potential producers, mainly in exchange for money. Would-be producers of goods and services also enter these markets to purchase the quantities of labour and resources that they feel they need to fulfil their production plans.

Once purchased by the producing firms these resources, or factors of production as they are also known, are combined together and transformed into goods and services for resale. This output is then offered for sale through the market, either to individuals, now acting as consumers and exchanging their earnings for goods, or to other firms, to re-enter the production process as additional inputs.

Developing this simple model of an economy one stage further it becomes obvious that the amount of output that can be produced in an economy over any specified period is a function firstly of the quantity of available factors of production and secondly, of the effectiveness or productivity of those productive resources. All production taking place in an economic system needs both labour and capital as inputs into the production process, together with the necessary resources to finance the time taken in the process itself. Labour as a factor or production includes the human effort, both physical and mental that enters production, whilst capital comprises the physical inputs needed to complete the process and includes non-renewable natural resources as well as man-made inputs.

Although all production needs both capital and labour, the quantities needed vary significantly between firms and are determined by such things as the nature of the output being produced, the state of technology, the size of the firm and the relative costs of the factors of production.

Classifications as broad as those of labour and capital are only useful as theoretical starting points. In a study of an actual economy one needs, in fact, to highlight the heterogeneity actually present within these broad categories. All land, for example, is not equally productive from an agricultural viewpoint, nor is it all equally well situated for the location of industry or for the provision of dwellings. Some areas of land have valuable non-renewable mineral resources, whilst other areas have none. Similarly, man-made capital is composed of a large variety of commodities that differ in terms of their physical characteristics, their life spans, their labour requirements and their specialized function. Labour is also heterogeneous. Some people may have higher levels of innate ability, particular physical skills, better education and training or simply a greater capacity for work, which makes them more valuable in the production process than others.

The actual role that is played by a factor of production in the output process, is to some extent shaped by the nature and quantity of the other available productive resources. A shortage of capital, for example, will tend to generate a production process that uses larger amounts of labour, and that is relatively unsophisticated in nature. Labour short economies, on the other hand, use much more capital-intensive, highly sophisticated techniques of production.

As output is produced, decisions are made by those who control the productive resources as to whether they should simply enjoy the fruits of their labours, or whether they should in fact save some of the present output and use it to expand their ability to produce output in the future. It is the aggregate outcome of these diverse decisions that largely shapes the economic path that is followed by an economy through time. Consequently the growth path attained in any market economy over a particular period is determined by the relative stocks of, and the distribution of the ownership of the productive resources of the economy, together with the patterns of economic behaviour of the groups of individuals who control these resources. The evolution of the development path of an economy is, therefore, a function of both the changes that take place in the distribution of assets as time passes and the economic behaviour of the major groups controlling the use of those assets.

Patterns of Economic Growth; the Supply of Resources, Social and Political Change

Economic evolution is necessarily accompanied by changes in the political and social structures of the society within which it takes place. Without such political and social evolution, the climate needed to maintain economic progress will be lacking and economic growth will eventually slow and perhaps even cease altogether. The relative supplies of the factors of production will have a significant impact on the patterns of all the facets of economic development that are taking place in an economy.

The actual nature and extent of the social and political change needed to maintain a given path of economic progress will depend upon the aspirations and the bargaining strength of the groups or alliances that currently predominate on the economic scene. In a capitalist market economy, the groups that will be in a position to influence social change through their economic position, will be those people who own or control the factors of production that are crucial inputs into the process of production. Consequently, the supplies of the factors of production, relative to one another, can exercise a significant influence on the way in which a society develops in the social and political fields, in addition to the direct influence that they exert on economic development patterns through the operation of the market.

Whilst some minimum rate of social change is necessary if the economy is to maintain a particular pattern of economic development, it is possible for the rate of social and political change to exceed this minimum rate or even to move in a direction different from the one needed to maintain the present growth patterns. When this happens, as it has to an increasing extent in many African countries in recent years, it is the degree and nature of the social change or political change that dictates the changes that take place in the economic structure. In such instances it is highly likely that the economic framework will be restructured in a manner that will further the economic interests of the groups that are newly politically powerful.

The interplay between social change, political change and economic growth is extremely complex and the ultimate outcome is conditioned by the relative strengths of these countervailing forces. Consequently, it is virtually impossible to develop a general theoretical structure which would permit one to predict either the rate of economic development from a given path of social change, or the rate of social change from a given path of economic development. One can, however, isolate some generalized relationships as a start in this direction. One can also analyse the course of change in a particular society, to determine which of the three influences, the economic, the social or the political, was the more dominant at a particular point in time and further to see how the influences have interacted with one another as the society evolved through time.

The following section discusses some of these generalized relationships with respect to economic growth through the capitalist mode of production; the mode most relevant to the South African economy.

Economic, Social and Political Change in A Market Economy: Some Generalizations

In a capitalist economic system there are two major economic classes, capital and labour and the division between them is determined by the nature of their access to control over the factors of production. A capitalist, in the pure sense of the word, is an individual who controls the allocation and application of capital, whilst a true member of the labour class has control only over his own labour power. In many modern, developed, capitalist economies, the dividing line between these two economic classes is no longer completely clear-cut, as in many instances workers have managed to obtain increasing control over capital, through saving from their wages and then buying themselves into the capitalist class, through the operation of worker committees or through the growing power of labour organizations.

In the early days of development through the capitalist mode of production, the class division is usually very clear and the way in which the society develops is to a large extent determined by the relative economic strengths of the two classes, which in their turn are a function of the initial sizes of the relative supplies of capital and labour, the way in which these relative sizes change as the capitalist economy expands and the social, legal and political environment into which capitalism is introduced.

When capitalism is introduced into either a feudal or a peasant economy, as was for instance the case in South Africa when minerals were first exploited in the late 19th century, one has a situation in which a well organized capitalist class faces virtually unorganized labour. Not only is labour unorganized in such a situation, but it is also likely to be politically and economically naïve, in terms of the new order that is developing in the society. Consequently it is highly likely that both the economic and political sources of power will be in the hands of the capitalist class.

The strong relative position of the capitalists often enables them to manipulate the market by political means and by so doing increase the rate of profit that they earn on their investments. If these profits are reinvested in the economy, the outcome is rapid economic growth. In many instances, however, the capitalist element is introduced into an otherwise relatively primitive economy from outside and in these cases the interests of such capitalist groups may well lie outside the domestic economy. If this is so, the foreign capital may choose to utilize its position of power to facilitate the export of profits earned, for investment in the country from which the capital originated. In such circumstances the introduction of capitalism is of very little benefit to the surrounding, more primitive economy and indeed may even lead to its growing impoverishment, rather than to an improvement in the living standards of the indigenous population.

Economic evolution requires that the profits earned by the infant capitalist economy are reinvested to foster the expansion of the sector. Political and social change under such circumstances, in the absence of revolution or growing outside pressure, will be unlikely to take place until the capitalist sector has grown to the point at which the supply of capital, relative to that of labour, becomes so large that labour is in short supply and its bargaining position becomes correspondingly strengthened. At this stage labour will be in a better position to force through the changes in the social and political structures that it believes will best enable it to satisfy its group aspirations. These changes can be seen as labour's price for continued co-operation in the process of economic expansion, as the alternative, labour unrest, will certainly slow down economic growth.

SOUTH AFRICAN ECONOMIC DEVELOPMENT 1860–1977

Introduction 1860–1910

The South African economy of today has its foundations in the discovery and exploitation of diamonds and gold, dating back to the latter period of the 1860s and the following fifty-year period. Prior to the discovery of these minerals, the economy was predominantly agricultural in nature and its rate of economic development very low and even non-existent in some areas. Capitalism itself was not firmly entrenched and the major portion of the region, now the Republic of South Africa, was organized on tribal or feudal lines. In the Cape Colony, some 'infant capitalism' was emerging which was largely based on the exploitation of agricultural products through export and ship chandlering.

The early years of the 1860s were a period of economic recession in South Africa and the economic prospects for the non-tribal areas were not particularly bright. The imminence of the opening of the Suez Canal was causing apprehension, particularly amongst farmers and traders in the Cape Colony, as it was rightly feared that the advent of the canal would substantially reduce the profits to be made from ship chandlering. In addition, the international price of wool, the colony's only export of any real significance, had dropped dramatically after the end of the American civil war. The poor economic outlook was compounded by a severe drought which affected major portions of the country. Not surprisingly, this was a period in which a large number of White settlers decided to go elsewhere in search of an easier existence, and in the early 1860s emigration exceeded immigration.

The discovery and subsequent exploitation of the significant deposits of diamonds in the Kimberley area and subsequently gold on the Witwatersrand, resulted in the transformation of the economy over the fifty-year period to 1915 and laid a solid foundation for the development of the economy as we now know it. The period 1865–1915 was a period in which there was a substantial change in the economic structure and one that saw the economy evolve from being almost solely dependent on agriculture, to become a capitalistic, modern economy that was based on a highly profitable mining industry, supported by an infant manufacturing sector and growing commercial and service sectors. This transformation was strengthened by the events that occurred after 1915 and the manufacturing sector in particular was stimulated by the two world wars and by the economic strategies adopted by successive South African governments over the period following 1910, the year of the formation of the Union of South Africa.

Growth and Change in Output, 1911–79

The period from 1911–79 was one in which South African output levels increased considerably. The annual average rate of growth of output, after adjustment for price changes, for the period as a whole was 3,8 per cent and Table 2.1 shows how this performance was spread over the different decades.

There have been five periods in which the rate of growth in output either halted or declined significantly. The first of these economic recessions took place in the period from 1920–22 and was largely the result of the combined influences of the substantial labour unrest, which took place on the Witwatersrand over this period and which culminated in the Rand Rebellion of 1922, and a general recession in the world economy. The second period of economic stagnation occurred during the period from 1928–32, the years of the Great Depression and the third took place over the period 1952–53, and was largely the result of somewhat over-zealous attempts on the part of the South African government to curb domestic inflation rates.

Table 2.1

THE GROWTH IN SOUTH AFRICAN OUTPUT, 1911–79

	1911	1920	1930	1940	1950	1960	1970	1979
Estimated Gross Domestic Product in 1970 Prices (R Million)	1 225	1 000	1 947	3 170	4 434	6 722	11 839	15 474
Growth Rate over Decade		−2,0	6,9	5,0	3,4	4,3	5,8	3,1
Share Produced by:								
Agriculture	21	22	14	13	18	12	8	8
Mining	28	18	16	13	13	14	10	13
Manufacturing	4	7	9	12	18	21	23	25

SOURCE: *South African Statistics 1978. Union Statistics for 50 years. Statistical News Releases.*

The fourth and the fifth periods of relative economic stagnation differ from the other three in that they both resulted mainly from political unrest within South Africa and, consequently, can perhaps be seen as the first indications that social and political change will increasingly become a pre-requisite for continued economic expansion in South Africa. The first of these two recessions took place in the early 1960s and was largely the result of the uncertainty generated by social disturbances in some African townships on the Witwatersrand, which led finally to the shooting tragedy in Sharpeville. The second period commenced late in 1974 and only started to abate in 1979. This recession was initially linked to a general world recession, but was greatly exacerbated by the political uncertainty that was triggered by further social unrest in the Black townships on the Reef in 1976. It was also fuelled by political disturbances in other parts of Southern Africa and by political pressure on South Africa herself, which adversely affected the inflow of both foreign capital and immigrants to the country, as well as by the generally poor economic climate present in the Western world as a whole.

The 68 years covered by the data in Table 2.1 have seen significant changes in the structure of the South African economy. Not only have the agricultural and mining sectors declined in relative importance, in terms of the share of total output that they produce, whilst industrial activity has correspondingly increased, but the nature of the industry within the country has also undergone very significant changes. In 1919 the production of metal products and machinery contributed only 3 per cent to the total value of industrial output; by 1976 this proportion had increased to 23 per cent. Similarly, whereas in 1919 the production of processed food, beverages and tobacco accounted for 33 per cent of the total value of manufactures produced in South Africa, by 1976 this subsector's share had declined to 14 per cent of the total.

The State and South African Economic Development

From an institutional viewpoint, modern South Africa has what is known as a mixed market economy. This is essentially a capitalist system of production in which private enterprise plays the major role, but does so in an economic environment that is managed by the state.

The state has played an important role in South African economic development since the early days of the exploitation of minerals – a period which saw it virtually assume the responsibility for providing an adequate supply of cheap labour for the newly founded mining industry. (Jeeves: 1974). Prior to 1924, the economic philosophy of the administration was essentially based upon the tenets of economic liberalism in all affairs other than labour matters.

1924 saw the coming to power of a coalition government based on the political alliance of White labour interests and those of White rural capital, and signalled a significant shift in the emphasis of state economic policies, from economic liberalism to those based upon economic nationalism and which entailed increasing state intervention into both agriculture and manufacturing. The economic role of the state began to become increasingly important. This trend continued and the private sector's freedom of action was steadily curtailed by the growing degree of state control over the economic environment that took place throughout the period to the present time.

Some of the increasing state controls, such as the measures that were aimed at soil conservation and pollution control, were designed to correct the market system's inherent inability to reflect the true social costs and benefits – operating as it does through the medium of individual decision making. Other controls, such as those imposed by the Group Areas Act and the Black Urban Areas Act, were based on ideological grounds and were related to the perceived need to separate South Africa's population groups. Still other measures, like the Black Labour Act and the Industrial Conciliation Act, were the result of a mixture of both these objectives.

Just as 1924 was a watershed year in South Africa in terms of the direction of government policy, so in retrospect may 1977 prove to have been similar. In this year, three Commissions were appointed by the government; the De Kock Commission, whose terms of reference were to investigate monetary policy; the Wiehahn Commission appointed to review the legislation administered by the Department of Labour; and the Riekert Commission, whose mandate was to examine a variety of legislation with a view to improving the utilization of manpower. The first reports of the Wiehahn and De Kock Commissions and the final report of the Riekert Commission were tabled in Parliament during 1979. The findings of these Commissions, together with the government's reactions to them, suggest that a major ideological shift with respect to state economic policy may be taking place. All three reports emphasized that the time had come for the state to play a less important role in shaping the economy, that the private sector should play a very much larger part in economic policy making, and that the market should be left to operate as freely as possible.

In addition, the recommendations made by the two labour Commissions and official reaction to them also suggest that there has been an ideological shift in respect to the race issue. Prior to the formulation of these proposed reforms, the underlying principle objectives of state interference in the labour market were the provision of a stable and cheap source of labour, the maintenance of 'industrial peace', and White supremacy. Whilst the first two objectives appear to have been retained, the third has clearly been rejected. The Wiehahn Commission commented explicitly on the race issue and stated that:

> The Commission accepted the premise that full involvement, participation and sharing in the system of free enterprise by all population groups with as little Government intervention as possible would not only give all groups a stake in the system, but would also ensure a common loyalty to both the system and the country. (R.P. 32/1979, p. 4)

– and further:

> South Africa should actively promote economic participation and freedom of competition within the South African labour system . . . the existing system will have to be modified in such a way that legal restrictions do not stand in the way of an individual's freedom to participate and compete. (R.P. 32/1979, p. 4)

The Commissioners clearly linked the rejection of continued White domination with the needs for the long term continuation of the free enterprise system. This again suggests that South African capitalism has now reached the point at which social and political reforms are a pre-requisite for further growth within the capitalist mode of production, and moreover, that the South African state perceives this and proposes to change its strategies to ensure, as far as it is able, the perpetuation of capitalism rather than that of White supremacy.

The Spatial Aspects of South African Economic Development

In common with most other developing nations a feature of South African economic development has been increasing levels of urbanization. In 1910, the year the Union of South Africa was formed, only 25 per cent of South Africans lived in towns. By 1970, however, this percentage had increased to 48 per cent and would without doubt have been considerably higher had South African Blacks been permitted to move freely within the economy.

Economic development in South Africa over the past century has been spatially uneven, largely because the present modern economic centres grew up around the mineral deposits and the sea ports handling the resultant trade flows. The extent of the spatial unevenness in economic advancement is clearly illustrated by the following data. In 1970 South Africa was divided for administrative purposes into 275 districts, 266 of which were White-dominated magisterial districts and 9 were designated as Black homelands and were largely controlled by Africans. In that year, only 21 of these 275 districts had productive capacities that enabled them to contribute 1 per cent or more to the total output of South Africa.

The actual concentration of economic activity is even greater than is suggested by the above statistics, as in 1970, nearly one fifth of South Africa's output was produced in the single largest district, Johannesburg. The richest ten per cent of the districts together produced nearly two thirds of the output and housed only 27 per cent of the population. At the other end of the wealth scale in 1970 were the 9 African homelands, which together produced only just over 3 per cent of the total output, but provided permanent homes for nearly two thirds of the population. (Nattrass: 1980a)

The Racial Aspects of South African Development

Largely as a result of being coupled to both the historical distribution of population and the institutional controls that exist over movements of major portions of the Black population of South Africa, the uneven spatial dimension to South African economic development has developed marked racial overtones.

Historically, South Africa's Black population was heavily concentrated in the North Western Border Areas and in the Eastern Seaboard Areas, both regions in which mineral deposits were not exploited. The spatial imbalance between Black population concentrations and the emergence of the modern economic centres was perpetuated over time by a growing network of legislation that controlled Black population movements, thereby limiting Black access to the regions of growing economic opportunity.

Within the modern centre itself the economic position of the Whites was also strengthened by the introduction of a number of legal measures, such as those relating to the reservation of particular jobs for Whites, the restriction of Black trade union rights and the controls that were imposed on the rights of Blacks to operate businesses. These influences further accentuated the racial character of the spatial inequalities and this was reinforced by the process of capital accumulation, in both physical and human terms. Wealth has concentrated in the hands of the Whites, who also enjoy higher average levels of education, better health facilities and better social security. Table 2.2 shows the estimates of the racial shares in total personal income in South Africa that have been made at different times over the period 1925–75.

Table 2.2

RACIAL SHARES IN TOTAL PERSONAL INCOME

Population Group	1924/25	1946/7	1960	1970	1975
African	18	20	19	19	24
Asian	2	2	2	2	2
Coloured	5	4	5	5	6
White	75	74	74	74	68

SOURCE: M. D. McGrath, *Racial Income Distribution in South Africa* Black/White Income Gap Research Report No. 2. Department of Economics, University of Natal, Durban, 1977, and J. Nattrass, 'Narrowing Wage Differentials', *South African Journal of Economics,* Vol. 45, No. 4, December, 1977.

From estimations that have been made by the author, it seems that since 1970 there has been a substantial redistribution of income at the margin from White to Black, but even after this redistribution, the average per capita White/Black income ratio in 1975 was 11:1. (Nattrass: 1977a). The approximate average per capita incomes per race group in 1975 implied by the data in Table 2.2 are, White, R2 500, Asians, R560, Coloureds, R430 and Africans, R200.

The distribution of income is mirrored by the occupational distribution of the race groups in the labour market, as we will see in more detail in the following chapters. Whites hold the majority of the key positions in the modern sector. In 1975, they filled 60 per cent of the professional and technical situations, 95 per cent of the managerial and administrative positions, 75 per cent of the clerical jobs and 60 per cent of the sales workforce. (Nattrass: 1977a). The rates of growth of the Black race groups in these categories over the period 1969–77 were, however, faster than that of the White in all categories other than that of managerial and administrative, which suggests that a change in the relative economic status of the population components will occur over time.

The average educational levels of the different sectors of the workforce also differ by race group. This racial educational disparity may militate against Black advancement, as it means that Black labour is often not a true substitute for the better educated White. Differences in educational levels are not the entire explanation for the racial occupational differences, however, as firstly, there are a large number of Blacks working in jobs well below their educational capability, and secondly, within each job category one finds a very wide range of educational levels.

Racial Inequality and South African Development: Two Alternative Views

It is obvious that the spatial and racial aspects of economic development are not independent of one another; the exact nature of the inter-relationship is, however, not clear and indeed has been the subject of a bitter dispute between the radical and the more orthodox economic analysts of South Africa.

Traditionally economists studying South African economic growth have argued that the high levels of inequality that persist are the results of spontaneous imperfections in the working of the market system in general and, more particularly, of those imperfections that are related to the practice of racial discrimination. The acceptance of racial discrimination as a way of life in South Africa, led successive governments to concentrate almost solely on improving the welfare levels of the Whites. As the South African black groups in general did not have franchise rights, there was no direct political pressure on the administration to adopt measures which might have led to a reduction in either the spatial or racial levels of inequality.

Some writers in this 'orthodox' school argue that racial inequalities of the magnitudes found in South Africa have been dysfunctional to South Africa's economic progress (Hobart Houghton: 1964) whilst others stress the role that economic growth can play as a liberalizing element in restructuring South African society. (O' Dowd: 1974, 1977)

The more radical analysts see the situation very differently and argue that racial discrimination was both introduced and fostered over the past century precisely because it was highly functional to economic progress through the capitalist mode. (Wolpe: 1972, Legassick: 1974). The radical school believe that the class struggle that is inherent in capitalism will always militate against the creation of what might be loosely termed 'a just society'. They further argue that poverty and inequality will not be eliminated in South Africa until both the political and economic systems are radically restructured.

It seems that both these schools of analysis have serious shortcomings. Those orthodox writers who basically argue 'leave it all to economic growth' may well be being too optimistic. Not only does such a view assume away the problems that are inherent in a developing capitalist economy, such as a growth in the concentration of power and growing inequalities in the distribution of wealth, but it also ignores the time horizon that may be involved and fails to take cognisance of the possible behaviour patterns of the groups whose status is dependent upon the maintenance of a 'no change' situation.

The radical school in its turn, arguing as it does that economic growth under a capitalist regime will not bring the type of change that it believes is necessary for the fulfilment of the aspirations of the majority, places too little weight on the power of the evolutionary forces within an expanding capitalist system to generate increasing economic and social justice.

Whether or not economic growth will bring with it a reduction in inequality and evolutionary social and political change, will be largely determined by the behaviour patterns of the major economic agents and by the changes that take place in the economic hierarchy itself, and it is to these aspects that this book attempts to address itself. The early chapters look at the role that the major factors, labour and capital, have played in the processes of production and distribution, whilst in the later sections, the analysis is broken down and the roles played by the different economic sectors are analysed.

THREE

The Labour Supply and South African Economic Development

INTRODUCTION

In the previous chapter it was argued that the contribution made by the productive resources to the output of any economy is a function of both the structure of those resources and their relative availabilities. In this chapter we will look in greater detail at the structure and availibility of one of the resources, namely, South Africa's labour supply.

The Determinants of the Labour Supply

When economists talk of the role that labour plays in the process of economic development they are talking of labour as an input in the production process and include both the mental and physical effort expended by people in the course of producing both goods and services. The extent to which labour, as a factor of production, can generate output in any economy depends upon:

1. The size of the labour input, that is, how many people are employed and for how long they work.
2. The productivity or efficiency of that labour input.

Labour productivity is determined by two things: firstly, the general level of knowledge that is present in the community and secondly, the extent to which the economy itself is able to make productive use of that knowledge.

The Extent of the Labour Supply

The extent of the labour supply, at any moment in time, is determined by the size of the economically active portion of the population, that is, by the number of people in the community who are both willing and able to work. This, in its turn, is dependent upon a number of factors, namely:

1. The absolute size of the population.
2. The rate of growth of the population.
3. The age structure of the population: in particular, how many people fall into the age category of 15–64 years, since it is these age groups that, in most economies, produce practically all the productive workers.
4. The social and legal institutions in the economy. For example, whether or not it is acceptable for women to work, whether or not certain occupations are restricted to members of a particular social caste, or whether or not there are legal barriers preventing certain individuals from entering specified professions or performing particular jobs.

Of these four elements the first two, namely the absolute size and the rate of growth of the population, are usually the most significant determinants of the size of the available labour supply. However, the direct relationships between changes in the population and changes in the extent of the labour input in the production process is far from being a 'one to one' relationship, as it is tempered by a number of other factors. Firstly, there is a time lag between an increase in population and an increase in the labour supply, a period during which children grow up and receive the necessary training to make them useful members of both the labour force and the wider community.

Secondly, populations can and frequently do, grow faster than job opportunities. When this happens the crucial factor that determines the rate of growth of the labour input into production is not the rate of growth of population, but the rate at which capital can be accumulated to create new jobs.

Thirdly, people both come into the economy from other areas and leave to settle elsewhere. Migration of this type affects both the calibre and the structure of the labour supply to a greater degree than it does the population structure. Studies of the migration process show that young adult men with higher than average levels of education are the most likely to emigrate. As a result, a flow of migrants has a very significant impact on the labour supply, as it contains a higher proportion of economically active people than a normal population. In addition, as the Nobel prize-winning economist, Simon Kuznets, has pointed out, migrants are 'typically outward looking, venturesome individuals, who, by definition, tolerate change' and so are particularly valuable in a dynamic situation. (Kuznets: 1965)

THE STRUCTURE OF THE SOUTH AFRICAN LABOUR FORCE

The Population and the Workforce

All South Africa's population groups contribute to her labour force, but as a result of differences in the demographic and social characteristics of the groups and in the institutions that govern their activities in the labour market itself, the nature and the extent of the contribution that each group makes differs quite significantly, as we shall see. Quantitatively, since there is an obvious link between population size and the number of people who will be both willing and able to work, one would expect that the racial contribution to the South African workforce would reflect the racial structure of the population, as indeed, broadly speaking, it does, as can be seen from the data in Table 3.1 below.

It is, however, interesting to note that whereas both the Coloured and the White groups form a larger proportion of the workforce than they do of the population, the African and Asian groups form a smaller proportion. This is mainly due to the high proportion of children in these latter two communities.

Table 3.1
THE RACIAL COMPOSITION OF THE WORKFORCE, 1975[1]

Race Group	Population		Workforce	
	Number	Percentage	Number	Percentage
African	17 500 000	71,0	7 002	72,0
Asian	729 700	3,0	221	2,0
Coloured	2 195 600	9,0	795	8,0
White	4 090 100	17,0	1 754	18,0
Total	24 515 400	100,0	9 772	100,0

1. Including Transkei and Bophuthatswana.

SOURCE: *South African Statistics, 1978.*

Population Growth, Economic Development and the Labour Supply

It is generally accepted that there is a relationship between changes in living standards and changes in population growth rates. Population growth rates reflect the combined effects of two other demographic variables, the birth rate and the mortality or death rate. It is argued that, as living levels rise from very low absolute income levels, the improved nutrition standards, sanitation and health care that normally accompany such increases, result in a dramatic reduction in mortality rates and a consequent, and equally dramatic, increase in population growth rates. The initial impact of economic development is, therefore, to increase the population growth rate. As development continues, however, the community becomes influenced by modernizing forces, particularly those that are linked with urbanization. These change family values and the size of the average family starts to decline, reducing the population growth rate.

Over time this second effect is the more powerful and the ultimate outcome of rising living standards is a low rate of population increase, such as those one finds at present in most of the advanced Western countries. According to the World Bank, in the United States the rate of population growth over the period 1970–1976 was 0,8 per cent, in the United Kingdom it was as low as, 0,1 per cent. In less developed countries it was much higher, being 2,7 per cent in Brazil and 2,6 per cent in Nigeria over the same period.

In South Africa over the period 1960–70 the estimated rate of growth of the population was 2,8 per cent, including the increases resulting from immigration. We saw in an earlier chapter that there are significant variations in the average standards of living enjoyed by South Africa's different population groups. In view of the above argument it is not surprising that there are also significant differences in the rates of growth of these groups and consequently in the rates of growth of their contribution to the potential workforce. The official estimates of the growth rates of the different groups for the period 1960–70 were: Africans 2,8 per cent, Asians 2,9 per cent, Coloureds 3,2 per cent and Whites 2,1 per cent.

A South African economist and demographer, Professor J. L. Sadie, made an intensive study of the racial variations in the demographic variables that have accompanied economic development. He concluded that the changes in the life styles and living standards of the communities had been such that amongst the White group, the decline in the birth rate could be dated back almost to the turn of the century. In the Asian community, however, birth rates did not start to decline until the 1950's, whilst in the Coloured group the change only took place in the late 1960's. The African birth rate has, to date, shown no tendency to fall and Professor Sadie argued on this basis that this group 'was still in the explosive (demographic) phase'. (Sadie: 1971). Table 3.2 illustrates these changes.

Table 3.2
RACIAL POPULATION GROWTH RATES, 1936–1970

	Average Annual Rate of Growth over the Period			
	1936–1946	1946–1951	1951–1960	1960–1970
African	1,87	2,18	2,39	2,65
Asian	3,31	3,59	2,94	2,60
Coloured	2,27	2,68	3,13	3,01
White	1,71	2,18	1,66	2,14

SOURCE: J. L. Sadie 'Population and Economic Development in South Africa', *South African Journal of Economics,* Vol. 39, No. 3, September, 1971, p. 206. (The figures include immigration.)

MIGRATION AND THE WORKFORCE

Economic development is essentially a process of structural transformation and labour migration is an integral part of such a transformation. As some areas expand faster than others, so their need for labour increases and if a local labour supply is not readily available, migrants will be attracted into the expanding region by the higher wages on offer there. Historically, industrialization has implied urbanization and a flow of labour from the agriculturally oriented rural areas into the growing towns. Although the major proportion of all labour movements are in the form of such rural-urban migration, this is not the only type of migration that goes with economic advancement. People also move internationally, seeking better economic opportunities or move from one urban area to another, typically, but again not exclusively, from a small town to a larger one.

Labour migration is a world wide phenomenon. In most areas it is a reasonably stable process; people migrate with their families from one area to another where they settle, and the wage earner seeks a new occupation. Such migrations normally lead to a lengthy stay in the host area and in many instances to the permanent resettlement of the in-migrants.

In some countries, however, a different labour migration phenomenon exists. Migration streams, both internal and international, are composed of two different classes of individuals; those seeking permanent residence in the area which they are entering and those who merely seek work for a limited period of time. When this period has expired the latter migrants return to their homes in the country or region from whence they came.

As far as the individual migrant is concerned permanent and temporary migration decisions are similar in many respects; such decisions normally arise from the same motives and are often differentiated only by quantitative differences in the strengths of the motives underlying the decisions. However, as far as the overall effects on the economies are concerned, the social and economic effects of temporary and permanent migration, for both the supplying and the receiving areas, are likely to be very different, as permanent migration implies:

1. The transfer of economically inactive persons as well as the economically active work seeker.
2. That the transfer of capital, both in terms of the assets that the migrants bring with them and the education incorporated in the migrant and his family, will be substantially greater than in the case of temporary migrants.

Both permanent and oscillating or temporary labour migration take place to a significant extent in the South African economy and they will be discussed separately in the following sections.

PERMANENT LABOUR MIGRATION IN SOUTH AFRICA

Internal Rural-Urban Migration

The twentieth century is a period in which dramatic changes have taken place in the structure of the South African economy, transforming it from an agriculturally oriented community to a modern industrial state. Development has, however, been spatially uneven with the main industrial activities heavily concentrated in the northern-central region of the country. This unevenness has generated a substantial shift in the distribution of the population. There has been a steady increase in the numbers of people living in the towns and a consequent depopulation of many rural areas, particularly those under White control. Table 3.3 shows how these movements have taken place.

Table 3.3
THE CHANGING DISTRIBUTION OF THE POPULATION

	Percentage of Group in Urban Areas		
	1911	1936	1970
African	12,6	17,3	33,1
Asian	43,2	66,3	86,7
Coloured	46,7	53,9	74,1
White	51,6	65,2	86,8
Total Population	24,7	31,4	47,8

SOURCE: *South African Statistics, 1978.*

The extent and the rate of urbanization differs amongst the population groups. The African community has urbanized more slowly and to a lesser extent than the other groups. This does not, however, mean that they do not participate actively in the modern sector workforce. What it does reflect is the nature of the impact that the process of industrialization has had on this population group. For a number of institutional factors, some of which were social, others cultural or legal in nature, the reaction of the African workforce to the growing industrial work opportunities was the creation of a substantial and ever increasing system of oscillating labour migration; a system in which the workers alone leave the rural areas to seek work in the growing modern sector of the economy, returning to their homes and their families when the demands of their work allow. By 1970 this stream of 'revolving' migrants had become so large that one and a quarter million Africans were away from their rural homes, working in the towns, on the census date in that year. (Nattrass 1976a)

African Rural-Urban Migration and the Growth of the Migrant Labour System

Why was it that, whereas the impact of the growth of the modern economy on the Asian, Coloured and White population groups, resulted in a substantial flow of families from the country districts into the towns, in response to the new opportunties that were created, amongst the African group it generated this massive stream of oscillating migrants? The answer is complex and will be dealt with more fully in the following chapter in which the historical evolution of the labour market is discussed. However, a brief review is pertinent here.

The initial discovery of diamonds at Kimberley and the subsequent opening of the gold mines on the Witwatersrand, resulted in a rapid increase in the need for labour in these areas, far greater than could be supplied by the relatively small population there. People, both Black and White, moved into the mining areas in large numbers. The Africans coming in were largely drawn from regions that were tribally controlled and the gulf between the ways of life in the mining towns and those of the tribal areas was initially so great that these migrant men did not, by and large, consider settling permanently in the new environment. Instead, they preferred to work only for a period long enough to enable them to accumulate the cash needed to purchase the goods that had attracted them to the area in the first place and to return home once they had achieved their target.

Continued contact with the growing modern economy, its work conditions, commodities and inhabitants reduced this initial cultural gap and, together with changing conditions in the African rural areas, lead to Africans settling in the towns in increasing numbers. Permanent resettlement was, however, never favoured by the authorities, who placed an ever expanding framework of control over the movements and rights of Africans in these areas. This culminated, during the late 1950s and early 1960s, in the present legislation, which virtually prevents a person born in an African controlled area from obtaining the right to settle permanently in the areas under White jurisdiction. Legislation, coupled with the lack of economic opportunities in the African rural areas and growing population pressure, institutionalized the migrant labour system. The present extent of the system and the way it has grown since the early days of the mineral discoveries are shown below.

Table 3.4

THE GROWTH OF THE MIGRANT LABOUR SYSTEM

Year	Number of Temporary African Migrants Absent from the Rural Areas of South Africa on the Census Day		
	Men	Women	Total
1936	409 000	67 000	476 000
1946	415 000	122 000	537 000
1960	671 000	216 000	887 000
1970	1 035 000	260 000	1 295 000
1975	1 232 000	303 000	1 535 000

SOURCE: J. Nattrass, 'The Migrant Labour System and South African Economic Development, 1936–70'. Ph.D. Thesis, University of Natal.

The stream of migrants moving between the modern economy and the rural areas grew over the period 1936–70 at an annual average rate of 3 per cent. However, the rate of growth itself increased, rising from a yearly average of 1,2 per cent for the period 1936–46 to 3,9 per cent over the ten years 1960–70, largely reflecting the growth in economic opportunities in the modern sector over these periods.

The contribution that the migrant labour system made to the labour supply in the modern sector, grew significantly faster than the system itself and averaged 4 per cent per year. This is because, from the labour supply viewpoint, not only did the number of migrants participating in the system increase, but they also increased the length of time that they spent working in the modern economy. The combined effect of these two influences was to increase the potential supply of man-years contributed by the migrant labour system from 6 million in 1936 to nearly 25 million in 1970.

The Migrant Labour System and the Structure of the Workforce

Apart from providing a substantial proportion of South Africa's labour force, the migrant labour system has also materially affected the structure of the workforce. We said earlier that labour migration was a selective process and that the groups that were particularly prone to migrate were the young, better educated males. These characteristics show clearly in the structure of South Africa's migrant workforce. The data below illustrate the changing age structure of this group and compare it with that of the settled African workforce for 1970.

Table 3.5

THE CHANGING AGE STRUCTURE OF THE MIGRANT WORKFORCE

| | Migrant Workforce | | | | Settled Workforce |
	1936	1946	1960	1970	1970
Percentage aged:					
Under 25 years	35	39	41	32	28
Under 35 years	72	77	75	71	50
Under 45 years	91	92	96	88	73
Under 55 years	100	98	99	97	90

SOURCE: Same as Table 3.4.

In 1970 the domestic migrant workforce was significantly younger on average than the settled workforce; the average age of the former being 25 years, against that of the latter of 35 years. Even though it was still relatively young in average terms in 1970, over the period 1936–70 the migrant workforce did shown atendency to age. Although the young age groups joined the system in increasing proportions over this period – a characteristic which tends to reduce the average age of the group – this tendency has been more than offset by a lengthening of the average period of time spent by an individual in the system. In 1936 there was a greater than 75 per cent chance that, by the time a migrant was 45 years old, he would have withdrawn from the system and been living permanently in the tribal areas. By 1970 this probability had decreased to 31 per cent.

International Labour Migration

Throughout the period of the development of the modern economy South Africa has relied extensively on the contribution that international migration has made to the labour supply. International migrants also fall into two classes, those who come with their families from other countries to make their homes permanently in South Africa, and those who enter alone as temporary migrants to work for a period and then return to their homes on completion of their work contract.

Permanent international migration has had a very significant impact on both the size and structure of South Africa's labour supply. Over the fifty year period 1925–75 approximately half a million people came into South Africa in this way, almost all of whom were White. The majority of these immigrants entered the country in their peak productivity ages, already educated at the expense of their home countries. If we take permanent immigration into South Africa in 1970 as an example – in this year 41 500 people came from other countries to settle in South Africa; of these 53 per cent were in the age group 20–40 years. Largely as a result of the age structure, educational levels and ethnic origins of the migrants, international migration has had a notable impact upon the patterns of evolution of the South African labour market. Being a significant source of supply of educated, skilled White labour, it has considerably reduced the pressure on both government and industry to advance members of the black population groups to the higher rungs of the job ladder.

Significant contributions to the early development of South Africa's modern economy have also been made by the considerable number of black permanent immigrants, starting with the slaves who were imported into the Cape Colony from further north in Africa and from Indonesia, and including the large numbers of Indians recruited initially as indentured labourers on the Natal sugar farms and the relatively small numbers of Africans who entered from the neighbouring states to settle permanently in South Africa.

South Africa has also relied heavily on the considerable number of temporary Black international migrants who enter the country for a relatively short period of time and who mainly work in the mining industry or in agriculture. Until recently foreign, temporary, Black migrants provided on average between three quarters and two thirds of the total number of Blacks employed in the mining industry. This contribution has been reduced in recent years. The growing political instability in Southern Africa has lead to the mining industry reducing its dependency upon labour supplied by foreign countries. By 1979 the contribution made by foreign Blacks to the industry's labour supply had dropped to 46 per cent.

Activity Rates: The Link between Population and the Labour Supply

The size of the supply of labour available for use in an economy, at a moment of time, is limited to the number of people in the economy who are both willing and able to work. This group is known collectively as the *economically active* portion of the population. The size of this economically active portion is determined by the age structure of the population as a whole, by the social, cultural and legal institutions in the economy and by the level of sophistication of the economy itself. The impact of the age structure is direct, since by far the major proportion of the economically active group is drawn from the people in the 15–65 year age group, the so-called productive years. The social, cultural and legal influences operate through the impact that they have on people's attitudes to work. The level of economic and technical sophistication will largely determine the average amounts of education required and supplied by the economy, which in their turn will affect the average age of entry into the labour market.

Table 3.6 shows the proportion of the South African population that was economically active (the activity rate) for each racial category in 1970 and the percentage of adults aged 15–65 years who were willing and able to work (the participation rate).

Table 3.6

ACTIVITY RATES BY RACIAL GROUP, 1970

	African	*Asian*	*Coloured*	*White*
Activity Rate	37%	29%	35%	40%
Participation Rate	70%	51%	69%	64%

SOURCE: *South African Statistics, 1978.*

It is interesting to see that the rank order of the groups alters with the measure of economic activity that is used. These differences in ranking reflect both the underlying age structures of the populations and variations in the group attitudes towards participation in the work process.

The age structures of the different racial communities in South Africa are given in Table 3.7. From these one sees clearly that the rapidly growing black groups have a much higher percentage of children in the total than the slower growing White group. Although age profiles can explain the differences in the activity rates, they do not explain the differences in labour force participation. Why is it, for example, that the participation rates of Africans are higher than those of Whites, whilst those of the Asian group are considerably lower?

Table 3.7
AGE PROFILES OF THE RACE GROUPS, 1970

Age Group	Percentage in Age Group			
	African	Asian	Coloured	White
0–14	43,0	41,0	46,0	31,0
15–64	53,0	57,0	51,0	62,0
Over 64	4,0	2,0	3,0	7,0

SOURCE: *South African Statistics, 1978.*

These differences can be partially explained by the disparities which exist between the race groups, in respect of the average length of time spent by one of their members in the education process. At present the average levels of education received by Africans are very much lower than those of the other groups. As African average educational levels increase in the future, so the participation rates can be expected to decline, as people stay in the educational process for a longer period and so delay their entry into the labour market.

Social and cultural forces also affect activity rates. Table 3.8 contains these rates by race and sex and the data show firstly, that men participate in the formal labour process to a greater extent than

Table 3.8
ACTIVITY RATES BY RACE AND SEX, 1970

1970	Activity Rates			
	African	Asian	Coloured	White
Men	49%	47%	46%	56%
Women	26%	11%	24%	24%

SOURCE: *South African Statistics, 1978.*

women, reflecting the woman's role as child bearer. Secondly, the activity rates of Asian women are particularly low when judged against those of the women in other groups. Since the rates of the Asian men are roughly the equivalent of those of the Africans and Coloureds, this difference in group attitudes to women and work accounts for the low overall participation rate of the Asian community. It is difficult to explain the relatively high level of participation by White men. The difference possibly reflects the impact of the racial disparities in economic opportunities on the average retirement age; because rewards are higher, a White man is prepared to work to an older age.

Labour Migration and Activity Rates

International labour migration, or the movement of people into South Africa from countries beyond her borders, has also had a substantial impact on the size and relative importance of the economically active section of the community. International migration on a large scale only affects two of South Africa's population groups, the Africans and the Whites. In the case of the former, legal immigration is virtually restricted to the men who are recruited from outside South Africa for work in the mining industry. Consequently, of this group, all are in the economically active category.

As far as the White immigrants are concerned, the impact, though somewhat less spectacular, is nevertheless similar. Over the period 1971–77, 387 000 immigrants entered South Africa of whom no less than 68 per cent were classified as being economically active.

THE STRATIFICATION OF LABOUR

One of the major characteristics of the South African economy is the extent of the stratification that has taken place in the labour market. On the demand side the market has been stratified by legislation limiting the access of particular groups of people to certain jobs and to certain geographical regions and by both sex and race discrimination practices. On the supply side the major decisive factors have been differences in access to education and training and the influence of the migrant labour system.

Education and the Stratification of the South African Labour Supply

At the beginning of this chapter we said that one of the major determinants of the contribution made by labour to the process of economic development, was the productivity of the labour force and that this was determined by the level of 'know how', the availability of capital equipment and the general levels of training and education of the workforce itself. In South Africa, educational and training stratification is not only race selective, but amongst the African population there is also a substantial difference in the average education levels of those living in urban and rural areas. The educational profiles of the different racial constituents of South Africa's workforce in 1970 are given in Table 3.9. There are several interesting features in the data in this table; firstly, the extent of the superiority of the average educational levels of the White group, of whom well over half had received full school education. Secondly, the extent to which the rural African workforce is relatively deprived in terms of education and finally, the fact that there appears to be, with the exception of the Asians, no sex differentiation in educational attainments. Women in all the groups, other than the Asian group, had educational profiles that were either equal to, or better than, those of the men in the same group.

The racial differences in educational attainments reflect the underlying distribution of educational and training facilities between the different population groups as well as the average levels of expenditure per pupil. Dr. E. G. Malherbe states that in 1973 the Government spent 72 per cent of the total expenditure on schooling on the education of White pupils, who formed only 22 per cent of the total school enrolment in that year. (Malherbe: 1977)

With differences in the average educational levels of the race groups of the magnitude of those illustrated in Table 3.9, it can in no way be surprising to find that Whites dominate the occupations that require a background of basic education. However, as we saw earlier, it is the African population group that forms the major and increasing proportion of the workforce. As this group's average educational levels are low, it would seem that South Africa could easily find herself in a situation in which the available supply of educated labour became insufficient to meet the demands of a growing and industrializing economy.

Table 3.9
PERCENTAGE OF THE ECONOMICALLY ACTIVE IN EACH RACE GROUP BY EDUCATION, 1970

Years of Education	African				Asian		Coloured		White	
	Urban		Rural							
	Men	Women	Men	Women	Men	Women	Men	Women	Men	Women
No Schooling	39,9	22,6	65,4	60,5	6,7	16,1	24,7	18,1	1,1	1,1
Primary only	42,1	48,0	28,9	31,6	34,7	40,1	43,3	48,9	3,3	1,7
Up to Standard 8	13,0	20,9	4,1	5,4	36,0	22,9	22,4	22,1	25,4	17,6
Up to and including Standard 10	4,7	7,2	1,2	1,7	19,2	15,5	8,2	8,0	54,8	64,1
Diploma and/or Degree	,3	1,3	,4	,8	3,4	4,6	1,4	2,9	15,4	15,5
Median Number of Years	3,0	5,0	nil	nil	7,5	5,8	4,1	4,6	10,4	10,6

In calculating these medians 'no education and level not specified' have both been treated as 'no education', imparting a downward bias to the median levels given in the table.

SOURCE: 1970 Population Census Report 02.05.07, *Levels of Education*, Department of Statistics, Pretoria, 1976.

In the past any potential shortage in the supply of educated and sophisticated labour was met by increased White immigration, rather than by black advancement. However, with the growing political instability in Southern Africa, White immigration levels have been significantly reduced, so the potential for black advancement seems better now than in the past, particularly since there has also been a rapid acceleration in State investment in black education at all levels.

Throughout the period 1948–60 public expenditure on African education rose at an average rate of only 5,4 per cent, scarcely faster than the population growth rate. Over the period from 1960–74, however, the average rose to 15,4 per cent – to nearly three times the earlier rate and it escalated still further over the period 1973–77 to 26 per cent per annum. The higher levels of expenditure are reflected in an increase in both the size of the student enrolment and the average length of stay in the schooling system. In 1976 approximately 72 per cent of the African children aged between 5 and 14 years, who were eligible for school, were, in fact, in the schooling system. The number of children enrolled in the tenth and twelfth year of school rose over the period 1970–75 by 18 per cent and 24 per cent respectively. Not only did more African children enter the schooling system, but those who did, on average, stayed in for a longer period of time.

Despite this recent increase in State expenditure on black education, the situation is still far from adequate. This is illustrated clearly by the fact that in 1970 just over one million South Africans had completed either the full school programme, or ten years with some tertiary training. Of these 88 per cent were White, 7 per cent African, 3 per cent Coloured and 2 per cent Asian. Despite the massive rate of increase in the number of African children entering the higher levels of school education over the period from 1970, in 1977 there were still only 11 000 African children enrolled in the final school year, which was the equivalent of one fifth of the number of White children in the same school standard. If the relatively disadvantaged position of the African group with regard to access to formal education is to be eliminated, it is essential that the rate of growth of State expenditure on such education is maintained at these high levels.

Racial Stratification in the Labour Market

Earlier it was pointed out that the relative educational profiles of the different population groups are such that they will ensure that Whites (and Coloureds and Asians to a lesser extent) will dominate all the jobs requiring a reasonably high level of formal education. The access of South Africa's black citizens to the upper rungs of the job ladder has been restricted even further by legislation that reserved certain occupations exclusively for Whites and which prevented blacks from being put into positions of authority over Whites. The combined effects of the educational disparity and the discriminatory legislation has been to confine Africans in particular, but also Coloureds and Asians to some degree, to the lower level jobs, as shown in Table 3.10 below.

Table 3.10

THE OCCUPATIONAL DISTRIBUTION OF THE POPULATION GROUPS IN 1977

Category	Percentage of the Race Group			
	African	Asian	Coloured·	White
All Economically Active	72,7	2,2	7,8	17,3
Professional and Technical	26,2	3,6	8,9	61,3
Managerial and Executive	,5	2,1	,8	96,6
Clerical	16,3	7,8	8,0	67,9
Sales	21,5	8,4	10,2	59,9
Production Workers	71,4	4,0	10,9	13,7
Unskilled	85,8	3,1	10,6	,5

SOURCE: *Department of Labour Manpower Survey No. 12, 1977.* The data in the table exclude employment in Domestic Service and Agriculture.

Over the period since 1970, South African blacks have, however, entered the higher job categories in increasing numbers and the White share of professional and technical jobs fell from 65 per cent in 1970 to 61 per cent in 1977, their share of clerical jobs from 85 per cent to 68 per cent and of sales from 67 per cent to 60 per cent. Despite the apparent upgrading of the non-White groups that has taken place, one still finds, however, that within the categories, Africans and Coloureds are clustered in the lower level occupations. For example, in 1977, 90 per cent of Africans in the professional and technical grade were employed as teachers or nurses, the equivalent percentages for Coloureds was 88 per cent, for Asians 62 per cent and for Whites 35 per cent. Similarly in the clerical occupations one finds a bunching of Africans, Asians and Coloureds in the lower clerical positions, such as storemen and filing clerks, whilst Whites dominate in the higher clerical occupations such as bank clerks, bookkeepers and committee clerks.

Quite apart from the racial stratification of South Africa's workforce there is also a significant degree of sex stratification in terms of access to the more productive jobs. Women of all race groups are relatively disadvantaged in the labour force and African women are particularly affected. In 1977 in South Africa's major metropolitan areas, although the educational profiles of African men and women were almost identical, only 12 per cent of the African men living in the urban areas were employed in domestic service or were unemployed, whereas 67 per cent of the African women living in towns fell into one or other of these categories.

EARNINGS FROM WAGE LABOUR IN SOUTH AFRICA

The occupational and educational stratification is reflected in the profiles of the earnings of the race groups. In 1975 average incomes per head of the various groups were Africans R200, Asians R560, Coloureds R430 and Whites R2 500. The differences in income per earner were less dramatic, but nevertheless still significant, as can be seen from the table below.

Table 3.11

AVERAGE EARNINGS BY RACE AND OCCUPATION, 1975

Category	African	Asian	Coloured	White
Professional and Technical	2 044	4 240	2 869	7 860
Managerial and Executive	1 409	4 963	1 979	7 860
Clerical and Administrative	1 913	3 704	1 772	2 750
Skilled Labour	2 008	3 990	2 248	⎫
Production Workers	1 629	2 829	1 383	⎬ 5 500
Unskilled Workers	956	2 015	924	⎭

SOURCE: *Bureau of Market Research Income and Expenditure Surveys No's. 27.1, 27.4, 27.7, 27.10* for African, Asian and Coloureds and unpublished estimates based on 1970 census data for Whites updated to 1975 by changes in consumer price index.

Racial earnings profiles for the country, as a whole, reflect the profiles within each sector of the economy, as well as the relative importance of the sector in the whole. Sectors vary quite significantly in terms of the payments that they make to earners in the different categories, as do the changes that occur in the sectors. The table below shows the ratio of the average earnings of Africans to Whites for 1960, 1975 and 1977 for four of South Africa's major economic sectors, mining, manufacturing, construction and agriculture.

Table 3.12
RATIO OF AVERAGE AFRICAN TO AVERAGE WHITE WAGES

	1960	*1975*	*1977*
Agriculture	–	1:13,4	–
Mining	1:15,5	1: 8,0	1:7,6
Manufacturing	1: 5,5	1: 4,8	1:4,4
Construction	1: 5,6	1: 4,9	1:5,2

SOURCE: *South African Statistics, 1978.*

Although the racial wage ratio has become smaller in all the sectors over the period 1960–77, the rate at which it has narrowed differed, whilst the ratio in the mining industry in 1977 had been reduced to nearly half its 1960 value, that in construction had been only marginally changed.

THE CHANGING ROLE OF LABOUR IN THE PROCESS OF ECONOMIC GROWTH

Although ultimately the characteristics of the supply pool of labour represent the limits within which labour can contribute to the process of production, in the short run the actual contribution made by labour is determined mainly by the nature and patterns of the job opportunities that are available to the potential labour force, that is by the patterns of demand of labour. As economic growth proceeds and the economy becomes increasingly sophisticated, both in terms of the products that are produced and the methods used in the production process, both the size and the structure of the job opportunities change. Changes occur in the number of jobs available, in the geographical distribution of work openings and in the nature of the jobs themselves.

As the economy becomes more industrialized, so the job opportunities in the manufacturing and commercial sectors of the economy grow relatively to those in agriculture and people move from the rural areas into the towns, in search of these new and more profitable work openings. In addition, as the growth process continues, production becomes more capital intensive as increasingly sophisticated methods of production are introduced. Concomitantly, the structure of jobs surrounding the capital alters. Over time, although more jobs are created in all categories, the rates at which they are created differ and manufacturing firms tend to employ a lower percentage of production workers and a higher percentage of service and clerical staff. Mechanization and automation also affect the structure of the skills in the labour force. As long ago as 1748, Adam Smith pointed out the benefits that accrue from specialization and the division of labour. The more capital intensive the process of production becomes, the greater are the possibilities for reaping these benefits.

With the increased degree of specialization, so the proportions of both highly skilled craftsmen and unskilled workers in the total labour force decrease relative to that of semi-skilled operatives. The demand for highly trained professionals, however, rises in line with that for production workers. In the United States the number of workers employed in these two categories quadrupled over the fifty year period 1920–70.

In South Africa similar trends are evident. In the twenty-four year period 1946–70 the number of economically active people in the economy rose by 188 per cent, but the number of professional and technical workers increased by over 300 per cent, as did the number of clerical workers. This process reflects not only the changes and modernization in the process of production that take place as an economy grows, but also the changes in the relative importance of the different sectors of the economy, which are characteristic of economic advancement.

Changes in the Sectoral Employment Patterns in South Africa

As the importance of the different sectors of the economy, in terms of their contribution to total output, alters as economic growth proceeds, these changes are reflected in the importance of the sectors as employers. However, although there is a linkage between changes in the patterns of output and employment, it is a relatively loose one, as both the amounts of capital needed to employ a man and his level of output differ between the sectors. In agriculture, for example, the amount of capital needed per worker is below that in manufacturing, as is the amount of output produced by each worker. As a result, as the manufacturing sector gains in importance as a producer, it will gain very much more slowly in the employment field. Nevertheless, as development proceeds there will be quite clearly defined changes taking place in the sectoral employment patterns. Agriculture will move from being by far the largest employer to become one of the smallest. The manufacturing sector will become increasingly significant throughout the industrialization phase and then, once a high level of economic sophistication has been reached, it will start to lose ground once more, this time to the service sector. The table below shows the changing employment patterns in South Africa for the census years 1921, 1951 and 1970.

Table 3.13

CHANGING SECTORAL EMPLOYMENT PATTERNS, 1921–70

Sector	Percentage Employed in each Sector		
	1921	1951	1970
Agriculture	63	34	33
Mining	10	12	9
Manufacturing	6	11	14
Construction		5	6
Electricity, Gas and Water		1	1
Transport and Communication	16	5	4
Commerce and Finance		7	12
Services	5	25	21

SOURCE: *1921, 1951 Union Statistics for 50 years.* 1970 *South African Statistics, 1978.*

The trends discussed earlier are clearly visible in the changes in employment patterns that took place between 1921 and 1970. The rate of change over the period was not constant and it would seem that, in employment terms, the period 1921–51 was a period which saw larger changes in the structure of the South African economy than the period 1951–70. Although this is true, one should not put too much weight on the data in the table, as they reflect not only the structural changes, but also the special role that the agricultural sector plays as a source of labour supply, which will be discussed more fully when we come to look more closely at agriculture itself. For our purposes now, it is sufficient to note that over this latter period, the African workforce increased more rapidly than did the number of jobs that were created in the modern economy. As a result a pool of African labour began to bank up in both the agricultural sector and domestic service.

The Racial Allocation of Employment by Sector

The racial composition of the workforce employed in the different sectors of the South African economy varies quite significantly, as can be seen from the data in the table below.

Table 3.14

RACIAL ALLOCATION OF EMPLOYMENT BY SECTOR: 1970

Sector	Percentage of Group Employed in Sector				
	Workforce	African	Asian	Coloured	White
Mining	8,0	11,0	–	1,0	4,0
Manufacturing	13,0	9,0	35,0	23,0	19,0
Construction	6,0	5,0	6,0	11,0	6,0
Electricity, Gas and Water	1,0	1,0	–	1,0	1,0
Transport and Communication	4,0	2,0	4,0	4,0	11,0
Commerce and Finance	11,0	6,0	30,0	12,0	27,0
Other Services	20,0	19,0	12,0	22,0	22,0
Agriculture	30,0	40,0	4,0	16,0	7,0
Unemployed and Unspecified	7,0	7,0	9,0	10,0	3,0

SOURCE: *South African Statistics, 1978.*

This difference in the allocation of the racial workforces between the sectors has had a significant impact on racial incomes. In a fully developed economy such as that of the United States, the average earnings of a man are not affected to any great extent by the nature of the sector in which he works; however, in South Africa this is not the case. The economy is not fully developed and the spatial aspects of the development that has taken place are very uneven. As a result, earnings in particular sectors and in particular regions are very much higher than those in others. For example, in 1977 average earnings per worker in the manufacturing sector were R3 086, whereas in the mining sector the average was R1 995 and in construction R2 517. As a result the sector in which a man is able to find employment is likely to exercise quite a significant influence on his earning capacity.

In South Africa the very low productivity sectors are Agriculture and Domestic Service and it is in these sectors that one finds high concentrations of African workers. On the other hand, Whites are concentrated in Manufacturing, Commerce and Finance and the Professional service occupations, all high productivity sectors.

Underemployment and Unemployment in South Africa

It is generally accepted that one of the basic human rights is the right to a meaningful job. Consequently one of the criteria used to assess the performance of a capitalist economy is the presence or absence of unemployment and underemployment. Unemployment occurs when a person who is economically active, is unable to find a job that he is prepared to take. Underemployment is a different phenomenon and is related to the large numbers of very low productivity jobs that are present in many countries. There are substantial definitional problems connected with the concept of underemployment, but loosely speaking, a person may be said to be underemployed if the output of the economy could be increased if he was transferred to another job. The sectors in which one usually finds evidence of underemployment are agriculture, particularly subsistence agriculture and domestic service, although in some countries the petty trading sector also contains significant amounts of disguised unemployment.

In South Africa, at the present time, there are significant numbers of people who are either unemployed or underemployed. The concentration of both unemployment and unemployment is heavier amongst the Black and Brown population groups than amongst the Whites. In 1978, for the four month period May to August, the official estimate of the average rate of unemployment amongst Blacks and Coloureds in South Africa was 10 per cent of the respective workforces. The equivalent figure for the White workforce was one per cent. The unemployment rate is significantly higher amongst women than men, averaging for the Black and Coloured groups 17,7 per cent, as against 6,7 per cent for men. Unemployment is also higher amongst the young age groups – those under 30 years of age.

Underemployment is prevalent amongst the African group and, indeed, has been estimated by Charles Simpkins to be greater than the unemployment amongst them. (Simpkins: 1978). African underemployment is concentrated mainly in the domestic service sector and in subsistence agriculture in the African homeland areas, although there is evidence that there is some surplus labour on White farms.

More serious than the absolute level of unemployment and underemployment is the fact that a number of researchers, such as Simpkins and Knight, have argued that there are indications that the two together are growing over time, rather than declining, as the South African economy expands. This means that although the people who have jobs will probably enjoy rising living standards, an increasing number of South Africans, mostly Blacks, will be excluded from an opportunity to share in the growing wealth of the country. (Simpkins: 1978, Knight: 1977)

Conclusion: Labour and Economic Development – An Overview

The three outstanding characteristics of the present South African labour market can be drawn from the discussion in this chapter so far. Firstly, the major proportion of the labour force is made up of members of the African population group. Secondly, the labour skills in the economy are largely monopolized by the White workforce. Finally, and indeed one might argue, almost inevitably, in view of the first two characteristics, there is a substantial gap between the average wages earned by White workers and those earned by Blacks. The view that the White wage advantage can be explained solely in terms of the relative scarcity of Whites, coupled with their superior education and training is, however, too simplistic.

In the early twentieth century South Africa's most pressing social problem was the growing numbers of almost destitute and largely uneducated Whites, who found it virtually impossible to obtain a job that would enable them to live amongst the rest of their fellow Whites. Consequently, one cannot simply explain the present labour market divisions in terms of the Whites' superior skills; one also has to explain how this difference in skill differentials itself came to have such a marked racial bias, since in the early stages of the labour market development, the unskilled labour force comprised both Blacks and Whites. An adequate explanation of the existence of the present South African labour market structures has to be sought in the realms of the evolution of the South African economy.

Differences in the way in which the population groups left the land to join the growing industrial workforce, differences in the extent of their access to political power and the manner in which the demand for labour has changed as the economy has become increasingly sophisticated, have all, in their own way, influenced the attainment of the present situation. The roots of the present labour market structure were planted in the early days of the first exploitation of minerals, with the growth of the migrant labour system, the creation of mine labour compounds and the reservation of certain specified tasks on the mines for Whites. These were watered and nurtured by government policies, such as those designed to eliminate the 'poor White' problem, to develop a viable White agricultural community and to ensure racial separatism, and it is to a discussion of these aspects that we turn in the following chapter.

FOUR

The Historical Background to the Racial Segmentation of the Labour Market

INTRODUCTION

Any capitalist economy seeking to grow and industrialize from a predominantly rural base, needs a stable and reasonably cheap workforce. The transition from a primitive economy, whether it is organized on tribal or feudal lines, to a capitalist market economy, essentially involves the separation of the major portion of the population from their dependence on the land, a process that is sometimes called proletarianization. In England the enclosures of the major part of many of the farmlands by the big landowners in order to grow wheat on a larger scale, dispossessed large numbers of peasant farmers of their land holdings. These people drifted into the growing towns and the subsequent industrial revolution and growth of capitalism that it engendered, took place by making use of these dispossessed people.

The South African economy is unusual in that the causes that separated labour from the land, in the early periods of the development of the capitalist economy, differed markedly between the races, as indeed did the extent to which they were separated from the land. Whereas the White working class emerged mainly as a result of the workings of the market system, action by the State was of considerable significance in the creation of a black industrial workforce. The process of the creation of a labour force, separated from the land, has been slow in South Africa and in some senses can be said to be still incomplete, notwithstanding the fact that the economy has now been predominantly capitalistic for over fifty years. The differences in the nature of the process of proletarianization and in the extent of its incompleteness are both reflected in the present structure of South Africa's labour market. They also largely explain why it is that paradoxically, an economy with a large potential labour supply has developed amidst cries of labour scarcity from miners, agriculturalists and industrialists alike.

THE CREATION OF THE WHITE WORKING CLASS

Prior to the discovery and exploitation of minerals, apart from some people who were engaged in trade and commerce, most South Africans – Blacks and Whites alike – made their living from the land. The opening up of the Kimberley diamond diggings, however, significantly changed this emphasis. Diamonds introduced new avenues for making money and the prospect of making what seemed from outside, as an 'easy fortune', attracted many South Africans to the diggings. However, it was not only South Africans who were drawn by the discoveries. The finds occurred in a period of world economic recession and growing unemployment and, as a result, many people from outside the country were also attracted into the area. Initially these people came in largely as prospectors and diggers working on their own account, but subsequently immigrants also came in as highly skilled wage labour, attracted by the very high rates of pay that reflected the rapidly growing demand for labour.

The Role of Immigration

The very significant role that White immigrants have played in South African economic development as members of wage labour, shows that one of the ways that the emerging mining and industrial sectors obtained a stable and competent workforce was by importing it from countries in which the process of the separation of labour from the land had already been largely completed.

Capitalism, White Agriculture and the White Workforce

A second source of supply of White labour for the developing capitalist economy was generated by the interaction between the capitalist sector and the basically feudally organized, White agricultural sector. This relationship had several different aspects to it.

Firstly, prior to the discovery of minerals, White farmers had, like their Black counterparts, been largely oriented towards production for their own and their family's needs. They were content to share their farm lands with their not so fortunate relatives, who lived on the farms as 'bywoners' and had little or no obligation to their landlord. Most farmers also shared their land with Black rent-paying or labour tenants.

'Farming on the half' was a common arrangement in these times. Under this system the Black tenant farmed his land, but paid the White landowner half of the crop that he raised as rent. Labour tenants were similarly obligated, but in this instance the Black farmer paid the White landlord his rent in the form of six months' labour service.

The growth of the mining areas led to a rapid increase in the demand for food and greatly increased the relative profitability of farming for the market. Many White landlords, anxious to reap the benefits from these new openings, sought to evict their 'land-using' tenants in order to free the land to grow crops on a commerical basis for their own account.

The White 'bywoner' was put into a particularly precarious position as a result of this switch, since, unlike the Black tenant, he usually refused to recognize any obligation to his landlord. Not only did his attitude often result in him being the first to go, but once evicted, he had no options open to him but to go to the growing towns and mining areas to seek work. Black tenants who were evicted had other possibilities; they could choose to 'squat' on unoccupied Crown Lands or to move into one of the areas that had been specially demarcated as 'African Reserve' areas. Whilst joining the industrial workforce was thus only one of three alternatives available to Blacks, it was the only possibility open to evicted Whites.

Secondly, the Roman Dutch Law's rules of inheritance, which prevailed in both the Transvaal and the Orange Free State, led to the continual sub-division of farms in those areas to the point that, with the existing farming methods of the time, the sub-divisions no longer represented economically viable, agricultural units. Conditions on these small holdings might well have been significantly improved if new farming techniques had been employed. However, at this time the average levels of education amongst farmers were low and the falling living standards made saving a virtual impossibility. These two factors together ruled out the possibility of the adoption of a farming technology more suitable to the new farm sizes. Living

conditions continued to deteriorate and finally the owners were lef
with no alternative other than that of leaving their rural homes tc
seek a living wage in the towns.

Had the farms that were deserted been bought by other farmers
conditions in the agricultural sector might have begun to improve
However, the remaining farmers were no match for the mining anc
land companies who were eager to acquire land, in the hopes of
finding further mineral deposits. These companies bought up the
farms that came onto the market and gradually accumulated vast
land holdings. The holdings, by and large, lay unproductive
effectively reducing the supply of available farmland, which exacerbated the situation.

Thirdly, the initial development of the early diamond and gold
mines led to the development of a substantial and highly profitable
'transport sector' that was based upon horse, donkey and ox-wagon
motive power. Many thousands of Blacks and Whites alike entered
this field and prospered. The continued development of the modern
capitalistic sector, however, led to demands for the construction of
an adequate railway system. Once this was achieved the railway put
most of these independent transport contractors out of business, as
the power of the ox and the ass proved to be no match for that of the
steam locomotive.

The Impact of the Boer Wars

The wars between the Boers and the British, particularly the second,
also contributed to the creation of a White working class. Farmers
and 'bywoners' both left the land to fight on one or other of the sides
in this war. Some historians, such as Donald Denoon, argued that
many of the 'bywoner' group chose to fight on the side of the British
in the hopes that, should the British be victorious, the Boer
landowners would be dispossessed and that they, the 'bywoners'
would obtain land grants. (Denoon: 1972). Other historians like
Stanley Trapido, however, point out that there is no real evidence to
support the view that the Afrikaner 'bywoner' was any less committed to the republican cause than the land owning, farming class
(Trapido: 1973). What is certain, however, is that in many instances
'the scorched earth' policy adopted by Kitchener in an attempt to
quell Boer guerilla activities, contributed to the growth of the White

urban labour force. Farmers and 'bywoners' alike, often found that they had no homes left to return to after the wars.

The Creation of the White Workforce and the 'Poor White' problem

The combination of all the varied forces that acted upon the relationship between White labour and the land, led to the development of a steady stream of White families, who left the land to start afresh as town dwellers. Exactly how large this stream was, is shown by the fact that, whereas in 1890, only 36 per cent of Whites lived in South African towns; by 1904 more than half (53 per cent) were urban residents. By 1921 this percentage had increased further and stood at 56 per cent.

So successful were these forces in generating a supply of White labour for the growing mining, industrial and commercial sectors of the economy, that there was little or no evidence that the supply was in any way inadequate, despite the growing demand over this period. Indeed, instructions given to would-be immigrants in *S. W. Silver and Company's Handbook to South Africa,* implied that, as early as 1891, there were already more Whites seeking work in the towns and the mining areas than there were acceptable jobs. Unemployment amongst Whites, particularly those with little education and virtually no industrial workforce experience, who were predominantly Afrikaans-speaking, increased throughout the first quarter of the twentieth century.

This growing unemployment, together with the poverty, social dislocation and misery that it caused, became South Africa's major social problem in these early years. The problem was intensified by the fact that increasing numbers of Africans were also entering the growing areas and were in competition with these Whites for the jobs that required little or no training. As the Blacks were largely migrant workers who had left their families behind in the Black rural areas, they were prepared to accept the jobs at a wage that was not only lower than the wage needed to sustain a 'White way of life', but also, in many instances, was too low to enable them to maintain both themselves and their family over any substantial period of time on the receipts from their wage labour alone.

The 'Poor White Problem', as it became to be known, grew steadily worse throughout the first quarter of the twentieth century.

It was only ameliorated over a number of years as a result of determined State action, designed both to create jobs for these people and to protect them from wage competition by Blacks. The problem was not effectively eliminated until the boom period of the 1960s. The means by which this problem was overcome will be discussed more fully when we consider how it was that the White labour force came to monopolize the elite positions in South Africa's job hierarchy. This will be done later in this chapter when we have discussed the creation of the black workforce.

THE CREATION OF THE BLACK WORKING CLASS

One of the rather surprising characteristics of South African economic development is the fact that, although it took place in a region in which there were always large numbers of relatively 'underemployed' Blacks, there is evidence that suggests that, in the early days, the supply of Black labour was insufficient to meet even the growing demands of the colonist farmers. It has been argued by a number of economists studying this phenomenon, notably Sheila van der Horst and W. Hutt, that it was a shortage at a particular price, and that had the settlers been prepared to offer higher wages, the normal market process would have generated an adequate supply of Black labour in the same manner as it did White. (Van der Horst: 1971, Hutt: 1964). This may well be so, but it leads on to an even more interesting question: Why was it that employers did not offer higher wages to Africans? Why did they choose instead to try to use the political machine to alter the conditions underlying the supply of Black labour to the point at which an adequate supply was forthcoming at the going wage rates?

These are difficult questions to answer in an entirely satisfactory manner, but there is little doubt that a number of factors all had some bearing upon this issue. In the first instance it must be remembered that South Africa was, prior to the mineral discoveries, essentially an agricultural country. Secondly, in the late nineteenth century, largely as a result of the outcome of a series of wars between the settlers who were seeking to expand their land holdings, and the African tribes who sought to protect the land they held, the African population living in the region that was to become South Africa, lived either on farms owned by Whites (as squatters, labour tenants or farmers on the half), in 'locations', areas set aside for their exclusive use, or in areas that were traditionally accepted as being under their control – even if this acceptance was somewhat loosely interpreted at times! These two factors, the dominant role played by agriculture and the extent of the African population's access to land, resulted in a situation in which, throughout this early period, average wage rates were low.

The Role of the Rural Areas in Determining the African Wage Rate

The demand by Africans for regular work amongst the White population was, prior to the opening up of the mining areas, generally limited to that by members of refugee bands who for one reason or another, had been evicted from the areas under African tribal control. All the other work provided by the African group in these early days, was done either on the basis of labour conscription by the colonial authorities, by Africans who were resident on White farms as labour tenants, or by voluntary migrants from the tribally controlled areas of Southern Africa. The labour conscripts worked for low wages and sometimes for no wages at all, and were allocated to the workbands by decree from their tribal authority. Likewise both the labour tenants and the rural-urban tribal migrants also worked for wage rates below the minimum subsistence level, although they did so for substantially different reasons. Africans living in the White owned farming areas were either rent-paying squatters, farmers on the half or labour tenants. The first two of these groups had no formal labour obligation to their landlord and paid their rent either in cash, largely earned from the sale of produce, or in the form of a half share of the output produced by them from the land they were leasing. Members of the third group, however, were bound to labour for six months on their landlord's farm in return for the right to settle, grow crops and graze their animals. These labourers received very low cash wages, as the farmer viewed the earnings that they made from his land during the other six months of the year, as part of his wage payment.

The men who came to seek work from the tribal areas also accepted very low wage rates. These migrants did not bring their families with them when they left the tribal areas to seek work amongst the White settlers and moreover, their families were not dependent upon the wages earned by them for their survival. Consequently such men tended to be target workers, who came into the area to earn sufficient cash to purchase goods that they wanted, that were not available in the tribal economy. Once they had earned sufficient to achieve their ends, the migrant workers returned to their families. These conditions explain why it was that a migrant would and, indeed, did accept a cash wage that was below the minimum level that would have been needed to maintain both himself and his family. He viewed his wage income only as a supplement to his major form of subsistence which was farming in the tribal areas.

The rural areas, both those under White and Black control, in an important sense, therefore, actually subsidized the labour costs in the growing urban areas, as it was the rural ties of both the migrant and the farm labourer that enabled the level of cash wage payments to be so low. When minerals were discovered the low wage structure that had persisted in the predominantly feudalistic agricultural sector and the small urban economies was carried over into the emerging capitalist economy.

The State and the Supply of Black Labour

A second important set of factors that had a bearing on the way in which an adequate supply of Black labour was generated, were the prevailing attitudes of the White settlers at the time. Prior to the mineral era, colonists had experienced periods in which there had been substantial shortages of labour and, as a result of these shortages, they had put pressure on the authorities to take action to alleviate the situation. In the Colony of Natal, for example, during the 1850s the colonists, in an attempt to increase the supply of farm labour, canvassed for the breaking up of the larger African locations that had been set up earlier by Sir Theophilus Shepstone, for an increase in the hut tax paid by Africans and for the exemption from hut tax for Africans who lived on White farms. They were largely unsuccessful in their efforts, but an ordinance was passed which attempted to limit the numbers of African squatters on the Crown Lands in Natal and in 1874 the hut tax was increased. Similar examples of official actions in the labour market can be found throughout the early history of both the Cape and the Trekker

Republics. Indeed, an infant system of labour bureaux was in operation in British Kaffraria during this period.

As a result of these early experiences the White community was slowly building up a set of values in which it was considered 'normal' that the State, rather than the private sector, should assume responsibility for ensuring an adequate supply of labour. To White South Africans, therefore, it seemed in no way incongruous that the period 1860–1924 should be one in which the role of the State in the labour market became increasingly significant.

The Mining Industry and the Supply of Black Labour

The second factor leading to the increase in the role played by the State in the generation of an adequate supply of Black labour was the cost structure in the growing mining industries. In a free enterprise economy for a given level of labour productivity measured in terms of the average output per worker, the lower the share of that output that is paid to labour, the higher is the share remaining for profits after the other costs of production have been deducted. Any increases in wage rates, therefore, have a very significant impact on profit earnings, unless the firm paying the increases manages to recoup some or all of its increased costs through increased product prices. This was a particularly important element shaping the actions of the early mining capitalists. Wages formed a high proportion of their costs of production and because they sold their gold on the world market at a virtually fixed price and so were not able to pass on increases in their costs of production, any increased labour costs reduced profit levels. Their profit position was limited still further by their heavy reliance upon foreign capital sources. This meant that the mines paid interest rates on their borrowed capital that were determined by the supply and demand conditions on the world money markets, which further constrained the opportunities to control their costs of production.

Unable as these early mining capitalists were to control either the selling price of their products, or the cost of their investment capital, it is not surprising that they sought to make use of every measure that they could command to prevent wage costs from rising. They joined forces with other interest groups and made use of their growing political muscle to influence the authorities. This resulted in a number of moves which improved the labour supply position, such as the passing of the Glen Gray Act in 1894, which imposed a 10/- tax on African men living in the district. Cecil Rhodes made no bones about the labour supply aspect of this Act, when he introduced it into the Cape Parliament. He spoke of 'the gentle stimulation of the labour tax' and argued that the tax would 'remove them [the African] from that life of sloth and laziness and . . . teach them the dignity of labour and make them contribute to the prosperity of the State and give some return for our wise and good government'.

Other actions by the authorities, aimed at improving the supply of labour in these early years were the importation of indentured Indian labour for work on the Natal sugar cane plantations in the latter half of the nineteenth century and the importation of Chinese labour for the gold mines by Milner just after the turn of the century. Apart from pressurizing the authorities to take action on the labour supply question, the mine owners also combined together to set up a system of recruiting African labour to work on the mines and extended the area from which such labour was recruited beyond the borders of South Africa to the regions now Mozambique and Malawi.

The Impact on the Labour Supply Position

Despite the variety of different approaches made by the authorities to the problem of increasing the supply of African labour over the period from 1860–1925, researchers such as van der Horst and Bundy, argue that these initial attempts of the authorities, particularly those based on the imposition of taxes or on increased rents, were largely unsuccessful. Africans over this period were able to meet the additional cash demands from the proceeds of the sales of produce. The growth of the mining areas offered profitable openings to African farmers, as well as to the Whites and both Bundy and van der Horst quote evidence which suggests that over the period between 1870–86, some African peasant farmers seemed to adapt to the improved market opportunities more quickly than the majority of their White counterparts. (Van der Horst 1971, Bundy 1972)

Over the period 1886–1913, however, the situation changed significantly, largely as a result of the combined influences of a number of factors. Firstly, not all African farmers were equally successful and those who failed sought wage labour amongst the Whites as a means of earning the cash needed to meet the obligations put on them by the White authorities. Secondly, the expansion of the areas under the control of the Whites, coupled with the natural population growth of the Blacks, led to increasing land hunger amongst the latter. Young men could no longer simply obtain a land grant from their tribal chief, but frequently had to wait until the death of a tribal elder freed the land they sought. Until they were able to obtain a land grant these young men formed part of a potential labour force for the growing modern economy.

The Market's Role in the Creation of the Black Workforce

The market system itself through the impact that it had on the forces operating on the boundaries between the growing capitalistic mining sector and White agriculture, in many instances affected the Black population in the same way as it did the White, with similar results.

The growth of the demand for foodstuffs in the mining towns and the increased profitability of agriculture led to the White farmers evicting, not only their White 'bywoner' relations, but also many of their Black squatters and rent-paying tenants. In addition, at this time, the erection of 'jackal proof' fencing closed off access to large areas of farm land and denied a way of life to a group of Black nomadic farmers who had previously wandered from farm to farm with their small herds. These groups became virtually destitute and in many instances nomads, evicted farm tenants and squatters alike sought their continued survival through participation in the wage labour system.

The population pressure on African land continued and like the White farmers, many Africans, through a lack of knowledge and capital, failed to adapt their farming methods to the changing conditions. Agricultural conditions in many African controlled rural areas started to decline and living levels were supplemented by the wages earned from short term work in the White economy. In many instances, the absence of the able-bodied men from these areas, away as migrant workers, undermined the agricultural potential of the Black farming regions still further, increasing the reliance of the community on the proceeds from migrant labour. This cycle leading from low productivity – to low farm incomes – to migrant labour – to still lower productivity and lower farm incomes, continued; and when coupled with increasing legislation that limited the access of Africans (particularly those who were not seeking work) to White areas, entrenched the system of migrant labour so characteristic of the modern South African economy.

Amongst the Africans, however, it was not only the farmers who failed who left the land; in some instances, particularly in the region of central Natal, successful African farmers were forced off the land by their White landlords who sought to farm the land themselves. The extent of the increase in demand for farmland by Whites is illustrated by the progress of events in Natal over this period. In 1875 Whites farmed 2 million acres, by 1893 this figure had nearly doubled and stood at 5,8 million acres and by 1904 Whites were farming over 7 million acres.

The position of the African farmers was further undermined by the severe rindepest outbreak which swept South Africa in 1896 and 1897. Both Black and White farmers suffered significant losses. In certain areas of Transkei Black stock losses were as high as 90 per cent and in a community which stored its wealth in the form of cattle holdings, this was a major economic catastrophe.

The growth of the railway system, which accompanied the early development of South Africa's modern economy, favoured the White farmers. It is a notable feature of South Africa's economic geography that the railways are distinguished by their absence in African rural areas. The lack of access to the railway system put the Black farmer at a severe economic disadvantage, as it was very much more difficult for him to get his produce to the growing markets of the Rand and Kimberley than it was for many of his White competitors.

Finally, towards the end of the fifty-year period following the initial discovery of diamonds, the conditions governing African access to land were significantly altered. In 1913 the government of the newly formed Union of South Africa passed 'The Native Land Act'. This act set out certain specified land areas, totalling just over nine million hectares, for the exclusive use of Africans, and prohibited the sale of land outside these areas to Africans, apart from land included in the 5–8 million hectares that were added as 'released areas' by the Bantu Land and Trust Act of 1936. The areas set out in the 1913 Act were already occupied by Africans and the effect of this legislation was to limit their rights to land only to those specified areas. Freezing the quantity of available land meant that, with continued population growth, agricultural conditions were virtually certain to deteriorate. African survival was likely to become increasingly dependent upon the earnings from wage labour, which indeed proved to be the case.

The 1913 Land Act also ended both the systems of squatting and share cropping by Africans on White farms, reducing both groups to the status of labour tenants. Some Africans affected by this legislation chose to resettle in the African areas, some to remain as labour tenants on the White farms, whilst others entered the growing industrial workforce. The ultimate effect of the Land Act was to increase the supply of African labour to mining, industry and agriculture.

THE RISE OF THE WHITE LABOUR ELITE

The conditions discussed earlier greatly increased the reliance of both Blacks and Whites on the earnings they could get from wage labour and generated a steady flow of labour to the growing industrial areas. This early labour market already exhibited the main characteristics of the present situation; skills were largely monopolized by the Whites, particularly the White immigrants who had been specially recruited for the mining industry and the wages paid to Whites were typically between four and ten times higher than those paid to the Black migrant workers. (Van der Horst: 1971)

There was, however, an element that was present in this early society that might have eventually eroded this initial labour market structure, namely the growing number of uneducated, poor Whites, who were being forced out of the rural areas into the towns. Had the market systems alone been left to solve this problem, the outcome, in all probability, would have been the creation of a multi-racial labouring class. However, this was not to be. The course of events in South Africa that accompanied the growth of the Trade Union movement and the consequent intensification of the economic class struggle during the early part of the twentieth century, resulted ultimately in State intervention. This intervention provided a solution to the Poor White Problem, which reduced the degree of competition between blacks and Whites in the labour market rather than allowing it to take its course. The role played by the franchise was to prove crucial in this struggle.

Some Explanations of White Labour Market Supremacy

There have been a number of explanations of the rise of the White labour élite, the best known of which are those offered by the economists Hobart Houghton and Horwitz. Hobart Houghton had this to say:

> The initial disparity between skilled and unskilled rates was the natural reflection of the relative supply and demand situations and was caused by the greater scarcity of skilled workers in an underdeveloped economy. But the distinction between skilled and unskilled soon became to be more or less identified with the distinction between the races and the operation of the market forces soon came in some measure to be replaced by the convention that the White man's wage was five to ten times the wage of a Black man. This convention was reinforced by Trade Union pressure for the White workers were more articulate and better organized than the Black. (Hobart Houghton: 1964, p. 140)

This reasoning, whilst it clearly covers most of the important relevant factors, does not offer an adequate explanation of the process that transformed the growing class of poor Whites, characteristic of the first quarter of the twentieth century, into the educated and highly paid workforce of the present time. Nor does it offer an adequate explanation of the persistence, over time, of the racial skill monopoly in South Africa.

Horwitz sought his explanation of the rise of White labour market elitism in the realms of the political struggle. He argued that unlike the emerging black workforce, the White group had the franchise and that they used this power to entrench their position even though, by doing so, they were seeking political institutions that would retard South Africa's future development. He saw South Africa's economic history as essentially being one of conflict between the dictates of the economy, driven by the needs of the growing capitalist system and the 'polity', whose actions were motivated largely by the ideologies of White supremacy and Afrikaner Nationalism. (Horwitz: 1968)

A third group of South African analysts, loosely termed 'the Neo Marxist School' argue forcefully that neither of these views is correct. They see the first of these explanations, that of Hobart

Houghton, as being too limited and economistic. With respect to Horwitz, they argue that whilst certainly both the economy and the polity have played their role in the creation of White supremacy, it is manifestly incorrect to see these two influences as being in any way in opposition to one another. This school argues that the expanding capitalist sector of the South African economy has used the polity to reinforce the position of both the capitalist class and capitalism in general, and further that the creation of a 'White worker élite' can be seen in terms of being almost a 'by-product' from this fusion of the economy and polity. (Davies: 1977, Kaplan: 1974). This view is also too simplistic, since whilst there is no doubt that the political power of the White worker stood him in good stead *vis-à-vis* the un-enfranchised Black, it should not be thought that White labour gained economic power at the expense of the capitalist class easily. It was in fact the result of a long and frequently 'bloody' battle waged between the White workforce on the one hand and the mining capitalists and the State on the other.

THE COURSE OF THE CLASS STRUGGLE BETWEEN WHITE LABOUR AND CAPITAL

Chinese Labour and the Colour Bar Legislation

The foundations for the creation of a White labour élite were laid in the early days of the mining industry and were initially based upon the Black/White skill differential. Time, however, started to erode this racial differential. Africans began to acquire skills on the mines and the numbers of uneducated and unskilled Whites drifting into the mining areas increased.

The advent of the second Boer War and the decision by the mining capitalists after the war to reduce African wage rates, severely disrupted the supply of African labour to the mining industry. The mining industry turned to the State to find a solution to this problem and Lord Milner, the British High Commissioner, anxious to improve the economic circumstances of the war-ravaged Transvaal, acceded to the requests from the industry to import Chinese labourers to work on the gold mines. White labour's price for their support of this policy was the introduction of the first legally sanctioned colour bar. This took the form of a schedule, which was attached to the Transvaal Labour Importation Ordinance and which set out the posts for which the Chinese labourers could be recruited, specifically debarring them from all skilled occupations. Although blasting on the mines had been restricted to Whites for some time prior to the ordinance, there were no other legal limitations on African access to jobs before this.

The Trade Union movement in South Africa also began to develop after the Boer War. The Transvaal Mine Workers Union was formed in 1902 and rapidly came into conflict with the interests of the mining entrepreneurs, who were, by and large, interested in lowering their average unit labour costs by replacing the high cost White labour with lower cost African or Chinese labour. There was, however, one mine manager, F. S. Cresswell, who was later to become the Minister of Labour, who argued that the solution to the mines' labour problem lay in running with 'an all White' labour force. He persuaded his mine owners to allow him to experiment on the Village Main Reef mine, but he failed to obtain the support of the other White miners, who objected to the employment of fellow Whites in the menial tasks that they had grown accustomed to seeing performed by Africans.

Strike Action by White Labour

Between the years 1907 and 1922, the year of the Rand Rebellion, there was a series of clashes between the mine owners and their White workforce. One analyst, Edward Roux, has commented: 'It was the traditional class struggle intensified and distorted by the peculiar racial and social conditions of South Africa.' (Roux: 1964). The major evident distortion, was the cleavage that was apparent between the black and White sections of the workforce. Strike action was undertaken on a number of occasions over this period by both black and White workers. However, notwithstanding the fact that both formed part of the same economic class, only on one occasion, in the 1913 strike on the New Kleinfontein mine, did black and White workers co-operate with one another and strike together.

The lack of co-operation, which was probably largely due to the attitudes of early White labour leaders such as Cresswell, resulted in employers being able to use black 'scabbers' to break White strikes and White 'blacklegs' to break black strikes. All the strikes by blacks and Whites alike were lost over this period, but the degree of government intervention needed to get the strikers back to work increased in strength and ferocity, until it culminated in the 'bloody' events of the Rand Rebellion in 1922.

The 1922 strike was precipitated by an announcement from the Chamber of Mines that they intended to repudiate an earlier agreement with White labour, the *status quo* agreement, which had fixed the ratio of black to White miners and, as a result of this repudiation, to lay off 2 000 White miners. Initially amongst the strikers there were three lines of thought – the first from a group oriented towards labour reform, the second from a group known as the Council of Action, whose interests lay in wide-spread political change and who included members of the Communist Party and finally those of 'The Commandos', bodies of strikers organized along similar lines to the Trekker Commandos, who were mainly Afrikaans speaking and who maintained close links with the rural areas. This latter group was actively anti-black in sentiment. The reformist group was largely swept aside by an alliance between the Council for Action and the Commandos, which lead to the rallying call of the Communist Party being rather oddly adapted to 'Workers of the world unite and fight for a White South Africa'. (Roux: 1964)

The strike lasted eight weeks and was followed by a two week armed rebellion. The Smuts Government finally subdued both the strike and the rebellion by a substantial show of force and with a considerable loss of life. Four of the leaders were tried and sentenced to death and went to the gallows singing 'The Red Flag'. It was at this point that the role of the franchise was to prove crucial.

Political Power and White Labour Supremacy

After an earlier strike in 1914 that was also suppressed by the government with the use of force, the Labour Party succeeded in securing a majority in the Transvaal Provincial Council with the aid of the votes of the White mine workers. The swing away from the Botha-Smuts Government continued and their chances in the 1915 general election looked relatively thin. However, the advent of the first World War enabled them to stage a 'khaki election' based upon a call to patriotism and thereby to defeat Labour soundly. In 1924, however, as Roux has pointed out, the situation was different:

> This time there was no war and there could be no lucky 'khaki election' to save Smuts and the mine owners from the Nemesis of defeat at the polls. (Roux: 1964, p. 147)

Smuts paid dearly for his suppression of the 1922 rebellion, as the 1924 election saw an alliance between White labour and Afrikaner agriculture come to power, which ended the political dominance of mining capital in South Africa and saw the start of the legal entrenchment of the White labour policy. The White workers had finally succeeded in transforming defeat on the workshop floor, into victory through the polling station. White labours' price for joining hands with Afrikaner Nationalism, was the entrenchment of the advantageous position of White labour, which meant State action to create jobs to eliminate the Poor White Problem. As a result of the alliance, the PACT government introduced three labour acts, which formed the foundation of the present structure of South Africa's labour legislation; the Industrial Conciliation Act, No. 11 of 1924, the Wages Act, No. 27 of 1925 and the Mines and Works Amendment Act, No. 25 of 1926. These three acts together legally entrenched the concept of White labour supremacy.

This government also introduced the 'civilized labour policy' effectively reserving certain public sector jobs for Whites only and giving preferential treatment to those industries employing a high percentage of 'civilized labour'. This part of the overall strategy was specifically aimed at ameliorating the economic position of the Poor White and resulted in the dismissal of a large number of blacks. Had black workers also held the franchise, there is little doubt that White labour would have been unsuccessful in its attempts to reconstitute itself as a labour aristocracy. It is also not at all certain that White labour would have succeeded in persuading the capitalist class to see them as separate from the black, had they not managed to turn economic defeat in the labour market into political success at the polls. The fact that White labour held the vote and black labour did not and indeed still does not, has undoubtedly helped to shape the present structure of South Africa's labour market.

The long term interest of South Africa's capitalist class may in fact have been well served by the dichotomization of the labour supply on racial lines. Kaplan has argued that the emerging South African capitalist class, whose activities centred mainly on local manufacturing, together with the White farming class, were prepared to pay the price of White entrenchment in return for the votes of the White labour movement. He argued that once it was possible to break the political hegemony of the mining capitalists, part of the large surplus earned by the mines could be, and indeed was diverted by the government to develop agriculture and to foster local industry. (Kaplan: 1974)

Even the mining industry gained in the long run as these events enabled them to treat the two elements in their workforce, African and White, in entirely different fashions, related to the conditions that governed their labour supply. Whilst additional White labour was attracted by increasing White wage rates, additional Black labour was obtained by improving the system of labour recruitment and by extending the geographical area from which such labour was drawn.

The Consolidation of the Situation – Legislation

In terms of the discussion in this chapter, it is apparent that the structures leading to the characteristics of the present labour situation had virtually all been established before the outbreak of the second World War. Consequently they can in no way be attributed to the policy of 'apartheid' masterminded by Dr. Verwoerd and introduced by the Nationalist government after its return to power in the 1948 general election. However, what can be attributed to the policies followed after 1948 is the extent to which the position of White labour was consolidated, by the amendments that were made to the labour legislation and the extent to which the institutions controlling the black labour supply were streamlined to improve their efficiency.

FIVE

Capital Accumulation and Economic Growth

THE ROLE OF CAPITAL IN ECONOMIC GROWTH

'Capital' is the composite name given by economists to all the 'man made' products that are used to produce other goods and services in the production process.

Viewed in this light it becomes obvious that a large variety of different commodities will fall into the category of 'capital'. Capital goods will include not only the obvious items such as plant and machinery and buildings, but also stocks of foodstuffs to feed workers engaged in time consuming production processes and expenditures on such items as schools, technical colleges and universities, in so far as the use of these training facilities increases the productivity of workers. The degree of heterogeneity found amongst the goods classed together as capital, makes it difficult to identify clearly exactly which goods comprise capital and to value them.

Broadly speaking, one could classify a nation's capital into three categories, productive physical capital, the capital embodied in people and social overhead capital. Productive physical capital comprises the machinery, equipment and buildings that are used in the production process, together with the stock of inputs on hand. Human capital, as the capital that is embodied in people is usually called, consists of the increased efficiency of a person that results from his education and training. Finally, social overhead capital consists of the capital in an economy that may not contribute directly or exclusively to production, but does improve the quality of life and includes roads, railways, power networks, schools, hospitals and the like.

Historically, economic development, measured in terms of increasing output or increasing output per head, has been accompanied by

78

the increasing accumulation of capital. In general terms, capital accumulation contributes to the growth of the economy's output in two ways: firstly, providing there are adequate supplies of the other factors of production available, it enables the process of *capital widening* to take place, i.e. it makes it possible to produce more of the goods and services that are already on the market. For example, one might duplicate an oil refinery or a clothing factory that is already in existence. Secondly, capital accumulation may enable an economy to enjoy the benefits from increasing specialization, through the process of *capital deepening*. In this case the additional capital is used not to build more of what is already in existence, but instead to introduce new and more capital intensive methods of production, which ultimately result in a higher output per man employed.

Broadly speaking, the process of capital widening is usually accompanied by a relatively rapid increase in the number of new jobs that are created in the economy and with slow or non-existent increases in both the average level of output per man (labour productivity) and the average wage rate paid. Capital deepening, on the other hand, generally results in a fairly rapid rise in labour productivity and in the average wages paid in the industry in which it takes place, and a much slower rate of growth of employment. Indeed, in some instances increasing mechanization may actually be accompanied by a fall in the level of employment. These differences are significant in the context of a growing economy, since they imply different rates of growth in job opportunities and in the standards of living of those employed. Consequently, the process of capital accumulation itself is one factor that determines the nature of the overall growth path of an economy through time.

The impact of the accumulation process may be increased or dampened by the relative rate of growth of the labour force. Again, as a generalization, in an economy like the South African one, in which economic growth has taken place with substantial amounts of surplus labour, capital widening will result in a growth process in which more and more people can share in the benefits. Capital deeping, on the other hand, favours those who are already employed and will act to widen the gap in the living standards of those who are part of the industrialized modern workforce and those who are not.

The specific impact that investment has on an economy over a particular period of time will also be significantly affected by a number of other things, such as the spatial allocation of the investment, the nature of the industries in which it is taking place, the size of the firms involved, the characteristics of the owners of the firms, the composition and availability of the other factors of production and in some instances, by the nature of the markets on which the final products are sold. As a result, if one really wants to know the impact that capital accumulation has had on a specific economy, one has to take a disaggregated view and consider the different aspects of the process separately.

Financing Increases in the National Capital

The accumulation of capital has a definite cost. The current output of a nation can either be used to satisfy the present needs and desires of its citizens or it can be set aside to provide for their future needs. If one diverts part of the present output to the production of capital goods, one is adding to the productive capacity of an economy in the future. However, the cost of creating more goods in the future is the production of less goods for consumption in the present time. Since investment carries a real cost, the decision to undertake it should be based on the same criteria as those applied to any other economic decision, namely, investment is only worth undertaking providing the benefits (the discounted stream of future consumption), are greater than the costs, those of foregoing present consumption.

The decision to transfer resources from present consumption to future consumption is known as saving and additions to the capital stock are only possible as a result of these savings decisions. If one takes the world as a whole, the amount of resources that can be transferred to the production of capital goods is limited to the amount of such resources that is not being used to produce consumer goods. However, any one economy can invest more than it saves over a particular period of time, if it is fortunate enough to attract into it the savings of the people, firms or governments of other countries.

CAPITAL ACCUMULATION IN SOUTH AFRICA

The Extent

A consistent set of estimates of South Africa's national fixed capital is only available for the period from 1946. Consequently for the earlier periods one is forced to make use of 'indicators' of capital accumulation, such as the value of plant and machinery in the manufacturing industry, or miles of road constructed. Table 5.1 contains a set of such indicators and shows the patterns that have occurred in their movements in South Africa for the periods 1919–50 and 1950–76.

Table 5.1

CAPITAL ACCUMULATION INDICATORS 1919–1950–1976

Indicator	Year			Average Annual Growth Rate	
	1919	1950	1976	1919–1950	1950–1976
Value of Machinery and Equipment in Manufacturing (R 000)	16 826	209 494	2 145 848 (1972)	8,8	10,2 (1950–1972)
Value of Machinery and Equipment used to generate Electricity, Gas and Steam (R 000)	7 716	70 769	1 513 971	7,7	12,5
Consumption of Electricity per Head (kwh)	167	733	2 903	5,1	5,4
Kilometres of Road	75 795	141 588	185 124	2,1	1,0
Number of Vehicle Licences	40 000	551 363	3 201 718	9,1	7,0
Number of Commercial Vehicles Licenced	905	110 086	761 253	17,4	7,7
Kilometres of Rail	15 182	21 239	21 726	1,1	–
Number of Locomotives	1 508	2 571	9 756	1,8	5,3
Thousands of Items of Mail Posted	216 656	643 415	1 550 833	3,7	3,4

SOURCE: *South African Statistics 1978* and *Union Statistics for Fifty Years.*

Although the indicators in the Table were partly selected for their availability, they are nevertheless instructive. The first indicator (the value of machinery and equipment in manufacturing) is a good surrogate for the amount of investment being diverted to generate increasing levels of industrialization. The second and third indicators, both of which relate to the production and consumption of energy, are reasonable surrogates for the extent of the usage of modern technology within the economy. The indicators relating to the growth of the transport system speak for themselves, whilst the last indicator (the number of items of mail posted) is relevant as a surrogate for the growth of the communication system; the level of education and the level of business activity.

There are two interesting aspects to the data in Table 5.1; the first of these is the fact that the behaviour of the indicators – value c machinery in manufacturing, value of machinery used to generat power, per capita electricity consumption, number of vehicle licenced, and number of items posted, support the hypothesis tha the South African economy has become increasingly sophisticate throughout this period of its development. Not only have all thes indicators grown rapidly over the period as a whole, but the rate c growth for the latter 26 year period was higher than that in the forme period in the case of the two energy components.

The second aspect of interest is the behaviour of the two indicator of social overhead capital, namely, miles of road and miles of rai both of which have extremely low growth rates throughout the sixt year period. This illustrates why it is that economies face suc massive capital demands in the early phases of their development Development in South Africa could not have taken place without th well established transport network that was, in fact, largely con structed prior to the period covered in the Table. However, once thi network was built, it was possible to use it increasingly intensively a the economy developed, and consequently little further investment i this type of social infra-structure was needed.

The Composition of South Africa's Fixed Capital Stock

According to the estimates that have been made, the value of South Africa's fixed capital stock at current prices was just over R38 billion in 1972; two and a half times greater than the value of production i South Africa in that year. (De Jager: 1973). In other words, for every R100 worth of output produced, R250 worth of fixed capital stock was needed. Machinery and equipment accounted for thirteen pe cent of the fixed capital; approximately half of which was employed in the manufacturing sector. Construction works such as roads, bridges, dams and irrigation projects made up 37 per cent of the fixed capital, transport equipment a further 7 per cent, whilst the balance of 43 per cent comprised buildings; roughly half of which were residential. (De Jager: 1973)

Over the twenty-six year period for which there is a composite estimate of the value and nature of South Africa's national capital (1946–72), it seems that the rate of accumulation of machinery and equipment was slightly faster than that of the other capital assets.

Machinery and equipment grew at an average yearly rate of 7 per cent in real terms, as against the averages for transport and buildings of 6 per cent and for construction work of 5 per cent. The relatively more rapid growth of machinery may be an indicator of a tendency within the economy to replace men with machines. However, one cannot be sure of this until one has compared the rates of growth of employment with those of investment in plant and machinery in the different sectors of the economy. Unfortunately, this data is not available for the economy as a whole, but can be obtained for selected sectors, in particular agriculture, manufacturing and mining, and consequently this aspect will be discussed in the chapters that deal specifically with these sectors.

THE OWNERSHIP OF SOUTH AFRICA'S FIXED CAPITAL STOCK

The Public vs. The Private Sector

Largely as a result of the very heavy capital demands made by the provision of the social infrastructure in an economy, the percentage of the capital stock owned by the public sector is usually considerably greater than the proportion of the total output that is produced by the sector.

Table 5.2

THE CONTROL OF SOUTH AFRICA'S FIXED CAPITAL STOCK

Year	*Percentage Capital Stock in the Hands of*		
	The Public Authorities	*The Public Corporations*	*Private Enterprises*
1946	46,0	3,0	51,0
1960	44,0	5,0	51,0
1972	47,0	7,0	46,0
1979	45,0	13,0	42,0

SOURCE: B. L. de Jager (1973). *Quarterly Bulletin of the South African Reserve Bank.*

The data in Table 5.2 show that the South African economy is no exception, approximately half of the capital stock has been under the control of the public sector throughout the thirty-three-year period covered in the table and the public sector share has shown a tendency to increase, mostly due to the increasingly important role played by the massive state owned iron and steel (ISCOR) and oil from coal (SASOL) projects over this period.

The recent increase in the share of the public sector as a whole and of the public corporations in particular is due to a number of factors; firstly, the arms embargo that forced the state to set up local capacity for the production of the country's defence needs which, although it is largely in the hands of the private sector, has had a significant government input through the public corporation, ARMSCOR. Secondly, the decision to decrease the nation's dependence on imported fossil fuels has led to a massive increase in the amount of state investment in the SASOL oil from coal project. Finally, the period 1975–79 has been a period of economic recession in South Africa and private sector investment was in general at a relatively low level over this time.

In 1979, however, the government made a number of statements which suggested that they intended to pull back their activity in the investment field in certain areas. These statements were made in the belief that the public and the private sectors compete with one another for the available investment funds. It was argued by the government advisers, that, in a situation of growing unemployment such as we have in South Africa at present, the private sector would make better use of these funds, since this sector was likely to create more jobs for a given input of capital investment than the public sector. If the government adopts positive measures to implement these views, the share of the public sector in the ownership of the nation's capital may start to decline again in the 1980s.

Foreign vs. Domestic Ownership of South Africa's Capital Stock

Both savings by South African residents (domestic saving), and the use of the savings of people in other countries (foreign capital inflows), have been significant sources of funding for South African capital accumulation.

Historically, South Africa is a country which has attracted large amounts of investment funds from foreign sources, and these date from the early stages of the development of the modern economy.

Although the diamond mines were sufficiently profitable to enable the industry to finance its development largely from its own surplus, the initial development of the gold mining industry required major injections of foreign capital. Frankel estimated that over the period from 1887 to 1934, the development of South Africa's gold mining industry absorbed £200 million, three-fifths of which was provided by foreign capitalists. (Frankel: 1938)

As South Africa's development has proceeded, so she has become increasingly able to provide the means required for her domestic capital formation from local sources. Over the ten-year period 1946–55 the total value of new capital formation in South Africa was R4800 million. Of this amount, 35 per cent was financed from foreign sources, whilst the balance came from within South Africa.

Over the last ten-year period for which data is available, 1966–75, the Republic's dependance upon net capital inflows from abroad appears to have diminished still further. The value of new capital created over this period was just over R21000 million and the funds to finance this expansion came from the following sources: 40 per cent from personal savings, 24 per cent from corporate retained earnings, 20 per cent from taxation, leaving only 17 per cent to come from direct contributions from abroad. The total contribution to South African capital formation over this period made by foreigners, is however, greater than this 17 per cent, as one must not forget that a proportion of the earnings retained by South African companies who have foreign shareholders, must also be considered as foreign capital.

Historically, foreign investors have been most heavily engaged in the mining sector. However, in recent years, foreign capital has gone increasingly into the manufacturing sector of the economy, and in 1973 the census of foreign investment showed that 40 per cent of this investment was to be found in the manufacturing sector and a further 25 per cent in the financial and business service sector, whilst only 15 per cent was still invested in mining.

A further factor that increases the impact that foreign investment has on South African economic development patterns, beyond that suggested by its quantitative value, is that such capital often brings with it access to foreign technology. Although this technology is often highly productive, in some instances its importation is somewhat of a mixed blessing. This is because this technology has largely been developed to suit the relative endowments of the factors of production in the country from which it originates. As the research and development processes that lie behind technological advances are in themselves usually capital intensive, such research tends to take place in countries that have an abundance of capital and are short of labour. This means that the origin of the technology is highly likely to impart a capital-using bias to it.

In a labour abundant economy like South Africa, excessive reliance on foreign technology that has a capital intensive bias can only exacerbate the relative over-supply of labour. In South Africa the link between foreign capital and the use of foreign technology is very much stronger in the manufacturing and business service sectors than it is in the mining sector. This is because South Africa is a major mining country and consequently is one of the major contributors to the technological advances that take place in that sector. As a result new mining technology is far more likely to be suited to South Africa's relative factor endowments than new industrial technology, the bulk of which is imported from the more advanced western countries. (Nattrass and Brown: 1978)

The 1970s have seen significant changes in the role played by foreign capital in South Africa. Not only did the rate at which foreign capital entered South Africa escalate sharply, but the destination and form of the major portion of the capital altered, as can be seen from the data in Table 5.3.

It seems that although historically, the major proportion of foreign capital has been directed towards the private sector of the economy, the most recent past has witnessed a significant shift towards the increased provision of foreign finance for public sector projects. In the years 1956–58 and 1964–66 no foreign capital was used to finance the expansion of the public corporations. In the three years 1974–76, on the other hand, over half of the total inflow of foreign capital was directed to this end. The compensatory movement was a reduction in the proportion of foreign capital inflows going to the private sector. However, so great was the increase in the volume of foreign capital coming into South Africa, that the annual average growth rate of the foreign funds flowing into the private sector was over 13 per cent between 1973 and 1978, despite the fact that the sector became less significant as an ultimate destination of funds.

Table 5.3
THE CHANGING ROLE OF FOREIGN CAPITAL

Destination	Percentage Share of Total Foreign Capital 1978	Annual Average Growth Rate 1973–1978	Three Year Average of					
			1956/58		1964/66		1974/76	
			Capital Inflow R Millions	Percentage of Total	Capital Inflow R Millions	Percentage of Total	Capital Inflow R Millions	Percentage of Total
Private Sector	66,3	13,3	25,3	64,8	43,7	92,3	316,7	33,7
Government and Banking	17,9	26,5	13,7	35,2	3,7	7,7	149,7	15,9
Public Corporations	15,8	28,9	-5,7	–	-2,0	–	47,3	50,4

SOURCES: Reserve Bank *Quarterly Bulletin*, December, 1979. *South Africa's Balance of Payments 1956–1975*, South African Reserve Bank, Pretoria, 1977.

The Sectoral Allocation of South Africa's Capital Stock

In Chapter Two it was pointed out that as the South African economy has advanced and modernized, substantial changes have taken place in its underlying structure. Notably, manufacturing output has become relatively more important in the national total, whilst that of the agricultural sector has concomitantly declined. These changes are reflected in the sectoral patterns of capital accumulation. In fact, because on average the amount of capital investment needed to produce a unit of manufacturing output is greater than that needed to produce an equivalent unit of agricultural output, the structural change in the capital stock is more marked than it is in output.

The data that is relevant to a study of the changing sectoral patterns of capital accumulation is only available for the period 1946–72. However, even over this relatively short time period one can see some change. The relevant data are given in Table 5.4. For example, the relatively more rapid accumulation of capital in the

Table 5.4

THE SOUTH AFRICAN NATIONAL CAPITAL: ITS SECTORAL ALLOCATION 1946, 1960, 1972

Sector	Per Cent of National Capital in Sector			Annual Average Percentage Increase 1946–1972 (in Real Terms)
	1946	1960	1972	
Agriculture	12	10	7	3,6
Mining	8	9	6	4,5
Manufacturing	6	8	9	7,9
Electricity, Gas and Water	5	7	7	6,8
Transport, Storage and Communication	23	21	18	4,8
Other	45	44	51	6,3
Value in Current Prices (R Millions)	3 008	12 262	38 399	5,7

SOURCE: B. L. de Jager: 1973.

manufacturing and power sectors that accompanies the process of industrialization shows very clearly in this table, as indeed does the relative decline in the importance of the agricultural sector.

Not only do the different economic sectors attract capital at different rates as the economy grows and modernizes but, because the technical conditions of production vary significantly between the sectors, they also use the new capital they obtain differently and achieve different final results.

Table 5.5 contrasts the changes that have taken place in the sectoral allocations of capital, labour and output in South Africa over the period between 1946 and 1970.

Table 5.5

CAPITAL ACCUMULATION AND USAGE BY SECTOR

Sector	Average Annual Growth Rate over the Period 1946–1970 in			Capital per Man (Replacement Cost Rands)	Capital per Unit of Output
	Capital Stock	Employment	Output		
Agriculture	3,8	2,6	3,1	965	2,3
Mining	4,9	1,5	5,1	2 169	1,7
Manufacturing	7,9	3,8	7,3	2 735	1,0
Transport and Communication	4,6	2,7	5,2	15 997	4,7

SOURCE: B. L. de Jager 1973 and *South African Statistics, 1978.*

The differences in the use made by the four sectors in the table of the new capital shows very clearly. Transport and Communication is a sector that uses relatively more capital intensive methods of production than the other three. The average cost of creating a job in this sector was nearly six times greater than in Manufacturing. Similarly, the capital output ratio was also very much higher in this sector.

Another interesting feature of the data in the table is the fact that although the average amount of capital required per man in both the mining and manufacturing sectors was more than twice that needed in agriculture, the capital requirements per unit of output in agriculture were higher than those in mining and manufacturing. In general the growth of employment over the period was considerably slower than that of both output and capital stock, which is an indication that the South African economy has moved towards more capital intensive methods of production, at least in so far as these four sectors are concerned.

However, it should be remembered that averages such as those we have been discussing in this chapter can be misleading as they can conceal differing degrees of heterogeneity, which in themselves are economically interesting. Agriculture is an excellent example as we shall see in Chapter 6. South African agriculture consists of two very different segments; the one, dominated by Whites, is based upon private ownership of the means of production and is modern, fairly capital intensive and geared towards commercial farming activities. The other is the domain of the Blacks and is tribally organized, based upon community ownership and oriented towards subsistence production. The use of averages to analyse the economic activities of agriculture conceal this vast divergence.

Differences within the economic sectors will be discussed in the following chapters that deal with the development and contribution made by the sectors themselves. However, it is not only the nature of the sector in which the capital is employed that determines the relationship between capital accumulation and the growth of employment and output; the size of the enterprise itself, in many instances, also appears to influence these relationships and it is to this aspect that we now turn.

The Size of the Firm, Capital Accumulation and Employment Creation

The size of the economic enterprise in which the capital is accumulated may affect the way in which this new capital is used. It is often argued, for example, that small firms use more labour intensive methods of production than large firms and that consequently an injection of capital into a number of small firms will create more employment than a similar injection of the total amount into a large firm.

This argument rests essentially on a belief (well founded on empirical evidence) that capital intensive techniques of production are more productive than labour intensive techniques as they are technically far superior and that they not only use less labour per unit of output than their more labour intensive associates, but also use less capital per unit of output. If capital intensive techniques of production are in general more productive than labour intensive techniques, a firm free to make a choice over a wide range of alternatives will choose the more capital intensive methods of production, since they are obviously more profitable. However, it is further argued that whereas large firms make their final choice from a wide range of alternative techniques and so choose the most economic (usually capital intensive techniques), small firms face a far smaller range, indeed one that is often limited to the more labour intensive production methods only.

The reasons advanced for the relatively disadvantaged position that small firms find themselves in are fourfold; firstly, it is generally the large firms which undertake the bulk of the research and development work that is done by private enterprise (Freeman: 1962, Mansfield: 1968). Consequently, as a result of their own activities, large firms are in a better position to expand the range of their choice than the smaller firms. Secondly, a number of empirical studies have found that large firms find it easier to raise the funds needed to finance the more capital intensive techniques than the smaller firms. (Penrose: 1959 Nattrass: 1972). Thirdly, large firms usually serve larger markets than the small firms and so are in a position to handle the output from the very much longer production runs that usually accompany the more capital intensive production methods. Finally, capital intensive production often requires a small cadre of highly qualified workers and the stronger economic position of the large firms may enable them to attract such people more easily.

A study undertaken of the relationships between the size of the firm and the capital intensity of its production methods in the manufacturing sector of the South African economy suggested that as far as the sector as a whole is concerned, there was a relationship between capital intensity in production and the size of the enterprise, measured in terms of output. On average, an increase of R1 in output was associated with an increase of 35 cents in the quantity of capital utilized per man year. (Nattrass and Brown: 1978)

There were, however, very significant differences within the sub-sectors of South African manufacturing. In the sub-sectors, Textiles, Rubber, Metal Products and Machinery and Electrical Machinery there was very little relationship between the size of the firm and the degree of capital intensity in production. Whereas in the Clothing, Wood and Paper, Printing, Chemicals, Non-Metallic Minerals and Base Metals sub-sectors, Brown found that the size of the firm seemed to be a significant determinant of the relative degree of capital intensity. (Brown: 1976)

The fact that the size of the firm is related to the amount of capital used per man, does not, however, necessarily mean that the larger firms in any one sector are capital intensive, relative to the smaller firms in another. Table 5.6 contains some estimates of the average amount of plant and machinery per man by firm size in 1976 for some of the sub-sectors in manufacturing, and illustrates this clearly.

The clothing sector, for example, is one of the sub-sectors in which changes in the degree of capital intensity is closely associated with changes in the size of the firm, but it is nevertheless still an extremely labour intensive sector, regardless of the firm size. The average capital required per man in the largest firms in this sub-sector was lower than that found in the smallest firms in *all* the other sub-sectors. The machinery sub-sectors, on the other hand, show little relationship between firm size and capital intensity, but even the small firms in these sectors use relatively large amounts of capital per man employed.

Table 5.6

AVERAGE CAPITAL LABOUR RATIOS IN SELECTED SUB-SECTORS IN MANUFACTURING 1976

Sub-sector	Average Capital Labour Ratios in Firms with Capital Stock of		
	> R10 000	R10 000 – R1 Million	Over R1 Million
Food	2 507	2 249	4 717
Textiles	1 119	1 201	2 333
Clothing	320	360	458
Wood and Furniture	685	1 239	2 401
Industrial Chemicals	636	2 158	4 013
Metal Products	1 827	1 459	2 408
Iron and Steel	–	1 403	19 352
Machinery	3 188	1 662	1 868
Electrical Machinery	3 643	1 074	2 912
Motor Vehicles	–	1 550	3 070
All Manufacturing	1 513	1 204	9 363

SOURCE: 1976 Census of Manufacturing.

An interesting feature of the data in Table 5.6 is the significant impact that ISCOR, the giant iron and steel public corporation, has had on the averages for the sector as a whole. The degree of capital intensity in the iron and steel sector was more than four times greater than the next most capital intensive sub-sector of those listed in the table. In 1976 the iron and steel sector alone contained 28 per cent of the plant and machinery invested in South African manufacturing and two sectors, chemicals and iron and steel, together employed 44 per cent of the total value of manufacturing's plant and machinery. There were in all 127 firms in the iron and steel sector and the six largest of these (of which ISCOR is the single largest), controlled 93 per cent of the total fixed assets in the sector.

There are, however, serious measurement problems in studies of this nature, since to make any meaningful comparisons between the sub-sectors, one has to assume that the economic conditions facing all of them are similar and that their assets have been valued on a common basis. If either or both of these assumptions fails to hold, this failure can cause significant difficulties. For example, 1976 was a recessionary year for the South African economy. One of the first sectors to reflect a recession is that of construction. A significant drop in construction activity in its turn, will affect the iron and steel industry, which may well then 'lay off' workers. Should this happen, it will have the statistical effect of significantly increasing the observed degree of capital intensity, whereas in reality there has been no change in production methods. Similarly, firm's assets are typically valued in terms of their depreciated original cost. This means that in times of inflation, identical plant that was purchased in different time periods will be valued differently. As a result, the 'vintage' or age of the plant also affects the observed value of capital. Consequently, one must exercise care when trying to interpret economic data of this type.

The Size of the Firm, Capital Accumulation and the Growth of Output

It is sometimes argued that the size of the firm in which the capital is being accumulated, may also directly affect the efficiency of the utilization of the new capital, measured in terms of output per unit of capital input. This is because large firms are in a position to benefit from what are known as 'economies of scale'. Pure economies of scale occur when the quantity of output per unit of the factor inputs rises with the size of the enterprise, even though the larger firms are using the same production techniques as their smaller associates. The cost savings that the large firm enjoys usually result from such things as economies in management and the better utilization of the physical environment within the firm.

Although the notion of 'economies of scale' is intuitively easy to understand, in practice the phenomenon is virtually impossible to isolate, as indeed are any benefits that may be emanating from this source. This is mainly because, as we discussed earlier, larger firms in general do not use the same production methods as the smaller firms. Consequently, any cost savings flowing from increases in output per unit of inputs, may well reflect the combined influences of scale and the use of more capital intensive production methods, which themselves may also be cost reducing. The problem of quantification is further complicated by the measurement problems that we discussed earlier, which will also affect any observations that might be relevant to an attempt to measure economies of scale.

THE SPATIAL DISTRIBUTION OF SOUTH AFRICA'S CAPITAL STOCK

As there are no official regional estimates of physical capital stock, one can only obtain a rather hazy picture of the spatial distribution of South Africa's national fixed capital, based on the incomplete evidence that is available. A selection of capital indicators, relevant to the distribution of privately owned capital, are given in Table 5.7 and they suggest that, not surprisingly, the allocation of capital is even more uneven from the spatial viewpoint than is the distribution of output.

On the basis of the capital indicators used in the table, it is clear that the major proportion of South Africa's privately owned capital is spatially located in the country's three major metropolitan regions. Between them they contained three quarters of all the plant invested in the South African manufacturing industry and, judging by the location of bank deposits, they were also the areas in which three quarters of the business transactions took place. Of these three metropolitan regions the Pretoria-Witwatersrand area is clearly the dominant one, as it singly contained 47 per cent of the manufacturing plant and accounted for over half of the nation's bank deposits.

Another estimate of the spatial allocation of capital stock in South Africa has been made by the author on the basis of the structure of the output in each magisterial district and Black State for the year 1970. This estimate was based on the assumption that the amount of capital needed to produce a unit of output in an economic sector was the same in all areas. In other words, taking agriculture as an example, it was assumed that it took 1,5 units of capital to generate one unit of agricultural output, irrespective of whether the district was situated in the relatively capital intensive farming areas in the Maize Triangle, or in a Black State. This type of assumption will tend to bias downwards the gap between the capital stock in the wealthy areas and that in the poorer regions. However, notwithstanding the bias, the average capital stock in the 27 districts which had the highest levels of average output per head, was *over 200 times greater* than the average for the 27 districts (including the Black States), which had the lowest levels of output per head. Indeed, the average for the richest 10 per cent of the districts was nearly five times greater than the average for the next wealthiest 10 per cent! (Nattrass: 1979e)

Table 5.7

INDICATORS OF THE SPATIAL ALLOCATION OF PRIVATELY OWNED CAPITAL STOCK

Area	Percentage of Total in 1972			
	Machinery and Equipment in Manufacturing	Mortgage Bonds (Registered Value)	Bank Deposits	Population (1970)
Pretoria-Witwatersrand	47	37	56	19
Durban – Pietermaritzburg	21	11	7	7
Cape Metropolitan	7	9	13	6
Total	75	57	76	32
Other Areas	25	43	24	68

SOURCE: 1972 *Industrial Census* and 1970 *Population Census Reports* and *Bureau of Market Research (1972A).*

Whilst studies of this type are somewhat simplistic, one can draw out a number of generalizations from them regarding the spatial distribution of South Africa's national capital. Firstly, that South Africa's urban areas are better supplied with capital than the rural areas, not only with respect to private sector capital, but also in terms of 'social overhead capital', which includes such things as roads, schools and hospitals.

Secondly, not only do the very large metropolitan regions dominate, but it also appears from a study undertaken by the Department of Planning that, certainly as far as the capital required to provide social services is concerned, large towns also fare considerably better than small towns. Taking Bloemfontein services as the equivalent of 100, the Department of Planning estimated a national hierarchy of towns in South Africa for 1970. Excluding the four major metropolitan areas, East London ranked second with an index of 99, Kimberley third with 48 and *90 per cent of the remaining 450 towns* had service levels estimated to be the equivalent of *10 per cent, or less,* of those in Bloemfontein.

Thirdly, since all of the ten districts that were under the control of Blacks fell into the poorest category, it also appears that the districts dominated by Whites are very much more favourably endowed with capital, than those under Black control.

The spatial allocation of capital is a very significant determinant, not only of the present relative economic positions of the different districts and regions within South Africa, but also of their future situation. An area that lacks capital is usually also short of physical infrastructure such as roads, the provision of an adequate piped water supply, a source of power and social services. The absence of these services makes it virtually impossible for private enterprise to locate any new investment profitably in these areas. As a result, the gap between the well and poorly endowed areas widens as capital accumulation takes place, unless this natural tendency is offset by vigorous government policy.

In South Africa, both the policies introduced in the 1960s to decentralize industry and the present government's stated intention to develop the Black States, can be seen as attempts to correct the spatial unevenness in the allocation of the nation's physical capital. Unfortunately neither of these policies has as yet been pursued with sufficient determination to make any inroads into the 'development gap' (the gap between South Africa's developed and underdeveloped regions). Indeed the recent tendencies seem to be for this gap to widen, rather than to narrow. Over the period from 1968–72 (admittedly a short period, but the only one for which data was available), the average yearly rate of growth in the average money value of output per head in the wealthiest 10 per cent of the districts, was 12 per cent. For the districts in the middle 60 per cent, it was 10 per cent, whilst in the districts in the lowest 10 per cent, it was only 5,6 per cent.

The spatial distribution of South African development is not independent of the way in which the economic structure itself has evolved. The impact of the exploitation of mineral discoveries on the spatial allocation of economic activity is obvious, but the nature of the economic growth in manufacturing and services will also affect the overall development of the country. In the following chapters, we will look at the way in which the development of each sector has affected South African growth patterns and so contributed to the characteristics of the economy of today.

SIX

Agriculture and
Economic Development

Introduction: Agriculture's Role in Development

The agricultural sector in any economy plays a vital role in the economic development process. In the early days of development, the agricultural sector dominates the economic scene being both the major producer and employer in the economy. As industrialization takes place, however, this situation alters and over time the sector becomes relatively less significant.

This change in the relative importance of agriculture and manufacturing implies that as the development process continues, productive resources must be transferred from agriculture to industry. Historically, the growth of the industrialized economies has been marked by a flow of both labour and capital from agriculture. This transfer of resources was largely accomplished because it was possible to increase the productivity of the factors of production remaining in agriculture and so to produce the increased output necessitated by the growing demand for food and inputs in the developing industrial sector, with smaller inputs of capital and labour per unit of agricultural output produced.

Agriculture in South Africa comprises two very distinct components; the subsector dominated by Whites and that under the control of Blacks. The roles that these two sub-sectors have played in the development of the South African economy have been very different. The White sector is by far the bigger of the two and has contributed both increasing amounts of output and substantial quantities of labour to the expanding mining and industrial sectors of the economy. In the Black sector, on the other hand, productivity levels have declined over time and, far from supplying food, the sector has gradually deteriorated to the point where it is a net importer of food. Consequently, this sector's contribution to South Africa's overall growth process has been largely in the role of a labour supplier.

Agriculture and Land Use Patterns in South Africa

The latest data on land utilization in South Africa in general, and agriculture in particular, relate to 1960 and 1965. In 1960 the estimated land surface of the Republic was 122 111 000 hectares, 87 per cent of which was classified as being used for agricultural and forestry purposes, 2 per cent was composed of urban areas, whilst a further 2 per cent was allocated for the purposes of nature reserves. The allocation of the agricultural land itself both between Blacks and Whites and between the various farming uses, together with the geographical patterns, were discussed in Chapter One and the reader is recommended to reconsult these sections briefly at this point for completeness.

There are three notable characteristics of the land allocation in South Africa; the first is the disparity in the allocation of land between Black and White South Africans. The second is the relatively low proportion of agricultural land that is under crops (less than 12 per cent of the total) whilst the third characteristic is that it is not only the distribution of land between Blacks and Whites that is uneven, but there is also a very uneven distribution, in terms of average farm size, in the areas controlled solely by Whites. In 1975, 26 per cent of farmers outside the Black areas controlled over 80 per cent of the area's farmlands and the largest 5 per cent of the farmers controlled 40 per cent of the land (Report 06-01-12: 1977). The large farms also dominated the marketed agricultural production. The Du Plessis Commission estimated that for the 1962/63 season, the largest 16 per cent of the farms produced 65 per cent of the gross value of agricultural sales in that period and the top 6 per cent; 40 per cent of the sales. (R.P. 84/1970)

SOUTH AFRICA'S TWO AGRICULTURES

Introduction

The two sections of South African agriculture are so different from one another that when one moves from a White-owned modern capital using farming sector to a Black subsistence oriented and tribally organized farming area, it is almost like stepping through a time warp. Because these sectors are so very distinct it is essential to consider both the characteristics and the extent and nature of the contribution that these two sectors have made to South African economic development separately. However, before we do so, it is useful to contrast their major characteristics to set the scene for the later discussion. Table 6.1 contains the relevant data.

Table 6.1

A COMPARISON OF SOUTH AFRICA'S 'TWO AGRICULTURES'

	Agricultural Sector	
	Black	White
Total Land Area (000 hectares)	15,076	87,795
Percentage cultivated	14%	14%
Employment (000) 1970[1]	1 103	1 126
Land per worker (hectares)	13,7	78,0
Output per man[2]	R65	R1 298
Output per hectare – cultivated	R34	R119

SOURCE: 1980. *Abstract of Agricultural Statistics, South African Statistics 1978.* (Lenta: 1977)

1. The 1970 Census classified all Black women living in the subsistence sector whose husbands were home working in agriculture as economically inactive, whether they were or not. This has lead to an underestimate of the size of the workforce in the subsistence sector, and a consequent overstatement of the average quantity of land per worker.
2. Subsistence based on Lenta's estimate for KwaZulu in 1971. (Lenta: 1977)

The vast differences in productivity levels between the sectors is evident in terms of both output per worker and output per hectare cultivated. The difference in terms of land is, however, lower than the difference in terms of labour, which is what one would expect since as one adds increasing quantities of labour to a fixed amount of land, although the returns per man added decline after a while, the output per unit of land continues to rise.

WHITE AGRICULTURE'S CONTRIBUTION TO SOUTH AFRICAN ECONOMIC DEVELOPMENT

We said earlier that the role of the agricultural sector in the process of economic development was to supply increasing amounts of both output and labour to meet the needs of growing industry. If there is not a significant increase in the levels of productivity in the sector, these two functions may conflict with one another, as it is not possible to produce more output with the same or a smaller labour supply unless one introduces new techniques that allow the sector to produce more output per man employed. However, if the rate of population growth is high enough to allow both the labour force in industry and agriculture to grow, this conflict will not materialize. At least not until the new sector has grown sufficiently for its labour requirements to have mopped up the surplus labour supply in the economy.

The Sector's Role as a Supplier of Produce

In White agriculture, over the period from 1911 onwards, not only did labour productivity in the sector rise, but in addition the resident population on the White farms grew more rapidly than farm employment. Both these elements enabled the sector to release significant quantities of labour without affecting the growth of output. The relevant data is in Table 6.2.

The growth rate of output in physical terms was relatively steady throughout the period, although it has picked up slightly in the most recent period. Overall, the ouput of food appears to have proceeded at a rate considerably above the rate of growth of population, which allowed for the increased use of agricultural products as inputs into manufacturing, an increase in agricultural exports and the increase local demand for foodstuffs following from both the rising population and the increase in average living standards.

Whether or not the rate of growth of agricultural output will continue to be sufficient to meet the growing needs of the modern economy without a substantial rise in food prices is, however, open to doubt. Black incomes have risen more rapidly than White in the most recent past and this trend is likely to continue. If it does, it will cause the demand for food to rise more rapidly than has been the case to date, as the proportion of any increases in income that are spent on food are very much greater, when incomes are low, than when the increases take place on incomes that are already relatively high. In addition, the demand for particular components of the sector's output, in some instances, may grow more rapidly than the supply,

Table 6.2
CHANGES IN AGRICULTURAL OUTPUT, EMPLOYMENT AND CAPITAL OVER THE PERIOD 1921-77

Year	Index of Physical Volume of Output 1958-60 = 100	Employment Indices (Including Casual Labour) 1960 = 100					Index of Capital Stock (Constant 1970 Prices)	Capital per man (Constant 1970 Prices) Rands
		Total Employment	Whites	Coloured	Asians	Africans		
1921	30	42	143	59	168	29		
1936	46	63	153	73	158	52		
1946	53	71	142	77	117	62	62	515
1951	73	82	123	76	109	77	69	470
1960	99	100	100	100	100	100	100	656
1971	144	179	83	98	59	181	154	660
1977	182	137	83	154		138	160	747
Annual growth rate								
1921-1977	3,3	2,1	-1,0			,8		
1946-1977	4,1	2,1	-1,7			,7	3,1	1,2

SOURCE: *1980 Abstract of Agricultural Statistics* and Nattrass: 1977b.

causing their relative prices to increase. This appears to have happened in South Africa as the data in Table 6.3 indicates.

Table 6.3
RELATIVE GROWTH RATES IN AGRICULTURAL COMPONENTS 1958–78

| | Annual Average Compound Growth rate 1958/59–1977/78 of | | |
	Horticultural Products	Field Products	Livestock
Volume of physical production	4,6	4,3	2,6
Volume of exports	5,1	6,4	,6
Producer average prices	5,2	5,0	6,3
Consumer price index			
all products		5,2	
food		6,0	

SOURCE: *1980 Abstract of Agricultural Statistics* and *South African Statistics, 1978.*

It seems that the increased output of the horticultural and field crop sectors of agriculture were sufficient to meet both the increase in the local consumer demand and that in export markets, as the producer prices for these components rose at almost exactly the same rate as prices in the economy as a whole. However, the growth of livestock production over the period was too slow, in relation to the growth in demand and the relative price paid to the farmer for livestock increased. (One should, however, bear in mind that the marketing of agricultural products is controlled, and it may be the activities of the marketing boards that have caused distortions in the normal operation of the market.)

The period 1919–76 was a period in which there was some change in the overall crop mix in the White farming sector. This is shown in Table 6.4. It seems almost ironical that crops should have become an increasingly important component of the agricultural sector's output over the period, in view of the forebodings of a 1940 Commission of Enquiry into Agriculture (quoted in Chapter One) which said 'South Africa must be regarded as a poor crop raising country'. (U.G. 40/1941, p. 7)

Table 6.4

THE CHANGING CROP MIX IN WHITE AGRICULTURE 1919–76

Year	Percentage of Total production		Percentage of Agricultural production				Percentage of Pastoral production	
	Agricultural	Pastoral	Maize	Winter Cereals	Vegetables	Fruit	Beef	Mutton
1919	44	56	39	26	5	6	23	16
1936	54	46	30	19	7	16	20	13
1951	50	50	30	17	6	15	18	11
1970	60	40	31	13	6	14	27	14
1976	62	38	32	13	6	12	29	12

SOURCE: *Handbook of Agricultural Statistics. 1978 Abstract of Agricultural Statistics.*

The bulk of South Africa's crop production takes place in the summer rainfall region. The Du Plessis Commission estimated that in 1965, as much as 70 per cent of the maize crop was grown in these areas, as was 45 per cent of the sorghum (millet or kaffircorn), 82 per cent of the sunflower crop, 23 per cent of the wheat and 32 per cent of the potatoes. The Commission also pointed out that over the period 1930 to 1968, the increase in maize output was largely due to an increase in the land area devoted to growing maize, rather than to an increased yield, as the area in which maize was planted grew by over 150 times over this period.

This report also commented on the relatively poor performance of the stock farmers, attributing it in general to poor management with respect to both the care and the quality of the animals selected, which together result in 'low yield and poor breeding capacity . . . as well as severe losses in weight and a high mortality resulting from diseases and exposure to harsh weather conditions.' (R.P. 84/1970, p. 93)

The Components of Growth in White Agriculture

All three of the major input categories, land, capital and labour have contributed towards the increase in White agricultural output over the period since 1911, although to a differing extent. Between 1930 and 1976 the total area controlled by farmers outside the Black rural areas rose by only 3,5 per cent. The total area cultivated, however, more than doubled over the same period. On this basis, it is clear that the increased utilization of land itself was a significant source of the increase in agricultural production in the sector.

Table 6.2 contains data relating to the growth in the input of both capital and labour for the years for which they are available. Capital in the commercial agricultural sector rose by an average of 3 per cent per year between 1946 and 1977, measured in constant 1970 prices and had nearly trebled in terms of its total real value over that 30 year period.

The labour input has also grown, but somewhat more slowly than capital, averaging 2 per cent per year. Consequently, the amount of capital employed per man in the sector rose, although relatively slowly, at just over 1 per cent per annum. It seems from this data, that the new capital injected into White agriculture was used over the period mainly to generate new jobs, rather than to employ new methods of farming which would replace labour.

Over the years from 1946 to 1977, farm output in the sector rose at a yearly average rate of 4 per cent. Taking the period as a whole, it would seem that 2 per cent of this increase appears to have been provided by the increased labour input and the remaining two per cent by the improved utilization of that labour made possible by the new capital. It is, however, apparent from the data in Table 6.2 that there has been quite a significant change in the economic behaviour of this sector in the period subsequent to 1970. From this year onward, total employment in White agriculture fell. Consequently, the increase in output, that took place after 1970, can be attributed to capital accumulation and the increase in labour productivity that it generated through the introduction of labour replacing technology. In more technical terms, over the period 1946–70 investment in commercial agriculture was predominantly of the capital widening variety, whereas after 1976 it seems that it was increasingly diverted towards capital deepening.

White Agriculture as a Supplier of Labour

Employment in White agriculture grew in absolute terms throughout the period to 1970 and from then on appears to have started to decline slowly. The sector, however, started to contribute labour to the rest of the economy from as early as 1946, as it was at that time that the rate of increase in job opportunities in the sector fell below that of the resident farm population. Estimates that have been made of movements of people in and out of White farms suggest that over the period from 1911 to 1973, approximately 240 000 Whites, 120 000 Coloureds and 383 000 Asians left these areas. As far as the African farm population is concerned, the picture is different. Up to 1960, White farms were net importers of African labour and an additional 290 000 Africans took up residence on White farms over the 50 year period 1911–60. After 1960, however, the situation changed significantly and the estimates suggest that as many as half a million Black workers and their families left the White farming sector in the period after 1960. (Nattrass: 1977b)

When one looks at the patterns of population movement in the White farming areas more closely, one finds that not only are there differences in behaviour with respect to the time periods considered, but there are also racial differences. Table 6.5 contains the relevant data.

Table 6.5

LABOUR MOVEMENTS ON WHITE FARMS 1911–76

| Period | Out Migration | | | | In Migration |
	Asian	African	Coloured	White	African
1911/1921	–	–	–	–	70 000
1921/1936	11 000	–	18 000	40 000	140 000
1936/1951	13 000	–	38 000	88 000	80 000
1951/1960	5 000	–	–	53 000	45 000
1960/1971	8 000	333 000	42 000	44 000	–

SOURCE: Estimated from data in Agricultural and Population Census Reports.

One can see from the data in the table that members of the White, Coloured and Asian groups started to leave the White farming areas in significant numbers as early as 1921, to be replaced in the main by the cheaper Black workforce. The period from 1960 onwards saw yet another change, as farmers substituted casual employees for their permanent Black workers and increasingly employed mechanized production methods.

Over the period 1960–71, it seems that roughly half a million full-time Black workers left their employment on White farms and were replaced by casual labour and by the increased employment of single migrant workers. When one remembers that each permanently settled Black employee probably has on average between four and six dependents, it is clear that the period 1960–71 was one in which there was a massive population resettlement. It may have affected over 1,5 million Blacks who had been previously resident on White farms. One million of these people appear to have moved into the urban areas, whilst the remainder resettled in the Black controlled rural areas. (Nattrass: 1977b)

The flows of temporary Black migrant workers in and out of the White farming sector are also interesting, as the sector both employs and supplies migrants. It has been estimated that in 1970, although the net flow of migrants from the White rural areas was only 12 000, this concealed a total flow that could have been as large as 700 000 people. The White farms employed just over 300 000 migrant men, mainly in the sugar belt, on the maize farms in the maize triangle, and on the fruit farms in the south eastern Cape. At the same time, the sector supplied a further 400 000 migrant workers to the urban areas. These crossflows of migrants are largely the result of the manner in which South African labour supply patterns were historically established. The areas using migrants have done so for the greater part of their existence, whilst in the poorer agricultural areas of the northern and western regions of Natal and the north eastern Cape, the farms have long been unable to generate sufficient work for their resident Black communities and have a history of supplying out-migrants to the towns.

The historical trends in the labour demand and supply patterns in White agriculture have been reinforced by well-established behaviour patterns on the part of both worker and employer, with respect to preferences for particular types of work, or for workers from a select location. For example, for many years the sugar farms in Natal have recruited the major portion of their cane cutters from Pondoland, an area in the northern part of Transkei. Inter-regional wage differentials have also been a significant factor in the generation of the cross-flows of migrant workers in the White farming sector.

It is clear that, over time, White agriculture has been a substantial source of labour for the growing modern economy beyond its

borders. It has been estimated that in 1970 as much as 24 per cent of
the White workforce employed outside agriculture, 33 per cent of the
Coloured, 41 per cent of the Asian and 20 per cent of the Black, either
originated directly in the White farming areas, or were first
generation descendents of such people. (Nattrass: 1977b)

Some radical analysts see White agriculture's role in the development process as that of a labour absorber and a food and capital
supplier (Legassick: 1974, Kaplan: 1974). Consequently these
writers see White farming as being in competition with the growing
modern sector for the available supplies of labour. Whilst this was no
doubt true in the very early days of South African capitalism – as
evidenced by the measures adopted to enable farmers to obtain
labour in the western Cape and the importation of indentured Indian
labour for the Natal cane fields – it has become less true as capitalism
has developed. Indeed, over the 50 year period considered here, it
is apparent that, far from reducing the available labour supply to
growing industry, White agriculture acted to increase it and did so
more intensively as time proceeded.

Over the 20 year period 1951–71, approximately 1 400 000
new jobs for Blacks were created in the sectors other than agriculture.
As foreign Black immigration declined over this period, the number
of new jobs available for South African Blacks was actually
1 500 000. These jobs were filled in the following way; 300 000 from
the natural increase of the Black population settled in the towns in
1951, 400 000 by the permanent movement of Blacks from the White
farming districts into the urban areas and the balance, 800 000, by an
increase in the flow of migrant workers from the Black rural areas.
This increase in migrants will also include a large proportion of
workers originating from the White farms, since of the 1,5 million
Blacks who left the White regions during this period, 500 000 settled
in the Black rural areas, some of whom will undoubtedly have joined
the migrant workforce.

With the continued capitalization of White agriculture it seems
highly likely that this trend will continue. Indeed, the present worry
to South African policy-makers is not the competition between
agriculture and industry for a limited labour supply, but the fear that
the White farming sector will expel its surplus labour supply faster
than it can be absorbed into the rest of the economy, aggravating the
unemployment position.

We saw earlier, in the data in Table 6.2, that although there had been quite significant capital accumulation in White agriculture, there was not a lot of evidence to suggest that farming techniques had changed to any great extent, as relatively little labour appears to have been replaced as this accumulation has come about. The current Economic Development Programme covering the period 1978–87 predicts that this tendency will continue and indeed that the rate at which labour is expelled from the sector will decline to an average of 0,8 per cent per year.

Structural Change in White Agriculture

The most significant changes in the structure of White agriculture undoubtedly occurred in the days of the early exploitation of minerals when farmers, who had previously largely been producing for their own use, saw the possibilities for profit that were opened by the growing mining towns. In Chapter Four it was pointed out that the period 1880–1925 was one which saw large numbers of Whites and Blacks dispossessed of their landholdings and a massive increase in the extent of the land that was cultivated by White farmers.

The period following saw a consolidation of the position rather than a continuation of the earlier trends. Table 6.6 contains data showing the growth in the area cultivated by Whites and in the average farm size over the 57 years 1919–76.

Table 6.6
CHANGE IN FARM SIZE 1919–76

Year	Number of White Farms	Average Farm size (1 000 hectares)	Area (1 000 hectares)	Percentage Change in Farm size	Percentage Change in Area
1919	78 086	992,6	77 504	– 16,2	– 11,4
1936	103 360	831,6	84 920	– 17,3	9,6
1951	118 097	736,5	86 979	– 10,4	2,4
1970	91 153	978,8	89 217	32,9	2,6
1976	75 562	1 134,4	85 719	15,9	– 3,9

SOURCE: Various Agricultural Censuses.

It is interesting to note that although there was net emigration by Whites from agriculture from 1921 onwards, the number of farms owned by Whites increased up to 1951. This seeming contradiction could be the result of any one of a number of things; for instance, the rate of out-migration may have been lower than the natural rate of population growth, or alternatively it may be due to the fact that in many cases more than one farm is owned by a farmer.

Of more significance, from an economic viewpoint, is the fact that whereas the average farm size declined from 1919 to 1951, it increased again quite sharply to be larger in 1976 than it was in 1919. South African White farms have always tended to be large on average by world standards; however, the average can be misleading as it conceals a wide variation of farm sizes within the sector. In 1975, for example, 5 per cent of the farms accounted for 40 per cent of the total farmland, whilst at the other end of the scale 24 per cent of the farms had land holdings of less than 50 hectares and together accounted for less than half of 1 per cent of the total White farmland.

As far as farming efficiency is concerned, both the very small and the very large farms give grounds for concern. The former because they seldom offer their owners a 'living' rate of return on their efforts and the latter because their sheer size frequently makes them a management problem.

White Agriculture as a Foreign Exchange Earner

One of the major functions of the agricultural sector in a developing economy is to earn the foreign exchange needed to purchase the sophisticated inputs that are required by the growing industrial sector and which frequently cannot be produced locally. South Africa needed to rely to a lesser extent on agricultural foreign exchange earnings than most developing countries, because she was able to use the massive foreign earning capability of the mining industry. Notwithstanding the contribution of the mining sector, White agriculture in South Africa has historically also been a significant net exporter and even at the present time the earnings from agricultural products sold abroad are substantial. In 1976, they accounted for 30 per cent of the earnings of foreign exchange, excluding the proceeds from the sale of gold.

The growth of the modern mining and industrial sectors has resulted in the growth in the export trade in minerals other than gold, and in manufactures. As a result, although the money value of South African exports of agricultural products grew on average by 6,7 per cent a year over the period 1925–76, agriculture's share in export earnings fell over that period, from 61 per cent of the total (excluding gold) in 1924, to 30 per cent in 1976. Major agricultural export earners in 1976 were sugar, maize, wool and processed fruits.

BLACK AGRICULTURE'S CONTRIBUTION TO SOUTH AFRICA

Economic Development

The major portion of Black farming activity takes place in the rural areas of the Black States. There is however, also some agricultural production by Blacks living on White farms, who have been given the right to cultivate certain portions of the farm as part of the reward for their labour. There are also a small number of Blacks who are independent farmers in their own right in White controlled areas.

From a purely climatic viewpoint, Black agricultural areas are very favourably situated. The Tomlinson Commission estimated that if the economic conditions in the Black rural areas were the same as those in White, the Black farming regions could produce more than 23 per cent of the country's total farm output. (U.G. 61/1961). At present, the estimated contribution of these areas to South Africa's total agricultural production is less than 6 per cent. Of the total agricultural production in the Black farm regions only about 10 per cent is offered for sale; the remainder being used for subsistence purposes by the farming families themselves. (Benso: 1976)

Black farmers have not always lagged behind their White counterparts. In the 19th century Black areas in South Africa were largely self-sufficient in foodstuffs and were marketing increasing quantities of produce in response to the high prices offered on the markets in the growing industrial areas. (Van der Horst: 1971). In the Natal Region, for example, in 1871 the acreage cultivated by White farmers was 38 000 acres, whereas Africans in the same year cultivated 137 000 acres; nearly four times as much. (Hobart Houghton and Dagut:

1972). In contrast, however, in 1945 Natal's Black farmers in the rural reserve areas produced only 25 per cent of the region's total output and by 1975 this percentage had declined still further to 17 per cent of the total. (Natal Regional Survey No. 7 and Report 06-01-12)

In general Black farming is organized on tribal lines with no security of individual tenure. The local chief has the power to allocate land and a married man seeking to set up home in the chief's area applies to him for the right to settle and for a grant of land. The agricultural land is traditionally allocated on a strip basis with the number of strips being largely determined by the availability of land. Grazing land is communal and even cultivated land may not be fenced, as once the crop has been harvested, it too reverts to the community for grazing purposes until the time comes to sow the next crop. There are differences between areas in respect of the organization of the community land. In particular many areas have reorganized in terms of the Central government's 'Betterment Schemes'. Under these schemes the land used for dwellings is centralized and the agricultural usage of the remainder is replanned by agronomists in terms of the environmental conditions.

In general, as we will see in the following sections, productivity levels in Black agriculture are low and the sector's major contribution to South African economic development has been as a labour supplier, rather than as a food producer.

Black Agriculture and the Food Supply

The major foodstuffs produced in the Black agricultural sector are maize, sorghum (millet), vegetables and wheat. Table 6.7 contains output data for three of these, maize, sorghum and wheat, for selected years over the period 1918–75.

From the data it seems that there has been virtually no change in the total volume of cereal crop production throughout the period covered in the table, although there was a change in the crop mix, as maize was apparently increasingly substituted for sorghum. This substitution was a retrograde step from the nutritional viewpoint, but was one that made a great deal of economic sense, as it meant the substitution of a less labour intensive crop for one needing a high input of labour in the face of an increasing shortage of suitable manpower, which was building up in the sector.

Table 6.7

PRODUCTION OF SELECTED FIELD CROPS IN THE AFRICAN RURAL
AREAS, 1918-75

Year	Production by Africans in African Controlled Rural Areas (tonnes)		
	Maize	Sorghum	Wheat
1918	261 339	119 464	9 643
1925	299 643	78 214	2 857
1935	193 214	54 018	3 393
1945	181 161	52 143	3 661
1955	259 553	62 410	5 000
1965	189 784	29 670	8 317
1975	326 800	46 423	9 543

SOURCE: Various Agricultural censuses.

Not only did the total output of the Black agricultural sector fail to expand to any great extent, but the same period of time saw a rapid rise in the rate of population growth in these areas. Between the years 1936 and 1975, the population in the Black rural areas almost trebled. With these rapid increases in the number of people dependant upon Black agriculture, the almost static sectoral output meant that, far from the sector being able to provide surplus output for the food needs of the growing towns, it was becoming increasingly unable to feed its own population. As a result, the people living in the Black rural areas became increasingly reliant upon the importation of food produced on White farms to maintain the population resident in the sector. (Simpkins: 1980)

The increasing dependence of the African farm areas on food supplies from outside is also illustrated by an estimate made of the ability of one of the Black States (KwaZulu) to feed itself in the years 1957-59 and 1971-73. It was estimated that in the first of these two periods, KwaZulu produced 38 per cent of its cereal needs, 12 per cent of its legume needs, 57 per cent of its tuber needs and 60 per cent of its meat requirements. By 1971-73, the position had changed and the region could only supply 30 per cent of its cereal needs and 33 per cent of its meat requirements. On the other hand, legume production had risen slightly to 13 per cent of the requirements and tubers to 69 per cent. (Lenta: 1977)

It is obvious from this data that one must agree with Brand's observation, namely that virtually the whole of the output contribution made by agriculture to South Africa's economic growth can safely be accredited to the modern, almost totally White-owned, agricultural sector. (Brand: 1969). Indeed one can go further and argue in terms of output or product that Black agriculture's contribution to South African economic development has actually been negative, since over a significant portion of the period the sector was a net importer of agricultural products instead of being the net exporter that development theory would suggest.

Over the years, a large number of varied opinions have been advanced as to why Black agriculture failed to modernize and to expand its output. These range from those placing the full responsibility for the failure on the limiting nature of the tribal system and communal land tenure (Hobart Houghton: 1964), through those who argue that central government policy has played a significant negative role (Bundy: 1972, Lipton: 1977), to those arguing that it is a necessary concomitant of the creation of cheap supply of Black labour. (Legassick: 1974). There is no doubt that all these elements have played their part in the creation of the present situation and as the labour component is a crucial element in the argument, a discussion of the reasons for the low productivity in Black agriculture will only be undertaken after the relationship between the sector and the labour supply has been discussed. It is to this aspect that we now turn our attention.

Black Agriculture and the Labour Supply

There is little doubt that the Black agricultural sector has made a considerable contribution to South African economic development as a source of supply of cheap Black labour. In 1916 the Beaumont Land Commission estimated that 55 per cent of the Black group was resident in what were then known as 'Native Reserve Areas'. (U.G. 19/1916). By 1936, this figure had declined slightly, but was still greater than half, at 52 per cent. By 1970 these areas were the home of 36 per cent of South Africa's population.

Over the past century Black agriculture has provided both permanent emigrants and continuously oscillating migrant workers to the growing modern economy. Between the years 1916 and

1951, nearly one million Blacks left the Black rural areas permanently to settle either on White farms or in the growing urban areas. In addition, the sector also provided a swelling stream of oscillating migrant workers, which by 1951 included some 650 000 people. (Nattrass: 1977b)

As we saw earlier, the general election in 1948 brought the National Party to power and heralded the years which saw the introduction of the legislation that was to be the framework of the policy of separate development. This legislation made it virtually impossible for rural Blacks to gain permanent residence rights in White controlled urban areas and it became increasingly difficult for Black families living on White farms to send out migrant workers. The combined outcome of the changes in legislation was to reverse the trends in the population movement and consequently the period from 1951–70 saw a significant flow of settlers into the Black agricultural areas, encompassing more than half a million people, with a concomitant increase in the size of the outflow of migrant workers. The stream of oscillating rural urban migrant workers from Black agriculture had grown to such an extent that on the census date in 1970 it included over 1,25 million people.

Exactly how important these migrants were in terms of the labour supply is shown by the fact that in 1970, 27 per cent of the total Black workforce, comprised migrants from the Black rural areas and the migrant men from these regions made up over 40 per cent of the Black male labour force employed in White areas. (Nattrass: 1976). From the viewpoint of the labour supply in the Black agricultural sector itself, the impact of the migrant labour system is just as dramatic; in 1970 more than half the adult men normally resident in the Black rural areas were absent as migrants and in some areas the absentee rate was as high as 70 per cent! It is obvious that male absentee rates of such magnitude will affect not only the labour input into agriculture, but also the productivity levels of the remaining labour supply, and we will discuss this in the following section.

The Migrant Labour System and Black Rural Productivity

It is the inability of Black agriculture to provide for its population that is a major force behind the migrant labour system. People leave the rural areas of the Black States to work as migrants in the modern economic centre because they and their families are unable to survive on what they can produce in their rural homes. However, the absence of large numbers of adults during the prime of their working life, places a very heavy work burden on those remaining behind; a burden so large in many instances that it cannot be dealt with.

The average absentee rate amongst adult working men in the rural areas of the Black States is over 50 per cent. Under these circumstances, the reallocation of work necessary to compensate for the absence of these able-bodied males often means that the young, the very old, the women who have the burden of raising children and those with less education are expected to be able to provide the workload of a very large percentage of the most productive members of the workforce. If this added work burden cannot be dealt with, certain tasks are neglected, which, over a period of time, tends to undermine the productive capacity of these areas.

Participation in the migrant labour system, whilst it may be essential in survival terms, also affects the productivity potential of the Black rural areas in a number of other ways and by doing so essentially perpetuates its own continuation.

Firstly, as was shown earlier in Chapter Three, the migration process is selective on the grounds of age and education, the migration propensities being higher than average amongst the young and the better educated. As youth is the innovator of most change, a high rate of absence amongst those aged under forty years means that it becomes increasingly difficult to introduce new techniques in an area so denuded of men in those age groups. In an African context where the man is traditionally the decision-maker, this effect is reinforced and the decision-making process in the rural areas becomes increasingly cumbersome as the proportion of males absent from a particular region rises.

Secondly, innovation in agriculture requires investment. Studies on the behaviour patterns of migrants suggest that they typically remit only between 20–35 per cent of their earnings to their rural homes. (Bureau of Market Research: 1971 a, b, c. Clarke and Ngobese: 1975). This low level of remittance to the rural areas, coupled with the low levels of productivity there, means that rural family incomes are too small to permit any substantial savings, making it virtually impossible for these families to finance investment.

Thirdly and probably most significantly, the prolonged continuation of the migrant labour system has socialized the rural communities into accepting it as a way of life. Boys growing up without their fathers take it as inevitable that they too will leave the rural areas. What limited investment funds that are available are channelled to providing the children with education that will suit them for a job in the cities, instead of to productive use in the rural sector itself. In one of the Black States, KwaZulu, over the period from 1936–70, investment in ploughs grew at only 0,8 per cent per year, in cultivators at 2,5 per cent and in cattle and sheep it did not grow at all. Investment in education, the passport into the city, on the other hand, grew at over 6 per cent per year on average throughout the period. (Nattrass: 1977c)

Through these relationships the migrant labour system reinforces itself. Low levels of productivity in the rural areas of the Black States cause men who have access to land, and women, to a lesser extent, to seek work to supplement their rural incomes. The absence of migrants lowers rural productivity and so perpetuates the need to migrate.

The normal route out of a cycle of this nature would be for those Blacks who have built up experience of life in the urban centres, to take their families with them to settle there permanently. The corresponding flow to the cities that this would produce would ease the population pressure on the land. Profitable opportunities would once again begin to present themselves in Black agriculture, encouraging investment and increasing productivity. The legal controls on Black population movements have, however, prevented this from happening. Migrants cannot take their families with them legally and are forced to continue to oscillate between their urban jobs and their homes in the rural areas. Population pressure on the land, far from being eased, increases; the number of landless families in these rural areas rises, and the land/man ratios continue to deteriorate, intensifying the problem.

Other Factors Contributing to Low Black Agricultural Productivity

A number of researchers who have studied Black agriculture have concluded that the persistence of the tribal system is the root cause of the sector's low productivity. Hobart Houghton stated this viewpoint quite explicitly when he said:

> The explanation would appear to be that the African peasants have failed to adapt their farming practices to modern requirements. General conservatism, the system of land tenure and certain social customs, like 'ukulobola', combine to perpetuate obsolete methods of farming. (Hobart Houghton: 1964, p. 71)

More recently, consultant planners to the self-governing Black State of KwaZulu argued that the five major reasons for low agricultural productivity in the area were (i) the tribal structure (particularly as it is not oriented towards production for the market and views land as a social commodity rather than as an input into the production of food), (ii) the tribal view that agricultural work is largely part of the women's role, (iii) the practice of accumulating wealth in the form of cattle holdings, (iv) the communal system of land tenure and (v) the poor land-to-man ratios. (Thorrington-Smith et al: 1978)

Although there is no doubt that certain aspects of the tribal system do exert a limiting effect on economic development, it should not be seen in any way as being the sole cause of the widening gulf between the productivity levels in Black and White agriculture. Certain aspects of central government policy-making over the past century have also contributed significantly to this growing differential. Merle Lipton states the following in answer to the hypothetical question as to why Black agriculture failed to develop alongside White:

> A large part of the answer is to be found in (a) overt political measures taken to coerce blacks into working for whites rather than producing on their own account, and (b) in the discriminatory allocation of economic resources, which has rigged the market against blacks so that it is not worth their while to put more inputs or efforts in to farming. (Wilson et al, p. 75)

The implication of past government policies for Black agriculture are discussed more fully in the following section which looks at the role the state has played in developing agriculture in South Africa in general. Briefly, however, Lipton argues that as far as access to land is concerned, the 1913 Land Act and its subsequent amendments entrenched an extremely unequal distribution of income between Blacks and Whites. From the capital formation viewpoint, the bulk of the very substantial amount of state assistance to agriculture has gone to the White farming sector. There has been virtually no attempt to offer profitable openings for Black agricultural savings which has encouraged over-investment in cattle with its concomitant environmental costs. Whilst as far as the labour input is concerned, increasing participation in the migrant labour system has led to the development of a situation in which the African farming sector is actually short of good quality labour. A study undertaken by Gill Westcott in the rural areas of Transkei in 1975 also suggested that a significant component of any increase in rural productivity levels was the presence in the homestead of an able-bodied man. (Westcott: 1977)

Another aspect discouraging agricultural improvement in many Black rural areas, is a lack of adequate marketing facilities. The discovery of diamonds in Kimberley saw the re-routing of the railroad previously scheduled to join Cape Town to Durban, to the diamond diggings in Kimberley and even today the Black rural areas are virtually devoid of rail transport. The road network is also heavily concentrated in the White dominated areas. These two aspects together mean that it is very difficult for a Black farmer to market any surplus crops he may grow, which over a period of time tends to discourage him from producing such a surplus.

THE STATE AND SOUTH AFRICAN AGRICULTURE

Since the formation of the Union of South Africa in 1910, government has played an increasingly large role in the development of the present structures in South African agriculture. There are basically two lines on which the government approach is based; the first is that of an actual financial input and the second is through control over the activities of people operating in the sector.

The State and Financial Inputs into Agriculture

Financial assistance to agriculture in South Africa is both significant in quantity and biased in terms of the race group of those receiving it. Its significance is clearly shown by the fact that State aid to White agriculture over the five-year period from 1965–70 averaged 19.3 per cent of the net farming income in these years. In other words, state aid on average provided one-fith of an average White farmer's income. (R.P. 19/1972). State aid to agriculture comes in a number of different forms, the largest of which are the payments made to stabilize the prices paid to the producers of the various products. In

1975 approximately 58 per cent of government aid to agriculture went towards price stabilization. Other major recipients were rebates on fuel (15 per cent), fertilizer subsidization (10 per cent), and soil conservation measures and the provision of water (13 per cent).

Government subsidies for farm improvements, whilst they certainly increase agricultural productivity, will also have a bias towards the wealthy (and therefore mainly White). Since farm capital improvements have to be financed, this implies either that the farmer must have accumulated savings or must have access to loan funds; both of which are easier for people who are already reasonably wealthy.

The allocation of state financial aid has been a factor encouraging the widening of the productivity differential between Black and White agriculture. Frankel estimated that between 1910 and 1936, the state spent R224 million on White agriculture (Frankel: 1933), whereas a similar estimate of State expenditure on Black agriculture over this period placed it at just over R1,25 million (Hailey in Horwitz: 1968), so the ratio of state assistance to White and Black farming over this period was a massive 197:1. Lipton quotes data which suggests that the situation improved after 1936. By the decade of the 1950s, she estimated that the differential had declined to an average of just under 14:1 and still further to just under 2:1 by 1973. (Lipton: 1977). She points out, however, that if one takes the aid in terms of per farmer rather in total terms, the gap will be considerably wider as there are many more Black farmers than White.

If the State was intent on narrowing the racial agricultural productivity differential, far from simply narrowing the subsidy gap, it would need to put a far larger share of the total State aid towards subsidizing Black farmers than it does to White. The political power of the White 'platteland' however, makes this change seem highly unlikely at present and it appears that the State will continue to act to widen the racial differential in agriculture, at least in the near future.

The impact of the State on investment in agriculture also operates through the behaviour patterns of the State owned Land Bank. The Bank was established in 1912 and to quote Wilson –

> The significance of the Land Bank Act lay not only in the fact that credit was made specially available to assist farmers, but even more important, that henceforth farmers were to look increasingly to the State to solve their problems. (Wilson: 1971, p. 136)

The Land Bank advances money to farmers either on mortgage bonds secured on the land or on the security of a hypothec on their movable property. The first category of loan virtually excludes Blacks who are prohibited from owning land by both the Land Act and tribal custom. The second category whilst it is not inherently racially biased will again tend to favour the more wealthy farmer, who is more likely to be White.

Over the past few years, attempts have been made by the State to rectify this situation. A number of Development Corporations have been set up whose mandate is to facilitate the development of the Black States. Although the major portion of their funds are directed towards the establishment of Commerce and Industry in these areas, loans are granted to 'progressive' Black farmers to enable the purchase of such things as tractors and irrigation pumps.

In terms of both the difference in the economic situations of Black and White farmers and in the relative numbers, it is clear that a great deal more must be done by the State to provide for financial assistance of all types for Black agriculture.

State Controls in Agriculture

The State has increasingly intervened in agriculture over the period since the formation of Union, and in this area too the impact of the interference appears to have been towards the widening of the gap between Black and White farmers. The most significant aspect of State interference from the racial viewpoint was without doubt the passing of the 1913 Land Act and its subsequent amendment in 1936. This Act entrenched the unequal distribution of land that was the result of both settlement patterns and acts of conquest over a significant period of time.

By forbidding the sale of land outside the specified reserve areas (and the subsequently added 'scheduled areas') to Blacks, the Land Act confined nearly 70 per cent of South Africa's population to 14 per cent of the land area – at least from the ownership viewpoint. Nevertheless, as Lipton points out, the allocation of farm land between the farmers of the different groups is less unequal than these statistics would indicate, as most of the land devoted to urban development is classified as White-owned.

When one looks at the racial land holdings in terms of an average individual farmer, however, the situation is once again worse due to the large numbers of Black peasant farmers. Lipton estimated the ratio of farmland available to Blacks and Whites at 1:42 and of cultivated land at 1:46 for the year 1970. (Lipton: 1977)

State control over the Black labour supply has also affected South African agriculture. Wilson argues that as far as White agriculture was concerned, State efforts in the period from 1937–66 to protect the economic position of Whites in the towns, had almost the opposite effect on their position in the White rural areas and this period saw the increasing substitution of Black workers for White on White farms. This, coupled with the protected and improved economic position of the urban White, lead to the 'beswarting van die platteland' (population of the country areas by Blacks). Whites left the rural areas attracted by the better prospects, whilst Blacks found it increasingly difficult to do so, hemmed in as they were by a growing network of legislation governing their freedom of movement. (Wilson: 1971)

The control aspects of the introduction of price stabilization schemes, through the creation of the various marketing boards, has also had unintended racial bias. The boards, in some instances, act as quality setters and by so doing either exclude Black produce altogether, or accept it into the lower quality grades with a consequent adverse impact on Black farm incomes.

State control over the marketing of agricultural products is very widespread and the Marais/Du Plessis Commission estimated that over the period 1967–70, 87 per cent of all such produce passed through the hands of the State Marketing Boards. The type of control and its extent differ between products.

Firstly, there are single channel fixed price schemes which cover such products as the marketing of maize, winter cereals and industrial milk. In these schemes, the marketing process is State controlled from the producer right through to the final consumer. The products falling into this category can only be marketed through the marketing boards and the producer is paid a fixed price dependent upon grade. Any losses sustained through exporting surpluses, are covered by price stabilization funds. According to the Commission, approximately 28 per cent of all agricultural produce is marketed under these schemes. (R.P. 19/72)

The second type of marketing scheme is that of 'revenue pooling'.

Here again, all produce is marketed through a control board but in this instance the board does not pay the producer a fixed price, but instead pays an advance payment on delivery of the produce and a final payment based on the revenue earned by the board once the entire crop has been sold. Fresh fruit, consumer milk, sugar and wine, are some of the products marketed in this manner, and roughly 21 per cent of farm production falls under this type of scheme.

In addition, there are also some products that are freely marketed, subject to a guaranteed floor price whilst others, such as canned fruit, are subject only to controls that are imposed to 'ensure orderly marketing' and adequate grading and pricing systems.

AGRICULTURE AND CHANGING LIVING STANDARDS

In a developing economy the role played by the agricultural sector in raising living standards and determining the distribution of income is problematic, largely due to the role the sector also plays as the absorber of all labour surplus to the needs of the growing modern industrial sector.

Agriculture and Surplus Labour

Table 6.8 contains data showing the age distribution of working Black men in the two agricultural sectors and the modern economy. It illustrates the labour-absorbing role of South African agriculture. (see over)

If agriculture obtained its labour supply on the same basis as the remainder of the economy, one would expect the age distribution of the workforce in the sectors to be roughly the same. Wage rates are higher in the non-agricultural sectors of the economy and consequently it is the employment patterns of those sectors that largely determine the sectoral age structures. Employers in the modern sector select the workers best suited to their needs, and those rural men who are not so employed, remain in agriculture. It is no accident that in 1970, 43 per cent of Black males employed on White farms and 70 per cent of those employed on Black farms, were in the age groups below 25 years. The excess weighting of these young age groups reflects the difficulties faced by young Blacks who are trying to enter the modern sector workforce. These young men, although classified as agricultural workers, are in reality more likely to be (as yet unsuccessful) modern sector work seekers.

Table 6.8

THE AGE DISTRIBUTION OF WORKING AFRICAN MEN IN 1970

Age Category	Percentage of each age group of total employment in the sector			
	The Modern Economy	White Farms	Subsistence agriculture	
			Farmers	Labourers
Under 20	7,3	32,0	–	45,3
20–24	18,0	10,9	17,9	24,8
25–34	30,9	17,8	11,8	18,1
35–44	22,3	15,9	18,0	6,9
45–54	14,1	12,4	22,4	4,9
55–64	5,6	7,5	18,2	–
Over 64	1,8	3,5	11,7	–

SOURCE: *1970 Population Census Reports.*

The other interesting feature of the age distributions given in th
table, is the relatively heavy weighting of the older age groups in th
category 'subsistence farmers'. This reflects the other major socic
economic role played by the Black subsistence sector. The lack of
well-developed system of social welfare for Blacks in the moder
sector of the South African economy, coupled with the lega
difficulty of obtaining permanent residence rights in the urban area;
has led to Blacks who work in the modern sector for the majc
portion of their working lives, retaining their land rights in the Blac
rural areas. These areas in a very real sense, therefore, provide
significant proportion of the social security needs of the moder
sector workforce. The higher weightings of the older age groups i
the Black farming category, reflect the fact that modern secto
migrant workers retire to those areas and do so on average aft
roughly 20 years of modern sector service. (Nattrass: 1976a)

Agriculture and Income Distribution

Over the period from 1921–70, the agricultural sector's share
national output dropped from 22 per cent of the total to only 8 p
cent (i.e. by nearly 64 per cent). The sector's share of employme
also declined but at a slower rate, from 63 per cent to 33 per cent. Th

suggests that relative to the average for the country as a whole, living standards in agriculture will have declined over the period.

Within the sector itself, however, there seems to be a good deal of variation as can be seen from the data given in Table 6.9, which covers the period 1960–75.

Table 6.9

AVERAGE GROWTH RATES OF REAL INCOMES OF SELECTED GROUPS IN AGRICULTURE 1960–75

Group	Average Annual Growth Rate 1960–1975
White Farmers	7,3
White Wage Earners	4,6
Asian and Coloured Wage Earners	9,5
Black Wage Earners on White Farms	9,1
Subsistence Farm Sector	
Total Output	3,4
Per Capita Output	nil
South Africa	
Per Capita Output	2,5

SOURCE: *S.A. Statistics 1978, R.P. 28/1979* and *Report 09-17-03.*

Output in agriculture grew in real terms at less than half the rate achieved by the economy as a whole. However, this relatively slow rate of growth of output was offset as far as the commercial agricultural sub-sector was concerned, over the period 1960–75 by the outflow of people and in this sub-sector per capita incomes rose faster than they did in the country as a whole.

Looking at the commercial farming sector alone, it appears that the living standards of all groups working in the sector rose on average. The slowest rate of growth in average living standards in the sector was that of White farm workers (a relatively small group of people), whilst the highest were those of the Asian, Coloured and Black workers. However, as far as these groups are concerned, the rates of increase in wages were from very low initial levels. In 1960, for example, average Black wage levels in commercial agriculture were R77, (in 1970 prices), by 1975, growing at an average yearly compound growth rate of 9,1 per cent, they had reached only R285 per year.

In addition, employment levels of all the groups declined over at least part of this period and indeed, in the case of the White, Coloured and Asian groups, did so throughout the period. As a result of this reduction in employment levels, the share of income earned in the commercial agricultural sector, that was paid out as wages to Black and White farm labourers, declined over the period 1960–75. This was because the gains from the wage rate increases were insufficient to offset the loss from the reduced employment. In other words, the increases in the living standards of those remaining in the sector were achieved as a result of the large numbers of people of all race groups who left the sector over this period.

Whether or not the people leaving White agriculture will be better or worse off will largely depend upon the sector in which they are re-employed. Whites leaving the farms in general move into the cities and obtain better paying jobs. Blacks, however, are unlikely to be as fortunate. The official route for a Black seeking to leave work on a White farm is for him to uproot his family, resettle them in one of the Black States and then endeavour to find himself work in the town as a migrant worker. As income levels in subsistence agriculture were virtually static over the period 1960–75, Black farm workers who were unable to join the migrant workforce seem almost certain to have been made worse off through their move from the White farms. On the other hand, those who finally obtain work in the modern sector will, in general, be better off financially, but will have to endure the social hardships imposed by the migrant labour system.

Not only were the Blacks who moved from White farming districts into the rural areas of the Black States likely to be worse off in income terms than they were, but the inhabitants of the subsistence agricultural sector as a whole also lost ground relative to the remainder of the economy over the period 1960–75. Real output in the subsistence sector grew more slowly than the total output of the economy, and the growth in output that was achieved in this sector, was offset by the increased number of people dependent upon it. As a result, real incomes per head in the Black rural areas were static throughout this period. Any increases in the living standards of these regions were due solely to the increased remittances sent back by the migrant workers.

The State and the Distribution of Income

On the production side, it was very clear that State policies regarding agriculture favoured the White farmer. On the income or consumption side this bias, whilst still present, is not quite as marked, as can be seen from the data in Table 6.10.

Table 6.10

ESTIMATES OF RACIAL CONSUMPTION OF STATE EXPENDITURE ON AGRICULTURE

| Year | Share Consumed by Race Group | | | |
	White	Coloured	Asian	Black
1949/50	45	18	4	33
1975/76	34	13	3	50
Population 1975	17	5	3	75

SOURCE: M. D. McGrath: 1979b.

On the basis of these estimates, although the major proportion of all State expenditure on agriculture accrues initially to White farmers, a significant proportion does in fact ultimately get passed on to Black consumers in the form of lower farm produce prices. The estimates contained in Table 6.10 also suggest that the proportion being passed on to Blacks rose between the years 1949/50 and 1975/76, from one third of the total State expenditure on agriculture to one half. (McGrath: 1979b). Part of this increase was the result of the increase in the Black group's ability to purchase farm products and part reflected the increased State expenditure on Black agricultural producers that took place over this period.

THE FUTURE

Agriculture is not only the source of supply of a crucial input, food, it is also a source of livelihood for nearly one third of South Africa's population. Over the period since the formation of the Union, the government has made a great effort to establish a viable, White, agricultural sector and in general, these efforts have been crowned with success. There are, however, still two significant areas of concern.

The first of these relates to the living conditions of Black workers on White farms, which on average are still extremely low. Not only are the money wage rates paid lower than those paid in the other sectors of the modern economy, but housing conditions are also in general poor and the distribution of social overhead capital for Blacks in these areas, such as schools, clinics and hospitals, is extemely sparse.

An increase in the real living standards of Blacks working on White farms will require a significant increase in the labour productivity levels in the sector. This, in its turn, will necessitate the upgrading of the Black worker himself. It is essential, therefore, that the government make a determined effort to extend the full range of public educational facilities to Blacks living on White farms. Education is the base upon which future progress in this sector will rest. The need for trained agriculturalists will become more and more pressing with time. With the present exodus of Whites from South Africa's rural areas and the growing pressure of population on the land in the Black farming regions, it seems inevitable that the future will see commercial farming passing increasingly into the hands of South African Blacks.

The second area of concern is that of subsistence agriculture. Although output levels have increased, the rates of growth obtained have not been sufficient to maintain the living standards of the people dependent on the sector. As nearly one third of South Africa's Blacks live in the subsistence farming regions, an increase in average Black living levels will effectively be dependent upon an improvement in the productivity levels of subsistence agriculture. This issue is of vital importance to the development of the 'Black States' and is taken up in more detail in this context in Chapter Ten.

SEVEN

The Mining Sector

INTRODUCTION

The mining sector has historically been the mainspring of South African modern economic development. The foundations of the present day economy were laid with the exploitation of the mineral discoveries of firstly, diamonds in Kimberley, and then gold on the Witwatersrand. Even today, more than a century later, the mining sector plays a crucial role in the continuing development of the South African economy.

The Importance of the Early Discoveries

Prior to the discovery of diamonds not only was the area now known as the Republic of South Africa mainly agriculturally oriented, but also in certain areas the White population was not firmly established. The historian Leonard Thompson commented on the almost total lack of development in the Trekker Republics of the Orange Free State and the Transvaal prior to the discovery of the mineral deposits, saying:

> lacking markets and separated from the colonial towns by great distances the republican Afrikaners remained essentially Trekboers . . . producing very little for exchange. (Thompson: 1969, p. 426)

Another historian, Denoon, argues that there is evidence to suggest that in the new settlement areas of those times, Whites were losing ground to Blacks in terms of their relative agricultural efficiency. He concluded his analysis with the comment:

> In the whole region north of the Cape Colony the African communities seemed likely to control and contain the White penetration of the interior and there was even the possibility that the extent of White settlement might have to be retrenched until such time as the White settlers became more productive. (Denoon: 1972, p. 64)

Hobart Houghton classified the economic climate in South Africa prior to the discovery of diamonds as being 'far from favourable' and pointed out that this was the result of the coincidence of a number of adverse factors, amongst them being the imminence of the opening of the Suez Canal with its consequent threat to the ship chandlering trade, the international economic recession, the drop in the price of wool which followed at the end of the American Civil War, a severe drought and Britain's attitude towards her relatively impecunious colony. (Houbart Houghton: 1971)

The discovery and exploitation of diamonds and gold led to an economic metamorphosis and the entrenchment of the White settlers throughout the region. The economist Frankel, commenting in 1938 on the overall importance of the diamond discoveries to the establishment of modern South Africa said:

> The miracle which Europeans in South Africa needed had occurred. The most effective means for obtaining surplus wealth had been found when the size of the industry is taken into account. The wealth accruing from the production of diamonds in South Africa has probably been greater than that which has ever been obtained from any other commodity anywhere in the world. (Frankel: 1938, p. 52)

The opening up of the Kimberley diamond mines in the late 1860s was followed in the 1880s by the discovery of gold, first in the Eastern Transvaal in the Barberton area and subsequently on the Witwatersrand. The impact of the development of these two highly profitable mining ventures on the South African economy was one of virtual transformation. Over the 60 year period from 1860 to 1920 the White population grew at a yearly average rate of over 3 per cent, reflecting the massive immigration that took place as people were attracted to the new openings.

The growth of the towns was even more spectacular. In 1860 roughly 13 per cent of the Cape population lived in urban areas. By 1904 this percentage had increased to 53 in the case of South Africa's Whites, to 51 for the Asian group, 37 for Coloureds and to 10 for the African group. Only a year after the discovery of diamonds, Kimberley was the largest town in South Africa apart from Cape Town and by as early as 1871, had a White population numbering some 50 000 people. Johannesburg, which did not exist prior to 1880, had over 290 000 inhabitants by 1921.

The transformation of the economic structure was equally dramatic. In 1865, 75 per cent of the workforce was employed in agriculture
and by 1921 this percentage had declined to 33 per cent; Government
expenditure grew at an average of approximately 5,5 per cent per
year over the period and the public debt by over 8 per cent. The value
of exports and imports also grew at an average yearly rate of 8 per
cent between 1867 and 1921 and the proportion made up of
agricultural products dropped rapidly as the products of the mining
industry became increasingly significant.

Quite apart from the economic revolution that took place in South
Africa as a result of the mineral discoveries, the exploitation of the
diamond and gold finds set in motion certain behaviour patterns,
particularly in the field of labour relations, that significantly affected
both the pace of South African development and the way of life of her
inhabitants and indeed continue to do so right up to the present day.

The impact that the discoveries of the first diamonds and
subsequently gold had on the emerging modern economy were
substantially different from one another in certain respects, although
they are often discussed together by analysts of the early development of South Africa. Consequently, one should be careful not to
generalize too quickly when one is discussing this topic.

THE DEVELOPMENT OF THE DIAMOND FIELDS AND SOUTH AFRICAN ECONOMIC GROWTH

The discovery of diamonds in the Kimberley area came at the end of a
period of severe depression and as a result, the discovery generated
an enormous flow of people to the area of the finds, who were intent
on recovering the economic status that they had held prior to the
depression.

De Kiewiet described the diamond fields as:

> South Africa's first industrial community. There South Africa
> really faced for the first time the modern problems of capital
> and labour. There South Africa confronted a new competition
> between its Black and White inhabitants, not for land or capital
> but for a place in industry. (De Kiewiet: 1941, p. 89)

Frankel argued that the most significant characteristic of the
diamond industry (and one which distinguished it from gold mining)

was its ability to generate surplus. (Frankel: 1938). The diamond industry developed largely through the process of reinvesting the profits that were earned in the industry. Indeed Frankel estimated that, prior to the attempt by Cecil Rhodes to amalgamate the diggings, for which he negotiated a loan from the international bankers Rothchilds, there was virtually no international capital invested in the diamond industry, and further that even by 1938 foreign investment in the diamond mines totalled less than £20 million.

In the initial stages, particularly in the case of the alluvial deposits, very little capital was applied to diamond mining. However, as the dry diggings began to go deeper and to cave in and fill with water, it became apparent that the answer lay in abandoning the initial mining techniques, which consisted of mining a 47 foot square claim with a 15 foot road servitude, and in the adoption of subterranean mining. With the change in the approach to diamond mining, came a significant increase in the size of the capital input needed for the mining operations.

By 1880 there were 12 companies in Kimberley with a total share capital of £2 500 000. De Beers itself was formed by Rhodes in 1880 to take over the combined claims of himself, Rudd, his partner and others, and had an issued capital of £200 000. Rhodes continued to consolidate claims and by 1885 De Beers had a capital of £841 550. Speculation hit the diamond industry at this time and in 1881, 50 companies were floated in six months, with an issued capital of £8 million – very little of which was actually subscribed. What was issued was, however, still practically all in the hands of the local capitalists.

At the same time as mining costs started to increase with the switch to underground mining techniques, competition between the mining companies lead to an oversupply of diamonds to the market and world prices declined dramatically. It became apparent to the leading capitalists of the time that it was essential to control the supply of diamonds to the market if the profitability of the industry was to be maintained. The output of the industry could only be controlled if the industry itself was controlled and to this end a bitter battle was waged between Rhodes, with his De Beers Group of mines and Barney Barnatoe of Kimberley Mines. In an attempt to finalize the control of the Diamond Diggings, Rhodes obtained a loan of £

million from Rothchilds and this enabled him to buy a large holding in the Kimberley Mine, thus transferring the effective control of the industry to De Beers Limited. By 1889, the industry had been finally consolidated into a monopoly, setting the scene for the control over the marketing of diamonds which was to continue up to the present time, subject only to some restructuring by Sir Ernest Oppenheimer in the 1920s.

The links established by Rhodes, through Sir Alfred Beit, with the foreign banking community, were to prove very useful in South Africa's subsequent development. They were particularly valuable to the mining entrepreneurial community when the time came to develop the capital hungry in gold mining industry.

Labour on the Early Diamond Fields

As the diamond finds occurred in an area that was relatively sparsely populated, the major proportion of the labour supply for the mines came in from other regions. Whites came from as far afield as the Cornish tin mines and in the main worked the fields on a regular basis, whilst Blacks came from a large variety of different areas in Southern Africa and in general worked on the diggings for a relatively short period of time. It has been argued that in these early days most Blacks who came into the area seeking work were 'target oriented', in that they came with the intention of acquiring a specific object or set of objects, rather than money and worked only for as long as it was necessary for them to earn sufficient to be able to purchase the desired commodities.

Guns were imported by the mine owners and sold to the Black workers. These proved to be an excellent means of attracting African labour, as many African Chiefs purposefully sent their young men to the diggings to arm themselves by working for a few months on the diamond fields. The importance of the gun as a means of attracting Black labour at this time is emphasised by the fact that Cecil Rhodes, who was elected to the Cape Parliament to represent the diamond area, made his maiden speech against a proposal to disarm the Basuto nation!

In the early days of the diamond diggings there were four clearly definable classes of people involved in the process of extracting diamonds, the diggers who were made up of both Black and White claim holders, White mine workers, a class of Black labourers who were the biggest proportion of the region's Black population and who came into Kimberley from a wide geographical area, and a class of convict labour supplied by the local jail. Sheila van der Horst reports that the average size of the labour force employed on the diamond fields between 1870 and 1880 was approximately 10 000 people. (Van der Horst: 1971). An on the spot observer, Matthews, estimated that over the period 1873–87, approximately 67 000 people passed through the Kimberley jail, which suggests that convict labour could have been quite significant in numerical terms. (Matthews: 1887)

The period from 1871–75 saw the gradual but continuous undermining of the position of the Black claim holder. White claim holders argued that their Black counterparts engaged in illicit diamond buying, and by providing a market for the stolen diamonds, encouraged the Black employees of the White digger to steal. They also alleged that employment of Blacks by Black claim holders encouraged vagrancy in the area. There were outbreaks of violence against Black claim holders instigated by Whites, which ultimately culminated in the Black Flag rebellion. However, Kallaway comments that by 1875 'the whole issue of Native claim holders appears to have evaporated' (Kallaway: 1974), and the issue had become one of Black labour rather than of Black mine-owners.

From the outset of the emergence of the modern South African economy, which commenced with the development of the Kimberley diggings, significant differences in the economic status of Black and White workers began to emerge. This difference was not limited to the length of stay on the mines. White workers, particularly those recruited from abroad, had a monopoly of the mining skills that were available, and so were able to command premium wages and in the 1880s the racial average wage ratio on the diamond fields was already as high as 5:1. (Van der Horst: 1971)

The 1880s also saw the introduction of the compound system for Black labour employed on the mines. These early compounds were totally closed and consisted of simple barracks in which the Black miners lived for the period of their contract. The concept was introduced to combat theft on the mines, and also to reduce the lost production time that resulted from drunkenness. According to official sources, prior to the introduction of the compound system, it was commonplace for from half to two-thirds of the African mine labour force to be absent at the beginning of the week, due to 'drunken excesses' over the weekend. Drunkenness leads to crime. In Kimberley in a population of 20–30 thousand people, there were 8 000 cases brought before the magistrate in 1882. This was regarded as 'average'. (Van der Horst: 1971)

By 1892 some 9 000 Black workers were housed in twelve closed compounds and the compound system effectively gave the White mining community almost the same degree of control over the 'free' Black labour supply as they were able to exercise over the convict labour force.

There is evidence that the introduction of the compound system did 'mitigate the evils arising from drunkenness and theft' and that both the mine-owners and the city dwellers benefited from the system. It has also been argued that that the miners themselves were better off, as their living conditions were improved and as their ability to purchase goods was limited to the range of goods provided in the company store, they saved more and returned home with a larger proportion of their earnings (in goods) than was the case previously. In support of this contention, it is pointed out that the diamond mines, unlike the later gold mines, have never had to tout actively for labour and to the present time have remained a 'popular' destination for migrant workers. (Hutt: 1964)

The Impact of the Diamond Discoveries on Relative Living Standards

The discovery of diamonds and the subsequent exploitation of the diamond fields, undoubtedly triggered the development of the modern South African economy. However, they also laid the foundation for the inequality that is characteristic of present South Africa.

The benefits from the diamond mines were unequally distributed. This unequal distribution had many facets. The distribution was unequal between the prospectors themselves, due to the nature of the finds' made on the various claims; between capital and labour due to the high rate of return on capital; between skilled and unskilled labour due to the shortage of skilled labour and the abundance of unskilled labour; and between Black and White members of the emerging industrial community due to the almost total monopoly of skills held by the latter.

Further, the historian, De Kiewiet, argues that had diamonds not been discovered, the development of the South African railway system, although it would undoubtedly have been slower, would have followed a route up through the eastern coastal belt. Had this in fact happened, it would have provided a large number of African traditional farmers with access to the major urban markets, which would have facilitated the development of a viable Black peasant farming community. As it was, White farmers, who enjoyed access to the expanding markets, prospered, whilst their Black counterparts were slowly placed in a less and less competitive situation and a growing gap began to open between their relative levels of prosperity.

THE DEVELOPMENT OF THE GOLD FIELDS

The discovery and exploitation of the gold bearing reefs on the Witwatersrand from 1886 onwards intensified all the tendencies and pressures introduced into the South African economy by the exploitation of the Kimberley diamond mines.

The Gold Mines and the Labour Supply
The Period up to 1970

Almost from its inception the gold mining industry relied heavily on the political machinery of the state to assist it in generating an adequate supply of low cost labour. (Jeeves: 1974). One might well wonder why it was that an industry emerging in an area in which there was apparently an adequate supply of labour should need state assistance. The reasons advanced are threefold. Firstly, African labourers were reluctant to accept jobs on the gold mines if they were able to obtain alternative employment. Secondly, the nature of the gold reef itself required the mining entrepreneurs to commit themselves to the size of the mine and the grade of ore mined in the initial development phases of the mine. This added to the risk factor, since a rise in the labour costs or a fall in the price of gold could put a low grade mine out of business. Finally, in the early stages of the industry, individual mines were unable to control the conflict and rivalry that developed between them over the available labour supply.

In an attempt to solve the labour supply problem, the gold mining entrepreneurs developed a centralized recruiting system to eliminate competition within the industry for labour and in addition, turned to the political system for help in increasing the supply of labour itself. In 1898, the central recruiting system, known as the 'Rand Native Labour Association', was formed, out of which were to grow the two associations – the Native Recruiting Corporation (NRC), which was responsible for the centralized recruiting of mine labour from within South Africa itself, Botswana, Lesotho and Swaziland, and the Witwatersrand Native Labour Association (WNLA), which recruited from geographical areas further afield. These two institutions were to control the recruitment of labour for the gold mines throughout the following 80 year period, combining once again in the late 1970s into one organization known as The Employment Bureau of Africa Limited (TEBA).

On the labour supply side the mining entrepreneurs turned to the state for assistance. Within the region that was to become South Africa, they lobied successfully for acts such as the Glen Gray Act passed by the parliament of the Cape Colony in 1894 and the Pass Law Bill passed by the Volksraad of the South African Republic in 1895. It has been argued that these attempts to increase the 'domestic' supply of labour through the use of the political machine were largely unsuccessful. Further, the true importance of the growing relationship between the then newly-formed Chamber of Mines and the state, lay in the fact that it enabled the Chamber to use the state to assist it to enlarge the area from which Black labour could be recruited for the mines, through the negotiation of labour contracts with countries beyond South Africa's political borders. (Wilson: 1972)

As early as 1898, some 60 per cent of the gold mines' workforce was drawn from Mozambique and although the relative importance of Mozambique as a source of labour declined somewhat over the first half of the 20th century, foreign labour as a whole remained of great significance to the industry, as can be seen from the data in Table 7.1.

There is probably no other issue that is so hotly debated by South African historians as that of the nature of the impact of the development of the gold mining industry on South African labour practices and on the wider aspect of the relative living standards of the different racial groups. Whilst all analysts agree that the roots of the present South African labour market were planted in the days of the early development of the mining industry, there is virtually no concensus regarding either the motives guiding the early mining pioneers, or the weight that should be placed upon the actions that took place in this initial period of development in relation to subsequent development, when determining the relative economic positions of the race groups.

Table 7.1

SOURCES OF LABOUR SUPPLY TO THE GOLD MINES

Year	South Africa		Foreign Black Labour			
			Mozambique		Other	
	Number	Percentage	Number	Percentage	Number	Percentage
1896	18 000	33,0	32 000	60,0	4 000	7,0
1906	18 000	22,8	53 000	65,4	9 000	11,8
1916	50 000	22,8	83 000	38,1	86 000	39,1
1926	84 000	41,3	90 000	44,5	29 000	14,2
1936	166 000	52,2	88 000	27,8	64 000	20,0
1960	145 000	36,0	95 000	24,1	158 000	39,9
1974	92 000	25,2	102 000	27,9	171 000	46,9
1979	216 000	54,0	39 000	9,8	145 000	36,2

SOURCE: 1896–1960 (Wilson: 1972), 1974 and 1979 kindly supplied by the Chamber of Mines.

Some argue that the introduction of the compound system, the creation of the centralized recruiting facilities and the expansion of the area from which labour was drawn was made necessary by the 'high leisure preference' of Africans and further that these activities should in no way be seen as exploitative. (Hutt: 1964), More radical observers, on the other hand, see these institutions as being the cornerstones in the edifice of the means for the exploitation of Black labour by capital. (Rex: 1974, Johnstone: 1976)

The debate is a longstanding one that has been extremely heated at times. However, when the debris is cleared away, one finds that the outcome is still inconclusive, as both sides tend to overstate their case. Nevertheless, regardless of the issues that are related to motives, the outcome of the introduction of the compound system, with the

onsequent institutionalization of the migrant labour system itself, is
ot still at issue. It has been adequately demonstrated that the cost of
lack labour to the gold mines actually dropped between 1911 and
931 and then once it had risen back to the 1911 level, remained
onstant right up to 1969, notwithstanding the fact that Black
mployment levels doubled over this period. (Wilson: 1972). Not
nly did Black labour costs remain constant over this later period,
ut the gap between White and Black earnings on the gold mines also
ncreased from 9:1 in 1911 to 18:1 in 1969. In addition, it is also an
ncontrovertible fact that the system of migrant labour, commenced
vith the discovery and exploitation of mineral and entrenched in the
nining industry by the creation of the compound system, is still, one
undred years later, the most outstanding characteristic of the South
.frican labour market.

he Gold Mines and the Labour Market After 1970

'he period following 1970 is one of dramatic change on the mine
abour scene. Table 7.2 shows the behaviour of the average wage
ates paid to Black and White workers on the gold mines for selected
ears from 1915–78 and highlights this change.

'able 7.2
,VERAGE REAL MINE WAGES FOR SELECTED YEARS 1915–78[1]

Year	Average Wage per Man[2]	Average		Black White Wage Ratio	Black White Wage Gap[2]
		White Wage[2]	Black Wage[2]		
1915	409	2 255	213	10,6:1	2 042
1935	434	2 331	233	10,0:1	2 098
1950	503	2 757	191	14,4:1	2 566
1960	544	3 275	194	16,9:1	3 081
1970	583	4 294	207	20,7:1	4 087
1976	1 012	4 836	614	7,9:1	4 222
1978	1 049	4 898	663	7,4:1	4 235

. All in 1970 prices.   2. 1970 Rands.

OURCE: *South African Statistics 1978. Union Statistics for 50 years.*

The table illustrates Wilson's conclusion, namely that Black miners' wages in real terms remained virtually unchanged throughout the period from 1915–70. The eight years between 1970 and 1978, however, show a very different trend. Black wages were on average more than three times greater in 1978 than they were in 1970. Similarly, the ratio of Black to White average earnings in mining which had increased from 1935 to 1970 to stand at a massive 1:2 declined sharply to 1:7,4. The size of the absolute gap in racial average real wages, however, continued to increase, albeit at a very much slower pace. Mining was the only sector in the modern economy in which this occurred over this period.

A significant change in the wage policy of the mines took place in 1972. Between March, 1973 and June, 1974 the starting wage for a Black novice miner on the gold mines rose by 140 per cent. The average wages paid to miners rose throughout the period 1971–79 and although the rate varied significantly in every year, the increase in money wages was greater than that of prices, and the real wages paid in the industry rose. The yearly percentage changes are given in Table 7.3.

Table 7.3
AVERAGE BLACK GOLD MINING WAGES 1971–79

Year	Percentage Increase in		
	Money Wages	Prices	Real Wages
1971	7,0	6,4	,6
1972	16,5	6,5	10,6
1973	36,5	9,5	27,0
1974	61,5	9,2	52,3
1975	67,5	13,5	54,0
1976	16,5	11,1	5,4
1977	11,8	11,3	,5
1978	15,0	10,1	4,9
1979	18,0	13,1	4,9

SOURCE: *Chamber of Mines 1979 Year End Review, South African Statistics 1978* and *Reserve Bank Quarterly Bulletin March, 1980.*

Why have Black mining wages risen so significantly in the period from 1971 to 1979 when they were virtually static from 1915–70? It is not possible to isolate any one factor as being either the single or even the main cause of the change in wage policy, as a number of different factors all appear to have some bearing on the issue.

Although one would normally assume that an increase in wages of such magnitude would reflect a growing shortage of labour, this does not seem to be the case. Although the estimates made of unemployment over this period differ in size, they do not differ in direction and all show rising unemployment levels in South Africa over this period. (Simpkins: 1978, Van der Merwe: 1977, Department of Statistics Current Population Survey). It has been suggested that despite the growing unemployment, the mining industry could still be short of labour as it requires a specific type of labour – in the main men who are physically fit and between 20 and 40 years of age. (Knight: 1977). This does not, however, seem to be the case either, as one of the characteristics of present South African unemployment is that it is quite heavily concentrated amongst Blacks in the younger age groups.

A factor that does seem to have some bearing on the issue, however, is the fact that growing political hostility towards South Africa has encouraged the mining industry to look to an increasing extent for its labour supply within South Africa's borders. This tendency was further strengthened by the withdrawal of the Malawian labour supply to the mines following an air crash, which took place in Francistown in April, 1974, in which a number of returning labour migrants lost their lives, and by the reduction in Mozambiquean labour, which occurred immediately following Frelimo's rise to power. Although the number of migrants from Mozambique subsequently increased, the impact of the temporary reduction was sufficient to change the attitude of the Chamber of Mines and an increased recruiting effort was launched within South African territory.

Initially this effort was directed towards the rural areas in the Black States, but subsequently the area was extended to include certain specified White urban and rural districts. The impact of the change in recruiting policy on the national composition of the mines' Black labour complement can be seen very clearly in the data in Table 7.1. In order to attract South African Blacks to the mines the wages offered had to be more competitive with those paid in the other sectors of the economy and this exerted a strong upward pressure on mine wages for Blacks. This argument may also explain why the increases tailed off somewhat after 1975. The years 1975 to mid-1979 were years in which the general level of economic activity were low and unemployment levels were increasing, which reduced the degree of competition between the mining industry and the rest of the modern economy for the available labour supply, lessening the pressure on mine wage rates.

Another factor that should be taken into account was the level of unrest in the mine labour compounds during 1974, which reached a peak in January, 1975. Although the Chamber of Mines came to the conclusion that the unrest was not related to conditions of employment, this conclusion has been questioned. (Horner and Kooy: 1980). It is probable that, no matter what the official view of the disturbances, mining employers had the costs of their continuation in mind when they were evaluating the potential for increasing wages.

The period from 1970 on was one that saw growing moral pressure for increased Black wages, applied to South African employers in all sectors of the economy. This pressure came from both within and beyond South Africa's borders and the mining industry, with its combination of high profitability and low average Black wage rates, was in many instances, the focal point. This too was an upward force on Black mine wage rates.

Finally, there is little doubt that the overriding influence was the improvement in the industry's 'ability to pay', that followed from the buoyant gold price, ruling from 1972 to mid-1975. The higher gold price put the gold mining companies in a position to meet the increased wage bills and this, coupled with a desire to increase the South African component of the workforce and the high levels of moral pressure on the industry, to pay more to their Black mineworkers, engendered significant increases in the wages paid to Blacks. (Parsons: 1980)

It is interesting to note that the opening of recruitment points, in areas in which such recruiting was not previously undertaken, had a significant influence in the domestic spatial distribution of the areas supplying mineworkers. One of the well established myths of the mining industry was that Zulu men would not work on the mines. The extension of the recruiting network into KwaZulu's rural areas saw this myth dispelled, as the number of Zulu's working in the industry rose substantially and has continued to do so up to the first quarter of 1980. This is not really surprising, since the extension of the recruiting system into the home region of the migrant lowers the cost of job search to a prospect mineworker and so is the equivalent to him of an increase in the wage rate that he is offered.

The combination of higher mine wages and growing unemployment in the remainder of the economy has greatly improved the relative attractiveness of the industry as a potential employer. The period after 1975 has seen a significant increase in the degree of stabilization present in the mines' Black workforce. Workers started to return to the mines in increasing numbers after the completion of their contract and by February, 1978, a spokesmen for the industry stated that the mines faced an over-supply of labour. This situation continued on through 1979 and was still the case in April, 1980. It has had the effect of decreasing the rate of labour turnover. In 1977, according to the Chamber of Mines publications, TEBA recruited 545 000 people in order to maintain an average workforce on the mines of 385 000 men. By 1979, however, they only needed to recruit 407 000 people to maintain a working strength of 430 000.

THE GOLD MINES AND CAPITAL FORMATION

Unlike the diamond mines which were sufficiently profitable in the early years to produce the major portion of the capital invested in the industry from the surplus earned, the early development of the gold mining industry in South Africa required large inputs of capital. This was largely due to the nature of the ore bodies themselves, which were on average low grade and found at deep levels. Gold mining was essentially an underground exercise from its inception and as a result its development made heavy demands on capital.

Since the economy was not, at that time, sufficiently developed to be able to provide this capital from domestic sources, the development of the gold mines saw the influx of major amounts of foreign capital and in this respect the international connections built up by the diamond magnates during the process of the consolidation of that industry were particularly important. The first attempt to float shares in London was undertaken in 1887 by Consolidated Gold-fields, (Rhodes and Rudd). This issue amounted to £100 000 and the prospectus included statements concerning the connection with and the success that the promoters had had in the diamond fields (Frankel: 1938)

If South Africa is to be considered a victim of economic imperialism (dominated by the more advanced countries), which itself is arguable, this came about through the dependence that arose from the links established during the early exploitation of the gold discoveries, rather than from that of diamonds. Between 1887 and 1934, some £200 million were invested in the gold mining industry, 60 per cent of which came from foreign sources. (Frankel: 1938)

It is interesting to note that whereas foreign investors supplied 60 per cent of the capital needs of the industry between 1887 and 1934, they received 75 per cent of the dividends that were paid out over the period. This suggests either that foreign capitalists had a higher success rate in the mining sphere than did South African local mining entrepreneurs, or that they were more reluctant to reinvest their earnings in the expanding industry.

The development of the gold mining industry has had an enormous impact on South African capital accumulation. Initially this took the form of the generation of a local industrial output that was closely allied to the immediate needs of the mining industry itself, such as the production of explosives, pit props, mining boots and food.

In some instances there was a direct link between the growing mining sector and infant manufacturing activity. Examples of this are the De Beers ownership of the explosives manufacturing plant set up at Somerset West in the Cape and the decision by Goldfields to move into the industrial sphere in 1919. (Innes: 1977)

It has been argued by some radical analysts that because the gold mining sector was predominantly owned by foreign capital, the industry initially strongly opposed the development of a local manufacturing industry, seeing it as being against the interests of its other foreign based industrial activities. (Kaplan: 1974). This argument has, however, been very convincingly undermined by Innes who argues firstly that the development of certain types of local manufactures were actually in the interest of the mining entrepreneurs, as they reduced mine operating costs and, secondly, that one of the major mining groups in the industry, Anglo American, was to all practical purposes locally orientated rather than foreign, orientated, since from 1924 on nearly 90 per cent of its total economic activities were centred in Southern Africa. (Innes: 1977)

The mining industry in general, and gold mining in particular, has also made a very significant contribution to South African capital accumulation through its capacity to earn foreign exchange. A country seeking to establish a manufacturing sector often runs up against a foreign exchange constraint. A developing economy seldom has the economic capacity to produce the capital goods needed by the growing industrial sector and so has to import them from the more advanced economies. Not only do such economies have high import requirements which have to be paid for in foreign exchange, but they also often lack the ability to export sufficient to enable them to earn the needed foreign resources. The South African economy has not had to face this dilemma, as the mining sector in general and the gold mines in particular have generated substantial foreign earnings. Table 7.4 shows the gold sector's contribution to exports.

Table 7.4

GOLD SALES AS A PROPORTION OF EXPORTS

Year (Three Year Average)	Exports in Value Term (R millions)		Percentage of Total that is Gold
	Total	Gold	
1911–1913	115 700	70 100	61
1930–1933	137 600	82 400	60
1950–1953	854 500	180 100	21
1974–1976	6 029 100	2 483 900	41
1978–1979	8 152 500	4 933 500	61

SOURCE: *Union Statistics for 50 years, South African Statistics 1978* and *South African Reserve Bank Quarterly Bulletin* March, 1980.

The mining sector's share of export earnings actually understates the contribution that it makes to net foreign exchange earnings because, unlike manufacturing, the sector makes relatively little use of imported inputs. Table 7.5 shows the contribution of the three major sectors of the economy to South Africa's net foreign exchange earnings in 1975.

Table 7.5

THE CONTRIBUTIONS OF MAJOR SECTORS TO IMPORTS AND EXPORTS
IN 1975

Sector	1975 Value of (R millions)		
	Exports	Imports	Contribution
Agriculture	597 8	142 0	455 8
Mining	3 342 5	1 130 5	2 212 0
Manufacturing	1 771 3	5 684 6	-3 913 3

SOURCE: *1975 Input Output Table.*

From the data in the table the dependency of the manufacturing
sector on the export earnings of the mining industry becomes very
clear. Of the total imports into manufacturing in 1975, R3 333
million, 59 per cent was in the form of machinery and equipment.
This highlights how dependent the further development of the sector
is on the economy's overall ability to earn foreign exchange. In 1975,
60 per cent of the South African demand for basic chemicals
(including oil) was satisfied by imported products, as was 62 per cent
of the demand for non-electrical machinery, 43 per cent of the
demand for motor vehicles and 42 per cent of that for electrical
machinery and equipment.

Had South Africa not had its very profitable mining sector,
progress in manufacturing would have been limited to the level of the
industry's own ability to produce capital goods, together with what it
could buy abroad with the proceeds from exports. What is more,
continued economic development in this country is still heavily
reliant upon the mining industry's ability to earn foreign exchange.

One of the most important sources of investment funds in an
economy is non-wage income, as the propensity to save from this
income is, in general, higher than that from wage earnings. The
mining industry has also made a substantial contribution in this area
as the industry's share of non-wage income has been very much
greater than its share of output over the past 20 year period. Table 7.6
shows the mining sector's contribution to non-wage income (profits)
in South Africa in relation to its contribution to output for the year
1946/1948, 1959/1961, 1969/1971 and 1975/1977.

Table 7.6

THE MINING SECTOR'S CONTRIBUTION TO OUTPUT AND PROFITS

Percentage Contribution to	1946/1948	1959/1961	1969/1971	1975/1977
Output	11,9	12,6	8,8	8,0
Profits	10,1	17,0	14,0	17,1

SOURCE: *South African Statistics 1978.*

The data in Table 7.6 shows how important the mining sector has been as a source of potential investment funds. Although the sector's percentage contribution to South Africa's output fell over the period covered in the table, from 12 per cent of the total, to 8 per cent, its share of non-wage income generated in the economy increased from 10 per cent to 17 per cent.

The mining sector has also been a significant source of funds for the state. In 1911, mining taxation comprised only 5 per cent of the value added by the sector (White wages taking a further 36 per cent, Black wages 24 per cent and profits 34 per cent). By 1936, the state's share of the value added had increased to 15,6 per cent and by 1946, largely as a result of Hofmeyer's war budget policies, had risen still further and stood at 25 per cent. Even though the period 1969–1978 was one which saw a decline in the state's share of the gold mining sector's value added from 24 per cent to 21 per cent, total state revenue from mining more than doubled over the period, growing at an annual average of over 13 per cent.

The final influence that the development of the mining industry has had upon South African capital accumulation relates to the impact that the sector has had upon South Africa's spatial development. The mineral deposits are not equally distributed through the space economy and by and large are in no way related to the historical patterns of the distribution of South Africa's population. The mineral deposits are concentrated in the northern and western areas of the economy, whereas the population densities are greatest in the eastern seaboard regions. The spatial dislocation between minerals and population meant that as the former were exploited in increasing quantities, so disparities in the level of economic development and in the per capita incomes in the different regions began to open up.

As time passed, so these spatial disparities were intensified by two factors that emerged on the economic scene. Firstly, the expanding mining sector began to attract industrial and commercial enterprises and these activities too were not equally distributed throughout the economic space, but tended to concentrate either on the Witwatersrand itself or at the seaports which were handling the trade to and from the gold fields. Secondly, South African modern economic development has been accompanied throughout by a steady growth in legislation limiting the movement of black South Africans, in particular those from the African group. This legislation has had the effect of legally entrenching the spatial dislocation created initially by the development of the mining industry and so has also entrenched a major source of the present differences in the life-styles of black and White South Africans.

STRUCTURAL CHANGE IN MINING

The Changing Structure of Output

Output from South African mining has grown spectacularly in both volume and value. Table 7.7 contains the relevant data.

Table 7.7
THE GROWTH IN OUTPUT OF THE MINING SECTOR 1915–76

Year	Value of Minerals Sold (R Millions)				Index of Physical Volume of Production 1970 = 100			
	Total	Gold	Diamonds	Coal	Total	Gold	Diamonds	Coal
1915	87,6	77,3	2,9	4,3		28,0		
1935	169,4	153,1	5,9	7,1		33,0		
1950	393,4	289,6	28,8	29,6	33,0	36,2	25,1	48,9
1960	856,7	536,0	33,9	55,1	61,4	66,3	41,0	70,5
1970	1 563,4	830,3	75,5	109,9	100,0	100,0	100,0	100,0
1976	4 468,6	2 380,2	215,1	517,8	96,1	71,1	102,4	137,2
1979	8 067,0	6 003,0		926,8	108,4	70,5		189,5

SOURCE: *South African Statistics 1978* and *Chamber of Mines Ninetieth Annual Report* 1979.

Over the period 1915 to 1978 the money value of South Africa's mining output rose by more than 90 times, whilst the volume of minerals produced increased by just under four times over the same period. The sector has benefited from a number of factors that have, over the period, combined to turn the terms of trade in the sector's favour. The average annual growth rate in the monetary value of minerals produced in South Africa for the period 1950–79 was 11 per cent. Over this same period physical output in the sector rose by an average of 4,2 per cent per year. This implies that increases in the prices of the sector's products grew on average at 6,8 per cent over these 29 years. Over the same period the wholesale price indexes for both local and imported goods increased at an average annual rate of 5,9 per cent – nearly one per cent less per annum.

As the mining industry expanded, so the structure of its output in value terms changed and the gold sector became on average less dominant. Table 7.8 shows these changes for the period 1915–79.

Table 7.8
CHANGES IN THE STRUCTURE OF MINING OUTPUT 1915–79

Year	Output in Value Terms as a Percentage of Total Mining Output				
	Total	Gold	Diamonds	Coal	Other
1915	100	88	3	5	4
1935	100	90	3	4	3
1950	100	74	7	8	11
1960	100	63	4	6	27
1970	100	53	5	7	35
1978	100	57	6	10	27
1979	100	74			
Average Yearly Percentage Increase					
1915–1979	7	7			
1960–1979	13	14			
1970–1979	20	25			

SOURCE: *South African Statistics, 1978, The Chamber of Mines Eighty-Ninth Annual Report 1978, Quarterly Bulletin of the Reserve Bank, March, 1980.*

In 1915, gold production accounted for 88 per cent of the value of minerals produced by the sector. By 1970 this percentage had dropped to 53 per cent. The period from 1969 to date has been one that has seen a massive increase in the world market price for gold and it is this that has enabled the gold mines to maintain their relative importance in terms of the value of the gold mined, despite the fact that the actual physical quantity of gold produced fell by nearly 30 per cent over the period from 1970–78. Indeed, the increase in the gold price during the year 1979 was sufficient to reverse the previous trend and to cause a significant increase in the proportion that gold forms of the total sector output. Average prices in 1980 were higher still and if they are maintained the relative importance of the gold sector may continue to grow.

Factors Affecting the Output of Gold

In view of the very impressive performance of the gold sector shown by the data in Table 7.7, it is rather ironical that the immediate decline of gold has been predicted at various times since the formation of the Union, starting from as early as 1920. In 1930, a government mining engineer went so far as to predict that the peak of gold production in South Africa would be reached in 1932! The life of the industry has been prolonged by a number of factors:

1. The discovery of new ore bodies, and of particular importance in this respect, was the discovery and exploitation of the gold deposits in the Orange Free State and on the West Rand.
2. Technological advances which have enabled the mining industry to extract ore under increasingly difficult conditions, such as at extreme, deep, levels or where there is excessive water.
3. The increases in the gold price which have occurred over the period. Although the international price of gold was fixed unchanged at 35 United States dollars per fine ounce up to 1968, the industry did enjoy some increases in the price of the commodity in terms of the domestic currency. These were the result of the devaluation of the South African currency on the international exchange market. Increases in the price of the metal not only increase the profitability of the mining industry, but also allow the mines to extract lower grade ore (that they would

otherwise leave) profitably and this extends the life of the mines themselves.

In 1968, measures were introduced into the international market that were designed to demonetize gold and to reduce it ultimately to the same status as that of other precious metals. These measures failed. This failure and other pressures generating international political and economic instability, combined to increase the monetary demand for gold and consequently its market price. Rather than demonetizing gold, the overall impact of the resulting instability in the international currency market was not only to increase the demand for gold, but also that for other precious metals. Silver and platinum in particular are being used increasingly as 'stores of value' in an inflationary world.

Quite apart from the growth in both the physical volume and the monetary value of gold production that has taken place over the past half century, the South African mining industry has diversified into the production of other minerals, both metallic and non-metallic. Diamond production has increased significantly, as has that of coal and iron ore. Unlike gold and diamonds which have always been predominantly export commodities, these latter minerals were initially developed to serve the needs of the local South African market. However, the more recent years have seen both coal and iron ore develop into significant export commodities.

The activities of the state in the development of industry in South Africa have had a vital impact on the mining sector and seem likely to continue to do so. The establishment of a public corporation to produce iron and steel (ISCOR) acted as an important stimulant to the production of both iron ore and coal and the latter industry has been further boosted by the growth of ESCOM, the public utility producing electricity and by the birth and expansion of SASOL, the state owned 'oil from coal' project. Uranium enrichment plants, which will also be state owned, are in the planning stages and when operational, these will generate a local demand for the uranium mined in South Africa.

Wages, Working Costs and Productivity in Mining

The changes that take place in the relationship between wages, other working costs and profits in any industry reflect both price and productivity influences. The following section looks at the changes that have taken place in the economic structure of two of the sub-sectors of the South African mining industry – gold and coal. These two sectors were chosen because they have exhibited very different characteristics as they have expanded. Together, in 1976, they accounted for 65 per cent of the sector's total output and 70 per cent of the sector's total employment.

Table 7.9 contains comparative data for these two sub-sectors for the period 1950–78. Over the 28 year period the monetary value of the sales of both sub-sectors grew at the same average yearly rate. The way in which this growth was achieved, however, varied significantly. Labour productivity on the gold mines, in terms of tons of ore milled per worker, was virtually static, whilst on the coal mines it increased at an average yearly rate of 3,6 per cent.

The nature of the gold-bearing reef in South Africa is such that it does not lend itself to the introduction of mechanized mining practices. With the exception of some significant advances that have been made in shaft sinking technology, techniques of production on the gold mines have remained virtually unchanged throughout the life of the industry. Output per man in terms of kilograms of gold, actually declined from 2,4 kilograms per man in 1970, to 1,6 kilograms per man in 1978. This reduction reflects the fact that the higher gold price enabled the mines to produce gold profitably from low grade ores, as the decrease in per man production of kilograms of gold was accompanied by an increase in per man production of tons of rock milled.

The increases in the gold price over the period after 1970 were large enough to allow significant increases in the average output per man in value terms, despite the fact that the production of gold itself declined. Increases in labour productivity, in terms of the monetary value of the gold output, rose by an average of 3 per cent per year over the period from 1915-70 and by a massive 21 per cent over the eight years from 1970-78.

On the other hand, unlike the gold sector, coal mining has seen almost revolutionary advances in mining technology that involved a considerable degree of mechanization. As a result of these changes in production techniques, the period 1950–78 saw a rapid increase in output per man in both physical and value terms. Over the 28 year period, employment on the coal mines grew relatively slowly

Table 7.9
OUTPUT, PRODUCTIVITY AND WAGES IN GOLD AND COAL MINING 1950-78

Year	Total Output				Output per Man						
	Physical Terms (Index 1970 = 100)		Value Terms (R millions)		Physical Terms (Tonnes)		Value Terms (Rands)		Average Wage Paid (Rands)		
	Gold	Coal	Gold	Coal	Gold	Coal	Gold	Coal	Gold	Coal	
1950	36,2	48,9	289,6	29,6	151	387	773	540	272	172	
1960	66,3	70,5	565,0	55,1	153		1 226	831	416	323	
1970	100,0	100,0	830,3	109,9	189	580	1 959	1 468	583	651	
1978	70,5	189,5	6 003,0	628,6	191	1 050	8 977	8 253	2 247	2 348	
Average Yearly Percentage Change											
1950–1978	2,4	5,0	11,4	11,5	1,0	3,6	9,2	10,2	7,8	9,8	
1970–1978	−4,3	8,3	28,1	24,4	,01	7,7	21,0	24,1	18,4	17,4	

SOURCE: *Chamber of Mines Annual Reports and South African Statistics 1978.*

averaging only 1,7 per cent per year. Over the same period, the physical quantity of coal mined grew at an annual average rate of 5 per cent and increases in labour productivity accounted for 72 per cent of these increases in output.

THE MINING INDUSTRY AND SOUTH AFRICAN LIFE-STYLES

The Industry and the Struggle for White Supremacy

With the benefit of hindsight one can see clearly that the discovery of minerals and the early patterns of development followed in the mining industry contributed significantly to the nature of the outcome of the struggle for supremacy that was taking place between Blacks and Whites in the early phase of the development of the South African economy. Denoon argues that the discovery of diamonds, and the subsequent political handling of the area which included the diamond fields, had serious implications for the African communities and stated:

> It was a disastrous coincidence that the mineral revolution should have started in an area where African societies were unusually weak since the disputes over possession of the diamonds created the precedent that African claims could always be ignored. (Denoon: 1972, p. 66)

The development of the gold mining industry also had a significant political and economic impact on the relative position of South African Blacks. At the time of the early mineral discoveries Whites in the region later to become South Africa, were politically organized into four separate states; the Cape Colony and Natal (both of which were under British control) and the two Trekker Republics, the Orange Free State and the South African Republic (later to become the Transvaal). From the political viewpoint the most important overall effect of the exploitation of the gold mines was probably the fact that the development of the mines generated an economic force that worked strongly towards the eventual union of the four, then independent states in South Africa, as the mines exerted a tremendously strong pulling force in terms of the flow of economic resources between these four states. (Horwitz: 1968, Thompson 1971)

Not only did the mines intensify the need for union, but they substantially strengthened the Transvaal's position in the pre-union negotiations. The improved bargaining position of the South African Republic was probably responsible for the fact that the final union agreement did not include a common set of rules for the granting of franchise rights. The northern states rejected out of hand the Cape Colony's franchise which, at that time, permitted a small proportion of Africans to vote, and their economic power prevailed. This opened the way for the eventual disenfranchisement of all South Africa's black citizens.

On the economic front patterns were also established in the early days of the mining industry that were to carry over into the lifestyles of modern South Africa. In the initial stages of the development of the diamond diggings there were a number of African claim holders. White claim holders were opposed to their Black counterparts, alleging that their presence encouraged vagrancy and diamond theft. By 1871 White views had prevailed on the diamond fields; in that year 'The Griqualand Masters and Servants Law' was passed. This law, ostensibly to limit vagrancy and theft, stipulated that contracts of employment had to be registered and that claim holders would only be legally recognized on the provision of proof that they were people of good character.

Although neither of these provisions in the Act had any overt racial characteristics, in practice the requirement of 'proof of good character' could only be supplied by Whites. Similarly, White workers on the fields, who were infuriated by a provision in the Act which gave an employer the right to search his employees, staged a successful strike against this right; the benefits of the strike were not, however, passed on to the Black mine workers.

As the diamond industry expanded increasingly sophisticated techniques were needed to extract the diamonds and these set up pressures for the amalgamation of claims. Capital requirements rose dramatically and ultimately it was the people who had access to capital, who came to control the industry.

Deep level mining also needed an input of skilled labour which was not present amongst the local workforce and so was specially imported, largely from Europe. Skilled labour commanded European standard wages which were high by local South African levels. The gap between the skilled and unskilled labourers wages was de facto also a gap between White and Black mineworkers, as in these early days a supply of unskilled White labour was virtually 'non-existent.

The discovery of gold and the development of the Witwatersrand mines intensified the tendencies towards racial economic inequality instituted by the discovery of diamonds. From the beginning gold mining required large inputs of capital and technology and as a result Blacks did not emerge either as mine-owners or as part of the skilled workforce. The knowledge gained by the mining capitalists on the diamond diggings was rapidly transferred to the gold fields and the economic position of the Whites was further entrenched by their virtual monopoly of the skills and expertise needed by the new mining enterprises.

The development of the mining industry also saw a rapid growth in Trade Unionism. Unions were present in the Cape Colony as early as 1850, but the movement as a whole only gained significance with the advent of the diamond and gold mines. The unions were, in the main, craft unions and consequently catered almost exclusively for the White worker. As the mining capitalists sought to lower their labour costs by fragmenting craft operations and substituting semi-skilled or unskilled Blacks for the White skilled worker, these early trade unions became involved in attempts to protect the economic position of their members, thereby introducing a racial element into the movement. (Katz: 1976)

Their first real successes came as as result of negotiations between themselves, Lord Milner and mining management, regarding the proposals to import Chinese labour for the gold mines, to relieve the shortage caused by the withdrawal of a large part of the African labour force in the early part of the twentieth century. As a result of these discussions, a number of jobs on the mines were formally reserved solely for the White workforce. The infant colour bar was strengthened by the requirement of the Transvaal Miners' Association that a prospective member be in possession of a blasting certificate. As Blacks were virtually excluded from the opportunity to obtain such a certificate, this membership provision limited union membership to White workers, thereby driving the wedge between Black and White workers on the mines in even more deeply.

The job colour bar in South Africa was legally entrenched for the first time in 1911 when the new Union parliament passed 'the Mines and Works Act'. From this point onwards for the next 67 years, White labour was to look increasingly to the state for assistance in upgrading its own position and to achieve this largely at the expense of the South African Black workforce.

The Mining Sector's Direct Contribution to Changing Living Standards in South Africa

Quite apart from the massive indirect impact that the mining industry has had on South African living standards through the effect that it exerted on the extent and nature of the country's economic development, the industry has also exerted a direct influence on the living standards of South Africans. The mining industry is a major employer and consequently, the allocation of the revenue earned by the sector between capital and labour, and between the different labour factions themselves, will affect the distribution of income in South Africa as a whole.

The dominant position of the sector as an employer can be seen from the following data. Prior to 1910 employment on the mines accounted for more than one quarter of all the work available, outside agriculture and domestic service, and 8 out of 10 mineworkers were employed on the gold mines. As the economy developed, so these percentages declined, but nevertheless, in 1950 mining employment still accounted for 18 per cent of modern sector jobs and the gold mines employed 74 per cent of all mineworkers. As late as 1970 mining employment still formed 13 per cent of the total. The share of the gold mines had declined to two-thirds of total mining employment and remained at that relative position through to 1978.

The Allocation of Revenue Earned by the Gold Mines

Table 7.10 shows how the revenue earned per ton of rock milled in the gold industry was allocated between wages, other working costs and profits for selected years from 1915-78. It is interesting to note firstly, that labour costs per ton milled having been relatively constant up to 1950, started to increase and rose very rapidly over the period from 1970-78. Secondly, profits per ton milled were roughly the equivalent of labour costs throughout the period from 1915 to 1970. However, once the world gold price started to increase rapidly

Table 7.10
THE RELATIONSHIP BETWEEN WAGES, ALL WORKING COSTS, REVENUE AND PROFITS IN THE GOLD MINING INDUSTRY 1915–78

| Year | Tons of Rock Milled per man | Per Ton of Rock Milled | | | | | | |
| | | Current Prices | | | | 1970 Prices | |
		Revenue R	Labour Costs R	Working Costs R	Profit R	Labour Costs R	Profit R
1915	105,7	2,9	1,1	1,9	1,0	3,7	3,4
1935	124,5	3,7	1,1	2,1	1,6	3,5	5,0
1950	151,0	5,2	1,8	3,5	1,7	3,3	3,1
1960	153,2	8,1	2,7	5,1	3,0	3,5	3,9
1970	188,7	11,2	3,1	7,3	3,9	3,1	3,9
1976	190,8	31,5	9,3	19,3	12,2	5,3	7,0
1978	191,1	52,7	11,7	27,1	25,6	5,5	12,0
Average Yearly Percentage Change							
1915–1978	,9	4,7	3,8	4,3	5,3	,6	2,0
1970–1978	,2	21,4	18,0	17,8	26,5	7,4	15,1

SOURCE: *Chamber of Mines Annual Reports* and *South African Statistics, 1978*.

after 1970, profits earned per ton milled started to outstrip wage costs and by 1978 were more than twice as great.

Table 7.11 shows the allocation of the net value added in the gold mining industry amongst the different groups who share in it; namely, the shareholders, White labour, Black labour and the state. Because of the extent to which the industry relies on foreign Black labour, the Black wage share has been further sub-divided into the wage earnings of South African and foreign Black workers.

Table 7.11
ESTIMATES OF THE ALLOCATION OF THE NET VALUE ADDED BY THE GOLD MINING INDUSTRY 1916–78

Year	Percentage of Net Value Added					
	Dividends	Tax	Wages	White Wages	Black Wages	South African Black Wages
1916	32	6	62	35	27	6
1936	33	18	49	28	21	11
1951	24	23	53	36	17	6
1961	29	20	51	34	17	6
1969	31	24	45	31	14	4
1973	34	25	41	25	16	4
1978	26	26	48	20	28	15

SOURCE: 1916–69 Wilson (1972), 1973–78 *South African Statistics 1978 and Chamber of Mines Annual Report.*

One can see very clearly from the data in Table 7.11 the powerful position that the White mineworkers had attained. Although they provided less than 10 per cent of the total workforce on the gold mines for the major part of the 60 years covered in the table, throughout the period up to 1973 they obtained, on average, almost one-third of the value produced in the sector. Black workers, on the other hand, provided 90 per cent of the workforce and received, on average, less than one-fifth of the sector's net value added.

One can also see from the data in Table 7.11 that the direct contribution made by the gold mining industry towards improvements in the living standards of South African Blacks has been very small. Over almost the whole period up to 1973 less than 6 per cent of the value added by the industry found its way directly into the hands of Black South Africans.

The situation changed quite dramatically in the years after 1973. Not only did the Black workers' share of value added almost double between 1970 and 1978, but in addition the relative weights of the national components of the Black workforce on the gold mines altered. The share of value added, paid to South African Black workers in the industry, almost quadrupled in only 5 years; rising from 4 per cent in 1973 to 15 per cent in 1978. This increased percentage share, coupled with the increased earning capacity of the industry, which financed the substantial gains in Black wage rates, created a situation in which the gold mines started to contribute towards improving living standards of South African Blacks in a direct and meaningful way.

Another major change in the structure of wage payments occurred in the gold mining industry after 1970. Over the period from the formation of the Union right up to 1970, the average wage paid to White mineworkers rose, whilst that paid to Black mineworkers actually fell in real terms. In 1915 the average real White wage was 10 times greater than that of Black mineworkers; this ratio increased steadily up to 1970 to reach a massive 21:1. The situation reversed in 1973 and by 1978 the ratio had fallen to 7:1 which, although it was still higher than the racial wage ratio in the remainder of the modern sector of the economy, nevertheless, represented a substantial improvement over the position in 1970.

Throughout the period to 1970 mining in general was a low wage sector for Black labour and the gap between White and Black average wage earnings rose steadily. This, coupled with the relatively small number of jobs provided for South African Blacks, suggests that up to 1970 the most likely direct impact of the mining industry on the racial income distribution was to worsen it. One could, however, only be certain of this if, firstly, the jobs held by non-South African Blacks were causing unemployment amongst South Africans, and, secondly, if average standards of living in the black rural areas were lower than the wage earning possibilities on the mines.

In the period after 1970, however, the employment practices in the mining industry will have had the effect of improving the relative living conditions of South African Blacks. The average racial wage ratio declined substantially, the average wage paid to Black workers rose and South African Blacks took up jobs, in what had become a high wage sector, at a very rapid rate. All these factors will operate to improve the overall racial distribution of income in South Africa.

Times had changed in the mining industry and the influential role played by the sector, together with its direct links into other economic areas, through the activities of the giant mining houses, made it likely that this change would spill over and flow through to the rest of the modern South African economy.

EIGHT

Industrialization in South Africa

INTRODUCTION

Although the exploitation of mineral resources has without doubt been the foundation upon which modern South Africa has been built, it is the process of industrialization which has generated the structure that now rests on those foundations. Indeed it was largely due to the determined efforts that were made by successive South African Administrations after 1924 to encourage industrialization and to develop a class of local manufacturing capitalists, that enabled South Africa to escape the ill effects of economic imperialism that were the concomitant of colonialism in so many instances on the African continent.

The development of a modern mining sector in an otherwise undeveloped economy, often leads to very little further economic development in the region. Indeed when it is undertaken by foreign interests, mining appears to provide an almost perfect means of transferring the investible surpluses that are generated within the economy supplying the minerals, to the country originating the investment. Until these surpluses can be re-diverted for use within the region itself, little economic development is likely to take place. The forces of the international market place are such that this diversion is usually not achieved without significant political intervention in the market. This needed intervention is often extremely difficult to engineer, as a lack of political sophistication amongst the native populace makes it relatively easy for the incoming foreign capitalists to set up a political system in which the interests of the dominant political group are largely coincident with those of foreign capital.

In South Africa the schism that developed between the Afrikaans and English speaking members of the politically dominant white group with respect to both their political and economic interests, paved the way for widespread economic development. These differences ultimately resulted in a situation which not only separated the sources of economic and political power from one another, but also enabled political means to be used to divert the investible surplus earned by the mining industry, for investment within South Africa itself. Once political power came into the hands of a group whose interests were mainly domestically oriented, it was possible to set the scene for the development of a modern industrial state.

The success of the industrialization process in South Africa owes a great deal to the rise of Afrikaner nationalism and in particular to the rather strange political alliance that took place in 1924 between White labour and White, Afrikaner dominated, rural capital and resulted in the formation of the PACT government. Not only did this alliance entrench the economic position of both White labour and White farming interests, *vis-à-vis* those of the South African Blacks, but the PACT government also embarked on a determined policy of industrialization. This was achieved through direct investment by the state and the creation of a wide ranging set of protective tariffs designed to raise domestic price levels to the point at which certain commodities, previously imported, could be profitably produced within South Africa.

The economic policies of the PACT government set the scene for the administrations that followed. Government intervention became an accepted feature of the South African market economy and the extent to which the government participated directly in manufacturing increased throughout the period up to the present time. The year 1927 saw the House of Assembly pass the bill which established the wholly state-owned iron and steel corporation, ISCOR and over the following half century, a number of other state enterprises were started such as FOSKOR, SOEKOR and the giant SASOL group. In 1977 the output of the public corporations contributed 11 per cent to the country's total manufacturing production.

THE LINK BETWEEN MINING AND MANUFACTURING

South African manufacturing has always been closely tied to the fortunes of the mining industry and even today the links between the two sectors remain strong. In the initial phases of industrialization, the products produced were closely allied to the needs of the mines and the subsequent development of manufacturing relied heavily on the economic resources that had been accumulated by the mining sector.

The foreign exchange earned from the sale of minerals financed the extensive importation of both capital goods and essential intermediate inputs that were needed by the growing industrial sector. The new sector also drew on the pool of skilled labour and the financial and business know-how that had developed as the mining industry expanded. Mining houses started to diversify their activities and moved into the industrial field, both directly and indirectly, allowing capital accumulated in the mining enterprises to be used to expand South African industrial capacity.

It was the links between mining and manufacturing that were also in part responsible for the foreign input that has come into South African industry. Periods of prosperity in the minerals market not only increased the surplus earned by the South African mines, thereby increasing the amount of domestic capital available for investment, but also attracted further foreign capital into South Africa, some of which found its way into the growing industrial sector.

Foreign links were also important in the provision of the needed increases in the supplies of skilled labour, managerial capability and, possibly most significant in terms of its overall impact on South African development patterns, for the technology used. In a nationwide survey of South African manufacturing industry undertaken in 1973, 73 per cent of the firms in the survey stated that over 90 per cent of the technology used originated outside South Africa. (Nattrass and Brown: 1978)

INDUSTRIALIZATION 1919-76: AN OVERVIEW

The Overall Performance of the Sector

Over the period from 1919 to 1976, the industrial output of South Africa grew at a yearly average rate of 5,9 per cent in real terms. There have been two periods of rapid industrial expansion, the period 1936-51, which included the second world war, and the period 1964-75. As the industrialization process gained momentum in South Africa, substantial changes took place in the manufacturing sector, encompassing changes in the range of commodities produced, in the size of the firms producing the products and in the techniques used in the production process itself. Table 8.1 contains data that illustrates these changes.

Table 8.1

THE GROWTH OF MANUFACTURING IN SOUTH AFRICA 1919–76

Year	Net Output (1970 prices) (R 000)	Employment	Average Value of Machinery per Man (1970 Rands)	Average Output per Man (1970 Rands)	Output per Rand Unit of Machinery (1970 Rands)	Wage Share per Rand of Output
1919	175 890	119 767	687	1 467	2 135	49
1936	342 938	218 966	667	1 567	2 349	44
1951	1 189 381	536 275	855	2 219	2 595	46
1970	3 101 889	1 095 557	1 481	2 831	1 908	47
1976	4 517 513	1 362 079	1 639	3 317	2 024	46
Average Yearly Growth Rate	5,9%	4,4%	1,5%	1,4%	,1%	

1. With the exception of 1976, the years represent an average of the three years surrounding the date specified.
2. The wholesale price index was used as the deflator.

SOURCE: *Industrial and Manufacturing Census Reports* for the selected years and *South African Statistics, 1978.*

The data show that as the manufacturing sector expanded, it became more sophisticated. On average, the amount of capital needed per man employed increased in real terms and output per man (labour productivity) rose correspondingly. This suggests that more mechanized methods of production were introduced over the period. On the whole, however, both the increases in the degree of capital intensity in production methods and in labour productivity were relatively low and, as we will see from the following subsection, on average the increases in output that occurred came mainly from the creation of new jobs, rather than from the introduction of more mechanized techniques. However, there may well be differences between firms and subsectors which cancel each other out and so are concealed in the statistics of this type.

In a market economy the continued inflow of new capital into a particular economic sector is largely dependent upon the rate of return that investors believe they can earn on their funds. Two indicators in Table 8.1 suggest that the real profit rate in South African manufacturing was maintained throughout the period under discussion. Firstly, the real value of output per rand unit of plant and machinery invested in the sector remained virtually constant. Secondly, the proportion of every rand earned from the output produced in the sector that was paid out as wages, was also extremely stable, notwithstanding the fact that the average real wage rates of both black and White workers rose over the time period; the former at a yearly average rate of 1,8 per cent and the latter at 1,9 per cent. The link between rising wage rates and increasing labour costs was broken, firstly, by the slight growth in labour productivity that took place and, secondly, by the fact that the firms in the sector substituted the lower paid black labour for the more expensive White labour as wage rates rose.

The Sources of Growth in South African Manufacturing

Increases in output in any sector can come from one of three sources; an increased input of the factors of production into the sector, from the improved usage of the factors already employed there, or from some combination of these two. The inputs of both labour and capital into South African manufacturing have increased substantially over the past 57 years and productivity levels of both factors have also risen, although relatively slowly, as can be seen from the data in Table 8.2.

Capital accumulation has obviously been of crucial importance to the growth of output in South African industry. When capital is invested in a sector, it can be used either to provide more output by using larger doses of existing production methods, (capital widening) or to introduce production methods that improve the level of output per man (capital deepening). In the first instance, the ratio of capital to labour remains the same and in the second case, the amount of capital per man increases.

In South African industry, by far the greatest proportion of new investment in the sector has been of the capital widening type, as the capital stock in the sector only increased faster than employment by

1,5 per cent per year. Put in another way, of the total annual growth in capital over the period, 75 per cent was used to create new jobs and only 25 per cent to introduce more productive production methods. Labour productivity growth rates were correspondingly low, whilst increases in employment were rapid.

Table 8.2

THE SOURCES OF GROWTH OF OUTPUT IN MANUFACTURING

Period	*Average annual growth rate of*			
	Plant & Machinery (in constant prices)	*Employment*	*Output per man (in constant prices)*	*Output per Rand value of Plant & Machinery*
1919–36	3,4	3,6	,4	,6
1936–51	7,9	6,2	,3	,7
1951–70	6,7	3,8	1,3	– 1,6
1971–76	5,4	3,7	2,7	,01
1919–76	5,9	4,4	1,4	– 0,1

SOURCE: Estimated from selected *Industrial and Manufacturing Census Reports.*

When one looks more closely at the periods within the total timespan, however, one finds that there is some evidence to suggest that the trend has changed as industrialization has continued. Between 1919 and 1936, all the new investment went to capital widening. Over the period 1936–51, a period of very rapid increases in output in the sector, 78 per cent of investment went to create new jobs and 12 per cent towards improving labour productivity. Between 1951 and 1970, the proportion of investment going to create new jobs decreased to 57 per cent and then increased again to 68 per cent over the 6 years to 1976.

As estimations of growth rates are extremely sensitive to the values in the two end periods used, data of this type should be treated with caution. For example, the relatively low proportion of capital used to generate new jobs over the period from 1951–70 and the increase that took place between 1970 and 1976 could both reflect a 'cyclical low' in employment in 1970. Nevertheless the general trends can be taken as being indicative and on this basis it does seem that over the past 25 year period, a greater proportion of the investment in manufacturing has been used for capital deepening, rather than for capital widening. This change in emphasis has had the effect of reducing the rate of growth of employment relative to that of capital accumulation, in comparison with that experienced over the period 1919 to 1951.

Changes in the Structure of the Manufacturing Enterprise

As industrial activity has expanded in South Africa, there have been some changes in the nature of the enterprises operating in the sector. The relevant data is given in Table 8.3.

Table 8.3

CHANGES IN THE STRUCTURE OF MANUFACTURING

	1916	1945	1960	1976
Number of Establishments	3 638	9 316	10 264	15 461
Average Number Employed per Establishment	24	39	63	88
Gross Output per Establishment (1970 Rands)	52 900	117 800	349 600	753 500
Average Investment per Establishment in Plant & Machinery (1970 Rands)	31 600	39 200	77 500	151 800

SOURCE: *Industrial and Manufacturing Censuses* for the selected years.

Between 1919 and 1976, the number of establishments operating in the manufacturing sector more than quadrupled. In addition, the average size of the establishment also increased substantially and a typical operation in 1976 employed nearly four times as many men as its 1919 counterpart, had five times the capital investment and produced an output that was 14 times greater.

STRUCTURAL CHANGE IN THE MANUFACTURING SECTOR

Changes in the Structure of Output

The period since the formation of the Union of South Africa is one that has seen a virtual transformation of the economy and nowhere is this transformation more evident than in the manufacturing sector. Not only has the sector grown enormously over the period, but it has significantly diversified its activities.

In the early stages of South African manufacturing the output of the sector was substantially geared towards the production of goods for the domestic consumer market and the mining industry. In 1919 the three sectors, Food, Clothing and Textiles, and Wood and Paper Products, together accounted for 57 per cent of the total manufacturing production. Two other important subsectors were Chemicals and Base Metals, both of which were strongly linked to the profitable mining sector. Factories making more sophisticated machinery were almost non-existent and contributed only 1 per cent to the sector's total output.

By 1976, there had been a significant change. The output from the Machinery-making subsector had grown at an average annual rate of 14 per cent throughout the period, to provide 13 per cent of the sector's total output. Chemicals and Metal Products had also become increasingly significant, as had the production of Electronic Equipment. What had been a sector largely confined to serving the more simple requirements of the domestic consumer market had grown into one that was capable of producing almost all South Africa's manufactured needs and was starting to break into the world market for these products. Table 8.4 contains detailed data relating to the nature of the changes that have taken place in the manufacturing sector over the period from 1919–76 with respect to the structure of output and employment.

Changes in the Components of Output

In a free enterprise system the pattern of goods and services produced in the economy by and large reflects the pattern of profitable opportunities for production. These, in their turn, mirror the relative availability of productive resources and the patterns of demands for the potential output. Over time a number of different factors affect production, working through either the demand or the supply side of the market.

Changes in population size and structure will affect the demand for final goods. An expanding population will be a force for the production of more of everything over time, but since a rapidly

Table 8.4
STRUCTURAL CHANGE IN THE MANUFACTURING SECTOR, 1919–1976

	Food, Beverages and Tobacco	Clothing and Textiles	Wood and Paper Products	Chemicals	Non-Metallic Minerals	Base Metals	Metal Products	Machinery Non-Electrical	Machinery Electrical	Transport Equipment	Other
Output											
1919	32	8	16	8	6	17	2	—	1	6	4
1936	25	12	16	8	8	15	2	—	2	7	5
1951	18	14	13	9	6	7	10	5	4	8	6
1970	14	12	12	10	6	9	9	7	4	8	9
1976	14	10	12	11	5	12	10	7	6	7	6
Employment											
1919	27	10	14	8	10	15	2	—	1	8	5
1936	21	17	13	6	14	13	3	—	1	8	4
1951	18	18	14	6	10	5	11	5	4	9	7
1970	14	19	13	5	7	7	10	6	4	8	7
1976	15	19	12	6	6	8	10	6	5	8	5
Black Employment											
1919	33	8	12	9	15	9	2	—	1	5	6
1936	24	11	11	6	20	13	4	—	1	5	4
1951	21	19	14	6	13	4	11	4	3	7	—
1970	16	23	12	5	8	5	10	5	3	6	3
1976	16	22	11	6	7	6	10	5	4	7	4

Percentage Contribution to Manufacturing Total

SOURCE: *Industrial and Manufacturing Censuses* for the various years selected.

growing population is also a youthful one, the immediate impact is to cause the demand for goods for the lower age groups to grow faster than the average. Similarly, if the rate of population growth starts to slow down and the population starts to age, one will find a reduction in the demand for these types of products and one will see things such as schools and universities being closed down.

There is also a strong link between rising income levels and changes in demand patterns. Once again, although the overall impact of an increase in income is an increase in the demand for goods and services, the impact on each class of products may well be different. Commodities have different income elasticities, that is to say that the demand for these goods respond in different ways to changes in incomes. Some goods, usually luxuries, are highly income elastic and the demand for these products rises proportionately faster than income. Other goods are what is known as income inelastic and in these cases the demand for them expands more slowly than income. The demand for some products actually falls as income levels rise and these goods are known as inferior goods, as they are only consumed because the purchaser cannot afford the more expensive substitute.

It is obviously very difficult to generalize on the likely relationships between rising income levels and changing demand patterns, as these are also significantly influenced by physical, social and cultural aspects. Nevertheless, there are some trends that have been observed to hold in a number of instances. Probably the most famous of these is the tendency known as Engel's Law, which states that as incomes increase, a proportionately smaller amount of income is spent on food. However, when incomes start to increase from very low levels, even this relationship does not hold and the demand for food often increases more than proportionately to the increase in income.

Another factor that can break the link between rising incomes and changing patterns of production is the opportunity to trade on world markets. If a country is particularly favourably endowed with some natural resource, it may well find it more profitable to exploit that resource, export it and then use the foreign exchange earned from the sales to import the goods that are not being locally produced.

The changes in the structure of South African manufacturing output that have occurred over the period 1919–76, reflect the influences of all these factors. The level of output has grown in all the sub-sectors of industry, but some sectors, notably Food, Wood and

Furniture and Base Metals, have grown more slowly than the sector as a whole, whilst others such as Machinery, both Electrical and Non-Electrical, Metal Products, Clothing and Transport Equipment, have grown faster than the average, due mainly to the fact that local production has been increasingly substituted for previously imported products.

Changes in the output of the Food and Beverages sub-sector reflect the combined influence of population growth, growing export opportunities and the possible operation of Engel's Law amongst the higher income groups. The real value of the sector's output grew at a yearly average rate of 4 per cent over the 57-year period, which was substantially above the rates of population growth. It was, however, also below the average for the sector as a whole and, as a result, the sub-sector's share in the total output of manufactured products fell from one-third in 1919 to only 14 per cent in 1976.

It is very interesting to note, however, that over the period 1970–76, a period which saw an increase in the previously very low black average incomes, the rate of growth in the real value of food and beverages produced in South Africa increased to 6 per cent, which was the average rate of growth for the entire industrial sector over this period.

Changes in the Patterns of Employment in Manufacturing

Although changes in employment patterns are related to changes in the patterns of the sector's output, they do not reflect output changes precisely, because the different sub-sectors in the industry use different techniques of production and so have different levels of output per man. For example, the share of employment in manufacturing that is accounted for by the clothing and textile sub-groups, is nearly twice as large as their contribution to the sector's output; in the case of the chemical industry the position is reversed.

The most rapidly growing sub-sectors, over the period, in employment terms, have been Machinery, Metal Products and Clothing and Textiles. As in the case of output, the period 1936-51 was the period which saw the most rapid rate of increase in employment in the manufacturing industry as a whole, with an average yearly rate of increase of over 6 per cent.

The racial composition of employment in manufacturing has also changed over time. Whites formed 37,5 per cent of the total in 1919 and by 1936 this percentage had increased to 40,6, reflecting the success of the PACT government's 'civilized labour' policy. The proportion of Whites in the sector's total labour force started to decline during the second world war and this trend has continued up to the present time; in 1976 Whites provided only 21 per cent of the sector's total labour force. The proportion of Whites employed in Paper and Paper Products, Base Metals, Machinery and Transport were all well above the sector average. On the other hand, Food, Textiles and Clothing, Wood, Furniture and Non-Metallic Minerals were sub-sectors that employed above average proportions of South Africa's other race groups.

The proportion of Whites employed in all sub-sectors, other than that producing Chemicals, has declined over time; the most spectacular change occurring in the Clothing and Textiles sub-sector in which, in 1936, the percentage of Whites employed was as high as 62 per cent and by 1976 had declined to only 7,4 per cent.

The substitution of firstly, Coloured and Asians for White and subsequently, Blacks for Coloureds and Asians, coupled with that of women for men in certain industries, enabled the manufacturing sector to keep the proportion of each rand value of output produced that was paid out to labour, remarkably constant throughout the period from 1919–76. Table 8.5 shows both the relative decline in the importance of the White workforce in each sector and the sectoral movements in labour costs per rand unit of output. From this data it seems that there is a good deal of variation between the different types of manufacturing activities in terms of both the proportion that Whites form of the total workforce and the average share of output, that goes to pay the wages of that workforce.

It also appears that there is no substance to the hypothesis sometimes advanced by South African businessmen that black labour is expensive labour, despite the low average level of black wages. Changes in labour costs per rand unit of output do not seem to be in any way related to the substitution of blacks for Whites. Indeed, there is not even a relationship between the actual percentage that is White and the wage cost per rand value of output. For example, the proportion paid out as wages per rand of output produced in both the metal products industry and the machinery sub-sector was 56 per cent in 1976 and the shares of Whites in the

Table 8.5
RACIAL SUBSTITUTION AND LABOUR'S SHARE PER RAND VALUE OF NET OUTPUT 1919-76

| | Sector as a Whole | Food Beverages and Tobacco | Clothing and Textiles | Wood and Furniture | Paper and Paper Products | Chemicals | Non-Metallic Minerals | Base Metals | Metal Products | Machinery | | Transport Equipment |
										Non-Electrical	Electrical	
Percentage of the Workforce that is White												
1919	37,5	23,5	49,5	35,5	61,8	25,1	11,5	60,6	35,5	74,7	69,2	55,5
1936	40,6	31,2	62,0	40,7	67,7	32,2	11,3	40,7	31,1	76,0	60,0	62,3
1951	31,9	21,8	28,4	22,8	51,4	29,6	13,4	38,7	30,1	45,7	47,7	47,7
1970	23,8	15,9	9,2	11,4	39,3	31,5	15,3	38,9	25,4	42,5	37,6	35,1
1976	21,2	15,4	7,4	10,9	37,1	26,8	4,1	38,5	23,8	38,1	32,3	31,8
Annual Average Rate of Change 1919-1976	-1%	-,7%	-3,3%	-2,1%	-,9%	,1%	-1,8%	-,8%	-,7%	-1,2%	-1,3%	-1,0%
Proportion per Rand Value of Output that is Wages												
1919	49,0	29,0	54,0	55,0	55,0	44,0	48,0	75,0	56,0	55,0	81,0	68,0
1936	44,0	28,0	58,0	59,0	52,0	32,0	40,0	51,0	59,0	75,0	60,0	56,0
1951	46,0	36,0	55,0	54,0	50,0	32,0	45,0	41,0	52,0	59,0	52,0	57,0
1970	46,0	34,0	48,0	49,0	46,0	31,0	40,0	49,0	57,0	64,0	54,0	55,0
1976	46,0	37,0	50,0	51,0	47,0	34,0	44,0	42,0	56,0	56,0	50,0	69,0

SOURCE: Estimated from various *Industrial and Manufacturing Census Reports*.

workforce in the two sectors were 23,8 per cent and 38,1 per cent respectively. Similarly, when one looks at the changes in labour costs through time in the sub-sectors, one finds that as blacks have been employed in greater proportions, labour costs per rand output increased in some industries and remained constant or declined in others.

Changes in Labour Productivity

Over the whole period 1919-76, labour productivity levels rose relatively slowly and the real value of output per man in the sector averaged an annual growth rate of only 1,4 per cent per annum. In a full employment situation this low rate of growth of productivity would be a matter for concern. However, in an economy like South Africa's, the slow rate of growth of labour productivity has allowed a larger proportion of the workforce to move from the low productivity subsistence sector to the modern economy and by so doing, to share in the growing income levels.

Over the same period the output from the sector grew in real terms at an average yearly rate of 5,9 per cent, 1,4 of which was due to the increase in average labour productivity, whilst the balance was the result of the creation of new jobs in the sector through increased investment. The extent to which increased employment and increases in productivity contributed to the growth in output differed between the major sub-groups in manufacturing, as can be seen from the data below in Table 8.6.

From the data in Table 8.6, it appears that four sub-groups had a rate of growth of productivity that was exceptionally low, measured in terms of the performance of the sector as a whole, namely Clothing and Textiles, Wood and Furniture, Machinery and Electrical Machinery. Jobs created in these four sub-groups over the period 1919-76 accounted for 38 per cent of all the new jobs created in South African manufacturing. Three other sub-groups, Chemicals, Base Metals and Non-Metallic minerals had growth rates in labour productivity levels well above those in manufacturing as a whole and as a result, these sectors together only accounted for 19 per cent of the increased employment created over this period.

Looking at the data in the table, it is clear that rising productivity levels in themselves are not the only causes of relatively slow growth rates in the number of jobs created in a sector. Five sectors, Wood and Furniture, Paper and Paper Products, Chemicals, Non-Metallic Minerals and Non-Electrical machinery, each contributed only 6 per cent of the new jobs created, despite the fact that in two of these sectors, Wood and Machinery, the increases in productivity levels were very low indeed. The link between labour productivity and job creation is broken by both the rate of growth of the sector and its size relative to other sectors. Indeed, it is the relative size of the Food sector that makes it an important source of job creation, despite its relatively low rate of growth of output and its relatively good productivity performance.

Table 8.6

CONTRIBUTIONS TO OUTPUT GROWTH IN THE SUB-GROUP, 1919–76

Sub-Group	Average Yearly Growth Rate in Output	Contribution Due to		Contribution by Sector to Jobs Created over the Period
		Increased Labour Productivity	Increased Employment	
Food, Beverages	4,3	23	77	14
Clothing and Textiles	6,4	14	86	19
Wood and Furniture	4,7	13	87	6
Paper and Paper Products	5,7	23	77	6
Chemicals	6,4	38	62	6
Non-Metallic Minerals	5,7	39	61	6
Base Metals	5,3	40	60	7
Metal Products	9,1	19	81	11
Non-Electrical Machinery	14,3	8	92	6
Electrical Machinery	9,1	15	85	7
Transport Equipment	6,2	27	73	8
Manufacturing in Total	5,9	24	76	100

SOURCE: Various *Industrial Manufacturing Censuses.*

Capital Accumulation in the Sub-Groups

Capital is a crucial input into production and capital accumulation is one of the cornerstones of economic expansion. As was explained earlier, an industry can expand output by using the capital that it accumulates to deepen its capital, i.e. to use more capital intensive methods of production or to widen it, as is the case when the additional capital is used to finance the hiring of more people, who will use the same methods of production. Here again when one looks at the sub-groups in manufacturing over time, one finds that they differ from one another both in terms of the extent to which they have accumulated capital and in terms of the way they have combined that capital with labour. The details are given in the Table 8.7 below.

Table 8.7
CAPITAL ACCUMULATION IN THE SUB-GROUPS, 1919–76

Sub-Group	Average Annual Growth Rate of				
	Capital (1970 Prices)*	Output (1970 prices)	Labour Productivity (1970 prices)	Capital per Man (1970 prices)	Employment
Food and Beverages	4,0	4,3	1,0	,7	3,3
Clothing and Textiles	5,1	6,4	,9	− ,3	5,4
Wood and Furniture	4,6	4,7	,6	,6	4,0
Paper and Paper Products	6,0	5,7	1,3	1,7	4,3
Chemicals	5,6	6,4	2,4	1,6	4,0
Non-Metallic Minerals	5,6	5,7	2,2	2,2	3,4
Base Metals	7,8	5,3	2,1	4,7	3,1
Metal Products	9,5	9,1	1,4	2,1	7,4
Non-Electrical Machinery	15,1	14,3	1,7	2,2	12,9
Electrical Machinery	8,7	9,7	1,2	1,2	7,5
Transport Equipment	6,6	6,2	1,7	2,2	4,4
Sector as a Whole	5,9	5,9	1,4	1,5	4,4

* The value of plant and machinery invested in the sector adjusted by movements in the wholesale price index has been used as a surrogate for capital.

SOURCE: Various *Industrial and Manufacturing Censuses.*

As it takes a greater number of units of capital to produce a given unit of output (i.e. the capital output ratio is greater than one), any structural change that takes place in an economy will show up more markedly in the changes in the patterns of capital accumulation than in the changing patterns of output. The structural transformation that has taken place in South African manufacturing as the economy has modernized, shows very clearly in the way that capital has accumulated in the sub-sectors. The rate of investment has been highest in the Machinery sub-sector, Metal Products and Base Metals and lowest in the sectors that were already relatively well established as early as 1919 such as Food, Clothing and Furniture.

It seems that the only sector in which the replacement of labour by machinery took place to any really significant extent, was that of Base Metals, as this sector had both the highest rate of increase in capital per man and the lowest growth rate in employment over the period. In the other sectors the rate of increase in capital intensity was moderate and indeed in the three sectors of Food, Beverages and Tobacco, Clothing and Textiles, and Wood and Furniture it was so low that it seems that virtually all the new investment in these sectors went towards the creation of new jobs.

On the basis of what is sometimes termed by economists as 'the law of diminishing returns', one might expect that as the capital labour ratio rises the returns in output terms per unit of capital (the output capital ratio) would fall. If capital and labour were simply substitutes for one another this would, no doubt, be the case. However, they also complement one another in the production process and as a result it is sometimes possible to substitute capital for labour and by so doing, increase the rate of return, in output terms, to both factors of production. This phenomenon is reflected in some modern production techniques and explains why it is that output on average has grown faster than capital accumulation in industries such as Chemicals and Non-Metallic Minerals, despite the fact that the capital labour ratio also increased.

It is, however, interesting to see that in general over this period the law of diminishing returns does appear to have operated in South African manufacturing, as the greatest gains in terms of output per unit of capital invested occurred in the industries in which the capital labour ratio was low and rising only very slowly, such as Food and Beverages, Clothing and Textiles and Wood and Furniture.

Capital Accumulation, Technical Progress and 'Learning by Doing'

One should not place too great an emphasis on growth rates that span a long term period, as they sometimes conceal fluctuations within the time span that may be more indicative of future behaviour patterns than the overall trend itself. This is particularly important when one is looking at capital accumulation as capital often embodies technical progress. This is the case, for example, when capital is used to incorporate new production methods and it takes time for the labour force to become accustomed to the new processes. As the labour force gains experience with the new methods, so they learn and labour productivity increases over time. This process is known as 'learning by doing' and it sometimes serves to break the direct time link between increasing levels of capital per man and increasing labour productivity.

Table 8.8 contains data relating to the relationship between capital per man and output per man over shorter periods in five selected sub-groups.

Table 8.8

MOVEMENTS IN CAPITAL PER MAN AND OUTPUT PER MAN IN SELECTED SECTORS

	Chemicals	Base Metals	Metal Products	Machinery	Transport
Capital per Man[1]					
1919–36	– 1,3	– ,8	– ,6	,3	– 1,9
1936–51	,2	3,5	6,9	13,4	4,3
1951–70	5,0	2,7	,6	– 2,9	5,1
1970–77	4,0	6,2	2,7	– 2,5	,4
Output per Man[1]					
1919–36	2,3	,8	– ,5	– ,5	1,2
1936–51	2,3	3,5	4,2	1,4	2,0
1951–70	2,4	,9	1,0	1,3	2,1
1970–77	2,6	5,9	3,6	5,4	1,2

1. All in 1970 prices

SOURCE: *Industrial and Manufacturing Censuses.*

From the data it seems that in the Base Metal and Metal Product sectors 'learning by doing' has not been an important source of increasing labour productivity, as in general the increases in output per man are linked directly to increasing amounts of capital per man.

On the other hand, in the three sectors, Chemicals, Machinery an
Transport Equipment, this link seems to be very weak indeed. This i
particularly true of the machinery industry which has a relativel
high craft component in its labour force and so appears to be we
placed to reap the benefits which flow from 'learning by doing'. Ove
the period 1951–76, labour productivity in this sector increased qui
substantially despite the fact that the amount of capital per ma
actually declined.

THE SPATIAL ASPECTS OF INDUSTRIALIZATION

Factors Affecting the Location of Industry

At a somewhat simple level it is possible to categorize industries i
terms of whether it is most profitable for them to locate close to th
market for their products, close to the supply of a major raw materia
or whether it makes little difference to them where they are situated
This latter class is sometimes referred to as 'footloose'.

Market oriented industries are usually one of two major types
Either they are producing commodities that are perishable an
difficult to store, or they are making products that are bulky t
transport in their finished form. Bakeries and butcheries ar
examples of the former class, whilst firms manufacturing domesti
appliances are in the latter category. Supply oriented industries o
the other hand are usually those which process bulky raw material
which would be expensive to transport, but which when processed
are relatively easy.

Industrialization tends to encourage agglomeration. This is be
cause by locating in an area in which other manufacturing firms ar
already situated, the new firm is able to enjoy the benefits of what ar
known as 'external economies'. An external economy is a factor
specific to an area, which enables a firm to lower its costs o
production, but over which it has no direct control. Examples of th
benefits which come from the physical concentration of industry ar
such things as: the ability to draw on a pool of relatively skille
labour that is already in the area, attracted by the other firms; th
existence of a better range of inter-firm services with a consequen
reduction in repair and delivery times which will lower costs o

production; and the existence of a better range of social services due to the relatively high concentration of population and economic activity which lowers the cost of such services.

The Location of Industry in South Africa

South African industry is highly concentrated from the spatial viewpoint. It has been estimated by the Bureau of Market Research that, in 1975, 81 per cent of South Africa's industrial output was produced in the four major metropolitan regions. Of the 272 administrative districts (263 magisterial districts and 9 African Homelands) in 1972, only 54 (i.e., 20 per cent), had industrial capacities large enough to enable industry to contribute 20 per cent or more to the district's total output.

Manufacturing activity is also strongly related to the absolute size of the economic capacity of a district. In the wealthiest 20 per cent of the districts (measured in terms of output per head), 56 per cent had industrial capacities large enough for industry to contribute 20 per cent or more to the total output. In the middle 60 per cent of the districts only 13 per cent were in this position, whilst in the poorest 20 per cent, which included all the African Homelands, only 4 per cent had industrial capacities of that relative size.

Although in absolute terms the Witwatersrand area is not large when compared to the massive urban industrial complexes like Detroit or Chicago, the relative concentration of economic activity in South Africa has been a matter for growing concern in official circles. There are a number of reasons for this.

Firstly, the Witwatersrand area has a water supply problem and it was felt that rather than undertake expensive schemes to transfer water into the area, it would be better to discourage further industrial expansion and to divert it to areas in which the water supply was adequate. The establishment of the growth points in Natal's Tugela basin were the outcome of these official views. More recently, however, the direction of official thinking on the water question was reversed and the Sterkfontein dam and pump storage facilities were constructed to enable, amongst other things, water to be physically transferred from the Tugela basin to the reticulation system feeding the Witwatersrand.

Secondly, there is growing concern regarding the strategic vulnerability of South Africa's industrial capacity and should the military situation deteriorate further, it will exacerbate this fear.

Thirdly, the physical dislocation between capital and labour in South Africa, together with government policy aimed at protecting the life styles of South African Whites, has led to the growth of a massive system of migrant labour with all its attendant social evils. In official circles it appears to be being increasingly recognized that the persistence of this system is beginning to undermine the security of the state, and that it is essential to provide jobs for Blacks in the areas in which they live, if the present government policy regarding racial development is to be maintained.

Finally, the spatial differences in living standards are vast. An estimate of the average income per head in the richest 10 per cent of South Africa's districts for 1970 was R1 215 whereas in the poorest 10 per cent of the areas it was only R100. (Nattrass: 1979e). The creation of a viable and healthy community requires that these differentials are narrowed and because of the vital role that industrialization plays in the creation of wealth, this again emphasises the need to decentralize industry. This is particularly important in a situation in which government controls on Black population movements act virtually to chain large numbers of Blacks to the poorer areas.

Government Policies to Decentralize Industry

The Tomlinson Commission, whose mandate was to study the economic conditions in the African Homeland areas with a view to recommending ways of raising living standards there and who reported in 1954, suggested that incentives should be given to encourage the location of industries in these areas. This recommendation was not accepted by the government who opted instead for a policy of 'Border Industries', by giving incentives to industrialists to locate their plants in 'Border Areas', (certain specified areas on the border of African Homelands) rather than within the homelands themselves.

In 1960, a 'Permanent Committee for the Location of Industry' was appointed to implement and administer the 'Border Area Policy'. Progress was slow initially and virtually the only areas that were developed in the early years were Hammarsdale, outside

Durban, Rosslyn, outside Pretoria and Pietermaritzburg, none of which were situated in the truly undeveloped areas of South Africa. The concessions offered to industrialists were numerous and ranged from assistance with the erection of buildings, through tax concessions, low-rate loans, transport rebates and assistance with the provision of housing for White personnel to the relaxation of the job reservation and minimum wage legislation. The concessions proved to be inadequate and were increased in 1964, in 1968, and again in 1972. Despite these increases, it was estimated that throughout the decade of the 1960s, the Border Area policy only succeeded in generating 11 600 jobs more than would have occurred through the spontaneous development of these regions. (Bell: 1973)

1967 and 1969 saw significant changes in policy emphasis. In 1967 the passing of the Physical Planning Act saw a 'stick' added to the 'carrots' offered by the Border Industry policy and this Act enabled the Minister of Planning to impose restrictions on the expansion of industry in the established areas. In 1969 the orientation of the decentralization policy was altered. The control on the establishment of White controlled industries in the Homelands was lifted and incentives were offered to White capital to establish industries within these areas on an 'agency basis'.

It was estimated by BENSO that in 1974 some 11 500 Blacks were employed in industries established within the Homelands on the agency scheme and a further 37 000 commuted to jobs established under the border areas scheme. (Benso: 1976). Over a period of 14 years, relatively little progress has been achieved in the decentralization of industry. It seems highly likely that despite government efforts, spatial inequality has widened in South Africa. Certainly over the period 1968–72 the growth rates of output were higher on average in the richest top 20 per cent of the districts and lowest in the districts that comprised the poorest 20 per cent. (Nattrass: 1979e)

THE MANUFACTURING SECTOR'S CONTRIBUTION TO CHANGING LIVING STANDARDS

The Allocation of Value Added by the Sector

A sector's contribution to the total output in an economy is measured by what is known as 'the value added', which is the sum of the wages and salaries paid out to the people employed in the sector and any other factor payments made, such as rent and profits. Over the period since 1919, the importance of manufacturing as a source of income to South Africans has increased dramatically. In 1919 the sector contributed only 7 per cent of South Africa's total production and by 1976 this contribution had increased to 23 per cent. The table below shows how this output was allocated between the factors of production in various selected years.

Table 8.9

FACTOR SHARES IN VALUE ADDED IN MANUFACTURING

Percentage Paid as	1919	1936	1951	1970	1976
White Wages	36,0	33,0	29,0	28,0	26,0
Other Wages	13,0	11,0	17,0	18,0	20,0
Rent and Profits	51,0	56,0	54,0	54,0	54,0

SOURCE: Estimated from various *Industrial and Manufacturing Censuses.*

As the sector grew and made increasing use of black labour, so the share of value added by the sector paid out to White workers declined and that paid to blacks correspondingly increased. The period that saw the most rapid change was the period which included the second world war. The demands of the war created a relative shortage in the supply of White labour and a consequent rapid increase in the rate of substitution of members of South Africa's other race groups for Whites in manufacturing. The increased share in value added paid to blacks reflected both rising average real Black wage levels and a rapid increase in the numbers of blacks employed in the sector. Real average black wages per man grew at a yearly rate of 5 per cent over this period and employment by 6,9 per cent, making the average yearly rate of growth in the real value of the total payments to black employees a massive 11,9 per cent.

The share paid out as non-wage income has remained relatively constant, particularly during the period following the second world war. Although the average capital labour ratio in the sector rose slowly throughout the period, the increase in labour productivity was sufficient to fund the increase in real wages, that took place over the period, without a reduction in the rate of return on capital. The average rate of increase in both capital and net non-wage income (profits) was 6 per cent throughout the period, which again indicates that the average rate of return per unit of capital invested in the sector remained virtually constant.

Of the profits earned by a sample of firms in the manufacturing sector over the 20 years from 1958–77, on average 35 per cent was retained within the firm for further investment in expansion and a further 35 per cent was paid out as dividends, whilst the remaining 30 per cent was paid to the government as taxation. If the sample is representative of the sector as a whole, it would seem that direct tax on the sector's earnings provides on average, approximately 12 per cent of the Central Government's current revenue.

The growth rate of real non-wage income earned in the manufacturing sector varied throughout the period. It was highest during the period spanning the second world war, 1936–51, and higher in the years 1970–76 than in the other two periods. Table 8.10 contains the detailed data. It is interesting that the two periods in which non-wage incomes grew most rapidly were also those which saw the greatest gains being made by both black and White wage earners in the sector.

There was also some variation between the subsectors, both in terms of the growth rates of profits (non-wage income) and wages and in terms of the way in which the value added was allocated between the two wage earning groups and the non-wage factor payments. The shaded figures highlight the period in which the growth rate of non-wage income was highest. In general a rapid rate of growth in profits led to an increase in the share of profits in value added. It seems that although both wage earners and capitalists benefited from the periods in which the sectors enjoyed improved economic conditions, profits took the greater share.

Within the two wage earning groups the White workers' share of the total wage earnings declined substantially in all the sub-groups other than Food, Beverages and Tobacco and Non-Metallic Minerals. White employment declined and White average real wage rates increased in all the sectors, but it was only in these two sub-groups that the decline in White employment levels was not sufficient to offset the increased wage payments.

The share of value added going to black workers increased over the period for the sector as a whole, but in a number of the sub-

Table 8.10
SUB-SECTOR PROFIT GROWTH RATES AND CHANGING SHARES OF WAGES AND PROFITS, 1919–76

	Sector as a Whole	Food Beverages and Tobacco	Clothing and Textiles	Wood and Furniture	Paper and Paper Products	Chemicals	Non-Metallic Minerals	Base Metals	Metal Products	Machinery Non-Electrical	Machinery Electrical	Transport Equipment
Growth rate in Real Value of Profits, Rents, Interest												
1919–1936	4.5	2.5	5.9	3.1	4.8	5.2	7.0	7.7	5.3	.2	11.8	7.0
1936–1951	8.4	5.3	10.5	8.7	7.1	9.0	6.2	4.3	21.3	46.7	15.9	9.3
1951–1970	5.2	4.1	5.3	4.0	6.2	5.9	5.2	6.0	4.2	6.4	5.6	5.2
1970–1976	6.5	5.6	2.5	3.0	6.0	8.4	3.9	14.1	7.7	11.1	14.1	2.8
1919–1976	6.0	4.1	6.5	4.8	6.0	6.8	5.8	6.9	9.2	14.2	11.0	6.5
White Wage Share												
1919	36.0	16.0	37.0	36.0	47.0	30.0	21.0	67.0	35.0	49.0	62.0	53.0
1936	33.0	18.0	42.0	41.0	45.0	23.0	18.0	40.0	38.0	69.0	52.0	46.0
1951	29.0	19.0	27.0	29.0	37.0	21.0	21.0	32.0	35.0	47.0	41.0	43.0
1970	28.0	18.0	16.0	21.0	32.0	21.0	21.0	37.0	35.0	49.0	39.0	39.0
1976	26.0	17.0	16.0	20.0	30.0	23.0	21.0	31.0	18.0	39.0	31.0	38.0
Black Wage Share												
1919	13.0	13.0	17.0	19.0	8.0	14.0	27.0	8.0	21.0	6.0	19.0	15.0
1936	11.0	10.0	16.0	18.0	7.0	8.0	22.0	11.0	21.0	6.0	8.0	10.0
1951	17.0	17.0	28.0	25.0	13.0	11.0	24.0	9.0	17.0	12.0	12.0	14.0
1970	18.0	16.0	32.0	28.0	14.0	10.0	19.0	12.0	22.0	15.0	15.0	16.0
1976	20.0	20.0	34.0	31.0	17.0	11.0	23.0	11.0	38.0	17.0	19.0	23.0
Non-Wage Share												
1919	51.0	71.0	46.0	45.0	45.0	56.0	52.0	25.0	44.0	45.0	19.0	32.0
1936	56.0	72.0	42.0	41.0	48.0	69.0	60.0	49.0	41.0	25.0	40.0	44.0
1951	54.0	64.0	45.0	46.0	50.0	68.0	55.0	59.0	48.0	41.0	47.0	43.0
1970	54.0	66.0	52.0	51.0	54.0	69.0	60.0	51.0	43.0	36.0	46.0	45.0
1976	54.0	63.0	50.0	49.0	53.0	66.0	56.0	58.0	44.0	44.0	50.0	39.0

groups, Chemicals, Non-Metallic Minerals and Electrical Machinery, the Black share fell over the period. In all sectors both black employment and black real wage rates rose, but in these three groups the increases were smaller than those that took place in the total value added.

The Contribution to Changing Living Standards

We noted earlier in this book that the share of total output that has gone into the hands of the South African black groups, (including Coloureds and Asians), was remarkably constant throughout the period up to 1970 and further, that this share rose quite significantly over the period from 1970–75. The wage income earned by the black population groups has been a crucial factor in determining these shares, as it forms the major component of black income. The earnings from the other significant source of black income, small scale agriculture, have declined in importance relative to the output of the economy as a whole over the period.

In 1960, wage income provided approximately 78 per cent of the total income earned by Blacks, Coloureds and Asians in South Africa. By 1970 this percentage had increased to 79 per cent and it was this increase that largely permitted the overall share of black factor earnings to remain constant over this decade. In 1975 wage income had increased to the point where it accounted for 84 per cent of the earnings of South Africa's black race groups and the black share of factor earnings had increased from 26 per cent to 32 per cent. Of the increases in factor earnings that took place between 1960 and 1970, it has been estimated that increased wage earnings accounted for 90 per cent and that they accounted for 94 per cent of the increases that occurred between 1970 and 1975. (Nattrass: 1977a)

Changes in wage income levels have two components; increases resulting from increased wage rates and those due to rising levels of employment. Both have been of significance in South Africa, particularly with respect to the contribution made by the manufacturing sector. Of the total increase in black wage incomes that took place between 1970–75, changes in the manufacturing sector's wage payments to the black group accounted for 28 per cent of the increase in their total income over the period. Of this 28 per cent, 61 per cent was the result of increased average wage rates, whilst the remaining 39 per cent originated from increases in employment levels. The sector accounted for 37 per cent of the increase in Coloured incomes; 64 per cent of which was due to higher wage rates and 36 per cent to employment, and for 45 per cent of the rise in Asian living standards: 73 per cent of which was due to rising wage rates and 27 per cent to increased employment. (Nattrass: 1977a)

In addition to the distribution of the wage bill between black and White workers, Table 8.10 contains the data showing the distribution of the value added by the various subsectors between the owners of labour and capital. The share of profits in value added varies between the subsectors and interestingly, with the exception of Chemicals, does not appear to be closely related to the average amount of capital employed per man in the sector.

The Racial Wage Gap and Living Standards

The difference between the average wage paid to Whites working in manufacturing and that paid to blacks (the racial wage gap or wage ratio) is also of importance in determining the relative living standards of the population groups. Detailed data concerning the magnitude and changes that have occurred in average racial wage rates and wage bills are given in Table A in the appendix and as can be seen from this table, in general the absolute value of the racial wage gap rose throughout the period.

The years between 1919 and 1936 were, however, an exception to this general trend and over this period the racial wage gap declined in both relative and absolute terms. One should not, however, interpret this change as representing a gain by the black groups; the contrary was in fact the case as the narrowing was due to the success of the 'civilized labour policy' that was introduced after 1924 and which caused poor Whites to be substituted for blacks in many of the lower paid occupations. This policy had the effect of lowering the average wage paid to Whites and it was this that accounted for the reduction in the racial wage differential.

The actual nature of the changes that led to a narrowing of the racial wage gap between 1919 and 1936, highlight the dangers that are inherent in the very common practice in South Africa of using either the relative or absolute racial wage gap as a measure of racial income inequality. Because the wage gap does not reflect either racial employment levels or changes in employment practices, it is an extremely misleading indicator of incomes in any society in which there is either substantial unemployment, or in which high and low productivity sectors co-exist with one another. In such situations an expansion of employment opportunities in the high productivity sector will be far more likely to contribute to a narrowing of the gap between living standards than a reduction in the wage gap in the high productivity sector.

The contribution that South African manufacturing has made to the narrowing of racial average incomes over the period 1970–76 illustrates this point from a different angle. The real value of the absolute racial wage gap increased from R2 665 in 1970 to R3 257 in 1976. Notwithstanding this increase, the sector contributed to a narrowing of the racial income gap through the contribution that was made to improving black living standards as a result of the increased number of job opportunities created for blacks in the sector over this period. The real value of the wage bill paid to black labour grew more rapidly than the White wage bill throughout the six years, averaging 8 per cent as against an average growth of 5,3 per cent per year in the White wage bill.

When one looks at the relationship between the racial wage gap and the relative performance of the black and White wage bills throughout the 57 year period, one finds that, although the real value of the black wage bill grew faster than that of the White wage bill over the period 1919–76 as a whole, there were differences within the time periods. Between 1919 and 1936, both the White/black average wage ratio and the absolute racial wage gap fell, but the White wage bill grew faster than the black. In other words, although the racial differences within the sector itself were reduced, nevertheless, the sectoral behaviour contributed to a growing gap in the average living standards of black and White South Africans over this period, as Whites entered this high wage sector faster than their black compatriots. After 1936, however, black labour entered manufacturing at an increasing rate and the expansion of the sector in general has been a force operating to reduce racial income inequality in South Africa.

NINE

The Economies of the Black States

INTRODUCTION

The concept that separate land areas should be set aside for Africans in South Africa dates back to a period before the founding of the modern economy and evolved from the policies followed by the early White settler governments. These governments set aside land known as 'native reserves', that were specified as being for the sole use of particular sections of the African population. The earliest of these was the reserve established by Sir Harry Smith, the then Governor of the Cape, for the Mfengu community.

The Mfengu, originally refugees from Natal who had been driven from their homes by Shaka, had settled amongst the Xhosa on the eastern frontier of the Cape Colony. After a frontier war that had taken place between the settlers and the Xhosa tribesmen during 1835 and 1836, Sir Harry Smith invited the Mfengu to cross the Kei River and to settle within the Colony itself. It was hoped by the Administration of the Cape Colony that the Mfengu settlement would act as a barrier between the White border farming community and the tribesmen living on the other side of the Kei River.

The example set in the Cape was rapidly followed in Natal. In this British Colony, by 1849 seven reservations for Africans had been established and by 1852 the area of the land so reserved totalled some two million acres. A century later, although the total number of reserves in the region had grown to 48, the total area had only increased to just over 2,25 million acres.

In addition to the the areas that were set aside for Africans within the regions that had been settled and colonized by Whites, other areas that were also solely occupied by Africans were those that, although they had been subdued by conquest, had not been effectively settled. These regions included the Zululand area in Natal, the African regions in Northern Transvaal and the Ciskei and Transkei areas.

GOVERNMENT POLICY IN RETROSPECT

The policy of racially segregating ownership rights to land was institutionally formalized in modern South Africa with respect to Blacks and Whites by the Union Government in 1913 when it passed the Land Act. This Act, together with the 1936 Bantu Trust and Land Act, limited African rights of access to land to certain specified geographical areas. By so doing, these Acts together effectively confined African land ownership (both tribal and private), to some 15 million hectares of land, or 14 per cent of South Africa's total land areas.

In these early years it was never seriously envisaged that the African population should remain limited to the areas that had been set aside for them. In 1916 the Commission investigating land allocation in South Africa (The Native land Commission), commented in its report that the areas to be set aside for African occupation in the Land Act, 'are almost fully occupied and do not offer more than limited opportunities for the introduction of Natives from outside'. (Knight and Lenta: 1980)

Two subsequent Commissions, the Economics and Wages Commission, reporting in 1925 and the Native Economic Commission in 1932, both pointed out that, in their opinion, the areas that were then set aside could not be developed to a point at which they could support their populations. Even the Native Laws Commission, reporting in 1948 well after the addition of the 'scheduled areas' to the Reserves in 1936, when commenting on the view that the Government should adopt a policy of total segregation between Black and White South Africans, categorically rejected the notion that the areas set aside for Africans could be developed to support all South African Blacks other than those working as migrants in the White areas. The Fagan Commission, as it was known, also rejected the idea that total segregation would become feasible if the Government were to buy up sufficient White land and transfer it to Blacks.

The 1948 general election brought the National party to power and heralded a complete change of direction with respect to the 'Reserve Areas'. Prior to 1948, the notion that the Black areas should be fully politically independent, had never been seriously considered. Some of these areas, however, such as Transkei and Ciskei had had a measure of political autonomy through the development of the

'Bungas', which were in essence a form of local government, more formally known as The Transkei (or Ciskei) Territories General Council and which had been established towards the end of the nineteenth century. However, the ascendancy of the National party in White politics brought new respectability to the views of the segregationalists and this concept was now seriously mooted in official circles for the first time. Racial separation ultimately germinated in the form of the policy of 'apartheid', or as it was subsequently relabelled 'separate development', that was proposed and introduced by Dr H. F. Verwoerd.

In terms of this segregationalist strategy it was envisaged that South Africa should be balkanized into a number of territories, that were to be delineated on an ethnic basis, with the ideal of allowing the right of self determination to each group, whilst preventing the possibility of the domination of one group by another. The decade from 1949 to 1959 saw the introduction of a number of measures designed to separate South Africa's racial groups and legally to entrench the position of the Whites in the heartland of the modern economy. The prohibition of Mixed Marriages Act of 1949, the Population Registration Act of 1950 and the Immorality Act were all aimed at establishing racial segregation at what Davenport has called the 'biological level', (Davenport: 1977), whilst the Group Areas Act of 1950, the Amendments to the Urban Areas Act that took place in 1952, 1957, 1964 and 1971, together with the various Acts designed to alter the labour market relationships, served to strengthen the economic position of the Whites.

The rural counterpart of the measures to separate the races in the urban areas was the 1959 Bantu Self-Government Act. This Act recognized eight separate African national units on ethnic grounds and set up the institutional machinery that would enable the eventual development of self-government entities based on these ethnic groupings. By so doing, the 1959 Act ushered on to the South African scene the Black Homelands or Black States as they are now officially known. (See Map 3, p. 17)

The actual establishment of the Black States implied that a transformation from the boundaries drawn conceptually on ethnic grounds to ones drawn on geographical lines had to be made. The physical and geographical mixes of South Africa's race groups and ethnic sub-groups, reflecting as they do nearly 2 000 years of population movements in response to a variety of physical and economic forces, have meant that the Black States that have been produced by this transformation, exhibit a number of unusual characteristics. The most outstanding of these is the extent to which these states are, in general, spatially fragmented. In 1979 only one of these states, QwaQwa, consisted of a single unit. Details of the fragmentation, the land areas and the population of the Black States are given in Table 9.1, whilst Map 3 shows their location, relative to the remainder of South Africa, in terms of the final boundaries that will result from the implementation of the 1975 proposals to consolidate the states to a greater degree than is at present the case.

Subsequent to the 1959 Act, a further ethnic group, that of the Ndebele, was recognized and at the present time it is envisaged that South Africa will ultimately comprise eleven separate political entities, ten of which will be Black States, whilst the eleventh will consist of the remainder.

THE GENERAL CHARACTERISTICS OF THE BLACK STATES

The separate land areas that at present comprise the ten Black States are largely composed of the most economically backward regions of the South African Republic. If one ranks the 263 White magisterial districts and then the nine Black States in terms of their average output per head for 1970, one finds that the Black States filled nine of the ten lowest positions in the rank order. Nonetheless, these areas housed approximately 35 per cent of South Africa's population.

In general, the land areas are rugged and the soils depleted due to overpopulation and poor husbandry in the past. Although Lebowa and Bophuthatswana have significant deposits of a number of minerals, notably copper, chrome and platinum, as far as is presently known the other eight Black States are not well endowed with mineral resources.

The majority of the people living in these areas depend upon the land and live in tribally organized societies. They grow crops mainly for their own use and keep cattle predominantly as a store of value and as a means of fulfilling their tribal obligations, rather than for commercial use.

Population densities in the Black States are high by South African

Table 9.1
COMPOSITION AND STATUS OF THE BLACK STATES IN 1979

Black State	Ethnic Group	Resident Population 1977 (000)	Land Area (000 Hectares)		Number of People per Square Kilometer	Land/Man Ratio (Hectares)	Number of Separate Land Segments		Political Status 1979
			1973	1975 Consolidation Proposals			1973	1975 Consolidation Proposals	
Transkei	Xhosa	2 434	3 871	4 501	47	1,59	2	3	Independent
Ciskei	Xhosa	534	942	770	57	1,76	26	1	Self-Governing
KwaZulu	Zulu	2 811	3 273	3 239	67	1,16	205	10	Self-Governing
Bophuthatswana	Tswana	1 222	3 799	4 043	24	3,11	19	6	Independent
Lebowa	North Sotho	1 435	2 248	2 518	49	1,57	14	6	Self-Governing
Venda	Venda	349	618	668	44	1,77	3	2	Independent
Gazankulu	Shangaan	345	633	741	40	1,84	4	3	Self-Governing
KaNgwane	Swazi	213	208	391	56	,98	3	1	Self-Governing
QwaQwa	South Sotho	92	48	62	53	,52	1	1	Self-Governing
Ndebele	Ndebele	75	20	73	63	,27	3	1	Limited Self-Governing

SOURCES: *Black Development*, BENSO, (1976) and South African Institute of Race Relations *Handbook on Race Relations (1979)*.

standards and have risen significantly over the period since the passing of the Land Act in 1913. The combination of high population densities, rapid population growth rates, the limited land area and the continuance of the tribal society has severely depleted the carrying capacity of the land in these areas. Low productivity in agriculture, when coupled with the importance of the sector, has resulted in a situation in which, in 1975, the average output per head for the Black States as a whole was only R75 for the year.

The Demography of the Black States

The major proportion of the population of the Black States constitutes Blacks. Although each homeland or 'Black State', has a dominant ethnic group, members of other groups are also found living in these areas. Population growth rates in the Black States are generally thought to be very high although, because there is not as yet a comprehensive register of Black births and deaths in South Africa, it is virtually impossible to obtain an accurate assessment. It is, however, usually accepted that the natural rate of increase in population in these areas is somewhere between 2,4 per cent and 2,8 per cent, which is very high indeed by international standards. Table 9.2 contains an estimate of the population changes that have occurred in the areas, now known as the Black States, since 1936.

The changes shown in the Table reflect the combined influences of the natural population increase and the extensive resettlement of sections of the African population that have accompanied the setting up of the system of the Black States, largely as a result of the so-called 'Black Spot' removals.

High natural rates of increase in the population mean high dependency burdens, as the major proportion of the population will consist of children. In the Black States participation in the migrant labour system exacerbates this problem; in 1970 half of the population enumerated in the Black States in the census was under 15 years old. For every 100 men who lived and worked in these areas, there were 320 such children, whereas amongst the Black population as a whole this ratio was only 100:189.

Men join the migrant workforce in very much greater numbers than women; in 1970 there were nearly four times as many male migrants from the Black States as there were female. Consequently,

the system also distorts the sex ratios in the Black States and adul
women outnumbered adult men by more than 3:1 in the age group
20–45 years, 1970.

An asymmetry in the demographic relationships of the magnitude
found in the populations of South Africa's Black States has both
social and economic side effects on the communities in which i
occurs. These will be discussed later in this chapter in connection
with the problem that the migrant labour system poses for the
economic development of these areas.

Table 9.2

THE POPULATIONS OF THE BLACK STATES, 1936–78

Black State	Population on Census Date (in 000's)					
	1936	1946	1951	1960	1970	1978
Transkei	1 135	1 231	1 241	1 372	1 727	2 484
Ciskei	245	264	265	319	526	554
KwaZulu	907	958	964	1 203	2 106	2 898
Bophuthatswana	210	243	257	396	877	1 273
Lebowa					1 086	1 471
Venda	471	557	583	832	269	358
Gazankulu					269	354
KaNgwane	N/A	N/A	N/A	N/A	N/A	N/A
QwaQwa	8	8	6	11	26	95
Total	2 976	3 261	3 316	4 133	7 003	9 707

SOURCE: BENSO Estimates given in *Black Development,* BENSO, (1976) and *Statistical Survey*
    of Black Development, BENSO, (1979).

THE ECONOMIC STRUCTURE OF THE BLACK STATES

Their Relative Economic Position in South Africa

It was said earlier that the Black States are largely composed of the
economically underdeveloped areas of South Africa. Notwithstand
ing this, however, in 1970 they housed more than one third of the
Republic's total population. Table 9.3 shows the estimated share o
each of nine of the ten states in South Africa's total output, income
and population in 1975.

Table 9.3

THE RELATIVE POSITION OF SOUTH AFRICA'S BLACK STATES IN 1975

State	Population (000)	Share of R.S.A. Population (%)	Gross Domestic Product (R1 000)	Share of R.S.A. Gross Domestic Product (%)	Net National Income (R1 000)	Share of R.S.A. Net National Income (%)
Transkei	2 306	9,6	210 356	,85	560 436	2,62
Ciskei	530	2,0	54 562	,22	120 900	,56
KwaZulu	2 663	10,5	180 977	,73	790 500	3,69
Bophuthatswana	1 158	4,6	188 288	,87	340 410	1,59
Lebowa	1 360	5,3	106 048	,43	339 500	1,58
Venda	331	1,3	21 138	,09	86 400	,40
Gazankulu	327	1,3	20 897	,08	107 600	,50
KaNgwane	202	,8	10,368	,04	34,500	,16
QwaQwa	88	,4	5 959	,02	16 500	,08
The Group as a Whole		35,8		3,33		11,18

SOURCE: *South African Statistics 1978.* Report 09.17.03 *National Accounts of the Bantu Homelands 1971–1975. National Accounts of the Republic of Transkei 1971–1975. Department of Statistics* and *1978 Survey of Race Relations.*

In 1975, these areas as a whole produced only 3 per cent of South Africa's total output. However, due to the fact that a large number of the citizens of the Black States worked outside these regions, as migrants or 'frontier commuters', the income received by people who were normally resident there was considerably higher than the output produced in the area, and made up 11 per cent of South Africa's Net National Income.

There is a considerable variation in both the domestic capacities of the States to support their populations and in the extent to which their citizens join the migrant labour system, which together result in variations in the average living standards in these areas. These variations are shown in Table 9.4.

There are two interesting aspects of the data in this Table; firstly, the differences between the areas in terms of domestic productive capacity (measured in terms of average output per head produced in the region) are greater than the differences in average living standards. This is probably because the lower productivity levels increase the pressure on individuals to find work in the modern sector, as members of the migrant or commuter workforces.

Earnings from these sources are used as means of counteracting the effects of relative local underdevelopment.

Secondly, when one compares the distributions of both average incomes and production in the three years given in the Table it seems that the gap between the state with the lowest average and that with the highest has widened in real terms over the 15 year period. However, not only has this gap widened, but the rank order of the states has also changed in each of the three periods included in the Table. This suggests that the most important determinant of the relative living standards in these areas has a random element and is probably the success or failure of the subsistence harvest, rather than the outcome of formal economic development in the areas. This view is further substantiated by the analysis of the economic structures of the regions, which is undertaken in the next section.

Table 9.4

AVERAGE OUTPUT AND INCOMES PER HEAD IN BLACK STATES, 1960–75 IN CONSTANT 1970 PRICES

Area	Average Output per Head (1970 Rands)			Average Income per Head (1970 Rands)		
	1960	1970	1975	1960	1970	1975
Transkei	38	50	58	81	155	163
Ciskei	29	39	66	75	123	159
KwaZulu	30	42	43	75	147	203
Bophuthatswana	38	59	104	88	159	183
Lebowa	33	36	50	83	94	172
Venda	33	25	41	83	143	171
Gazankulu	33	31	41	83	164	216
KaNgwane	33	26	32	83	125	112
QwaQwa	45	50	43	80	120	125

SOURCE: Estimated from official data in Department of Statistics Reports 09.17.01, 09.17.02 and 09.17.03 and *Black Development* BENSO, 1976.

The Structure of the Economies

In the discussion earlier concerned with the nature of the evolutionary process in a capitalist market economy, it was argued that the distinguishing characteristics of an underdeveloped economy were the persistence of non-market oriented economic activity, the predominant position held by the agricultural sector, in terms of both its contribution to the total output and to employment, and the relative unimportance of both the manufacturing and the business service sectors of the economy. Table 9.5 below shows the magnitude of these indicators, from the output viewpoint, in the economies of the Black States in 1975.

Table 9.5

THE ECONOMIC STRUCTURE OF THE BLACK STATES IN 1975

State	Percentage of Total Output Contributed by							
	Subsistence Activities	Commercial Agriculture	Mining	Manufacturing	Construction	Trade and Business Services	Community Services	Other
Transkei	45,9	1,0	–	3,4	2,7	13,1	25,5	8,4
Ciskei	21,6	1,9	–	,7	12,3	10,4	44,7	8,4
KwaZulu	35,1	4,6	,4	2,1	6,1	11,2	34,0	6,5
Bophuthatswana	13,7	,9	45,7	6,7	3,3	12,5	16,7	,5
Lebowa	21,9	4,2	27,3	2,6	3,3	5,7	31,5	3,5
Venda	42,8	3,8	1,7	3,1	2,0	4,8	40,8	1,0
Gazankulu	23,9	7,1	,2	3,2	8,3	7,8	45,1	4,4
KaNgwane	53,4	7,4	–	1,2	,6	15,8	20,9	,7
QwaQwa	22,0	1,9	–	1,0	6,0	7,1	49,3	12,8

SOURCE: Report 09.17.03 and Report 09.17.01, *National Accounts of the Bantu Homelands,* Department of Statistics, Pretoria, 1978. Transkei, Department of Statistics Unpublished Estimates.

In terms of the data presented in Table 9.5 it is obvious that, in output terms, the Black States are still very underdeveloped. They are heavily dependent on the output from agriculture in general and on subsistence production in particular. This view is strengthened when one considers the employment position, as the majority of the workforce in all the states was employed in the low productivity subsistence sector. Even in Bophuthatswana and Lebowa, states with relatively well developed mining sectors, 48 per cent and 67 per cent respectively of the local workforce was employed in agriculture in 1970, and in KwaZulu in 1975, the percentage of the labour force employed in agriculture was as high as 78 per cent! (Thorrington-Smith: 1978)

The Performance of the Subsistence Sectors

The economic performance of the subsistence sectors in the Black States is of crucial importance to the well-being of the majority of the people living in these areas. In 1970, 92 per cent of the population of the Black States were rural dwellers and the major proportion of the output produced by them was for their own subsistence rather than for the market.

In the discussion on the role of the agricultural sector in the development process, data was given that showed conclusively that over the period 1918–75, the output from African agriculture was virtually stagnant and that consequently, in the face of growing population numbers, the sector's ability to feed the community dependent upon it, declined over this period. There are, however, quite significant differences between the Black States, in terms of both their ability to feed their resident populations and the performance of their subsistence sectors over the 15 year period 1960–75, as can be seen from the data in Table 9.6 below.

Table 9.6

GROWTH IN SUBSISTENCE ACTIVITIES IN THE BLACK STATES, 1960–75

State	Average Subsistence Output per Head (in 1970 Rands)			Percentage Growth in Real Value of Subsistence Output	
	1960	1970	1975	1960–1975	1970–1975
Transkei	23,7	23,2	27,2	4,5	9,5
Ciskei	17,5	12,1	21,1	3,3	8,0
KwaZulu	21,7	18,1	17,6	3,8	3,7
Bophuthatswana	27,9	14,0	15,5	1,9	5,9
Lebowa	⎫	12,4	17,4	⎫	3,1
Venda	⎬ 16,4	9,7	17,4	⎬ 6,9	17,0
Gazankulu		8,7	10,0		6,8
KaNgwane	⎭	17,9	19,8	⎭	11,8
QwaQwa	–	16,2	10,0	–	–2,6

SOURCE: Reports 09.17.01 and 09.17.03 *National Accounts of the Bantu Homelands 1969–1970 to 1973–1974 and 1971 to 1975, Black Development in South Africa, The Official Year Book of South Africa, 1974,* Department of Information, Pretoria, 1974.

Data relating to non-marketed economic activity should always be treated with circumspection, as it poses difficult valuation problems. Data relating to subsistence activities are doubly suspect, because they are also extremely difficult to identify let alone evaluate. For example, the lack of a piped water supply in nearly all the rural areas of the Black States means that providing water for the household is a time-consuming task. It is clearly an economic activity, forming part of the production of the subsistence sector, but it is difficult to decide how much time has actually been spent on water carrying, since it will obviously vary from one household to the next and will be affected by such things as household size, household needs and the distance from the dwelling to the water source. Assuming one can overcome this difficulty, one still has to decide what value one should place on time spent in this way.

A further problem arises when one comes to consider output performance over time. Growth rates are very sensitive to the values at either end of the period over which they are estimated. Since a major component of subsistence output is the production of food and the agricultural sector is very prone to climatically induced fluctuations, subsistence sector growth rates are very sensitive to good and bad harvest years.

Bearing these problems in mind let us now try to assess the data in Table 9.6. The first thing that strikes one forcibly is the very low level of output in the sector in all the Black States and their obvious inability to support their population in terms of food. The highest average level of output per head in the subsistence sector was that in Transkei, but even there average subsistence production reached only R23 per head per annum and was clearly too low for an individual to survive on alone.

Although there was an increase in subsistence production in terms of total output over the 15 year period in all the areas, in some the increase was insufficient to maintain the 1960 real per capita levels, due to the combination of low rates of output growth and high population growth. The period from 1969 onwards was a period which saw an exodus of Blacks from the White farming districts. The majority of these people resettled in the Black States and partly account for the high rates of population increase.

Low levels of labour productivity in subsistence agriculture were well established before the system of self-governing and independent

'Black States' was set up. They are the outcome of the interaction of a number of interrelated factors, such as the persistence of the tribal system of social organization, the limited land area, increasing population pressures, poverty, poor average educational levels and probably the influence that is at present the most significant, that of the nature of the labour linkages between the Black rural areas and the modern economy operating through the migrant labour system. The historical events that lead to the establishment of the migrant labour system were discussed in Chapter Four and the nature of the links between the increasing participation in the migrant labour system and the low levels of labour productivity in the subsistence sector in Chapter Six. Although these arguments are highly relevant to the present situation found in the rural areas of the Black States, they will not be repeated here and the reader is instead referred back to these earlier chapters.

THE DEVELOPMENT OF A MODERN ECONOMY IN THE BLACK STATES

Modern economic development in the Black States has proceeded relatively slowly. Prior to the creation of the Black States in their present self-governing form, very little effort was made by successive governments to develop these areas. The period 1970–79, has however, seen a significant change in policy. Development corporations have been set up to encourage the development of private enterprise through the provision of finance and training. The grants from the central government to the local state authorities have also been significantly increased, enabling these local governments to move ahead with infrastructural investment to a greater degree than was previously possible.

The provision of a minimum level of infrastructure is a prerequisite for development through the capitalistic mode of production, particularly in an area that is competing for private enterprise investment with more advanced regions in the same geographical region. Development in the Black States has, to date, been slow and until the backlog in infrastructural investment has been made up, will probably remain so. Up to 1975, the latest year for which data is available, public sector activities dominated the economies of the Black States as can be seen from the data in Table 9.7 below.

Table 9.7

THE GOVERNMENT AND THE MODERN SECTOR IN 1975

State	Percentage Share of	
	Total Output that is Monetized	Public Sector in Monetized Output
Transkei	54	60
Ciskei	78	82
KwaZulu	65	66
Bophuthatswana	84	
Lebowa	78	45
Venda	57	73
Gazankulu	76	68
KaNgwane	47	61
QwaQwa	78	82

SOURCE: Report 09.17.03 *National Accounts of the Bantu Homelands.*

In 1975 on average some 70 per cent of the total output of the Black States was produced in the modern sector, the remaining 30 per cent being production for home consumption in the subsistence economy. Of the 70 per cent which was modern sector production, more than two thirds originated in the public sector, and was mainly the result of service sector activity rather than government enterprise activity. The mining, manufacturing, construction and trade sectors of all the Black States were relatively small as will be seen below where they are discussed separately.

Mining

Mineral deposits are not equally distributed amongst the Black States. Bophuthatswana and Lebowa both have significant deposits and the mining industry is well established in the former. In 1975 approximately 68 000 people were employed on the mines in Bophuthatswana and there are 26 mines operating in the State. Ironically, the mining industry in Bophuthatswana does not employ a large number of people living in the region, but instead makes significant use of migrants drawn from other areas. It was estimated by the Buro vir Ekonomiese Navorsing Saamwerking en Ontwikkeling (BENSO) that in 1975 only 1 per cent of the Blacks employed in the platinum mines in Bophuthatwana were of Tswana origin.

The three states on the eastern seaboard, KwaZulu, Transkei and Ciskei are not well endowed with minerals. In 1975 there were 9 very small mining operations being carried on in KwaZulu employing just over 100 men altogether and no operating mines at all in Transkei and Ciskei.

The development of the mines presently operating in the Black States has been undertaken by private enterprise using capital drawn from outside, mainly from South Africa. Consequently the benefits to the Black States accrue in the form of wage payments, ground rent, royalties and taxes, rather than in the form of profits.

Manufacturing

The manufacturing sectors in the Black States are small. Although it has been central government policy to encourage the decentral-ization of industry in South Africa since 1960, in the initial stages of the formation of the Black States, White capital was not permitted to enter and was limited to setting up industries in the so-called 'Border Areas', which were situated close to the Black States and intended to provide employment for their citizens. 1968 saw a change in government policy and from then on White capital could be used within the Black States subject to certain provisions.

Neither the efforts made by the central government to encourage the decentralization of industry to the Border Areas, nor those of the Black States to attract private sector capital into the States them-selves can be said to have been successful in terms of job creation to date. BENSO estimated that by March 1974 some 63 000 Black workers were employed in industries that had been established under the various facets of the decentralization schemes. This means that only approximately 4 500 jobs a year have been created since the inception of the programme.

In output terms in 1975, modern manufacturing contributed only just over 5 per cent of the total output produced in the Black States and mining, manufacturing and construction together produced only 10 per cent of the output. Trade and financial and business services provided a further 9 per cent.

The development in these sectors has also been mainly undertaken by private enterprise, although a number of tripartite agreements have been signed, such as those signed by the KwaZulu Government, by means of which it is envisaged that the enterprises will be initially owned by a partnership consisting of capital from outside (again mainly South African), the KwaZulu Government and the KwaZulu people.

BENSO in their review of Black Development in South Africa, remark that Black entrepreneurial participation in the industrial development of the Black States has so far been limited and that Black businessmen tend to concentrate their activities on producing products for consumption within the Black areas, such as bread, maize, flour, furniture, candles and clothing. (Benso: 1977)

Construction

This sector is considerably larger on average than the manufacturing sectors in the Black States, as can be seen from Table 9.5. The sector's size and growth, to a large extent, reflects the activity of the large public sector in these areas.

A great deal of public activity has been directed towards the creation of townships and the building of schools, hospitals and roads, all of which stimulate the construction sector. Unlike manufacturing, the major proportion of the construction sector is controlled by the public sector and not by private enterprise. For example, in 1974 in Ciskei some 3 800 people were employed in the sector, of whom 82 per cent were government employees; in KwaZulu in the same year 56 per cent of the construction workers were employed by government.

Commerce and Trade

It has been estimated that in 1974 there were nearly 10 000 commercial enterprises in the tertiary sector of the Black States, of which 82 per cent were in retail trade and 52 per cent (63 per cent of the retail traders) were general dealers. Most of these enterprises were owned and operated by Blacks. (Benso: 1976)

Although Black traders have been protected from competition by

Whites within the Black States, they are in fact, in many regions, particularly in the urban areas adjoining White towns, facing strong competition from White traders operating outside the Black areas and there is a significant leakage of Black State income through this medium.

In output terms the sector is of considerable significance, being the largest source of value added in the Black States outside the subsistence sector and the Government.

The Public Sector

The data in Table 9.7 show very clearly how dominant the public sector is in the Black States. To a certain extent this dominant position of the public sector is a reflection of the generally low levels of development in the other areas of these economies.

The role of the public sector in fostering economic development is crucial in any economy and in backward areas, where there is usually a significant lack of infrastructural investment, this is even more true. It was said earlier that an adequate level of infrastructural investment is vitally important, since without it it is virtually impossible to generate meaningful levels of private sector investment. Consequently it is not enough that a high proportion of economic resources are in the hands of the public sector; it is also crucial that these resources are used to finance investment projects.

In 1970 only 24 per cent of public sector expenditure in the Black States was on capital projects. Although this percentage had increased to 35 per cent by 1975, by general South African standards this was still too low, as the average for the country as a whole for the same year was 54 per cent. Despite the fact that government spending in the Black States almost trebled over the five years to 1975 in terms of public investment projects, the gap between the Black States and the remainder of South Africa continued to widen. Table 9.8 gives the share of government expenditure on investment and current running expenses for the separate Black States.

As can be seen from the data in the table, the public sector investment rate varies quite significantly between the regions, from as high as 50 per cent in KaNgwane in 1975 to as low as 27 per cent in Kwa Zulu in the same year. One of the factors that makes it difficult for governments in underdeveloped areas to maintain a high level of investment is the limit imposed by their own current expenditure

Table 9.8

GOVERNMENT EXPENDITURE IN THE BLACK STATES

State	Percentage of Expenditure that is			
	Current Expenditure		Investment	
	1971	1975	1971	1975
Transkei	63	65	37	35
Ciskei	67	68	33	32
KwaZulu	73	73	27	27
Bophuthatswana		67		23
Lebowa	69	63	31	37
Venda	84	67	16	33
Gazankulu	66	56	34	44
KaNgwane	46	50	54	50
QwaQwa	61	55	39	45
South Africa	49	53	51	47

SOURCE: Report 09.17.03 *National Accounts of the Bantu Homelands.* Transkei kindly provided by Transkei Department of Commerce and Planning. *Statistical Survey of Black Development,* BENSO 1979.

which is often related to the size of the population. Table 9.9 shows the level of government expenditure per head of the population of the States for 1975.

Table 9.9

PUBLIC EXPENDITURE PER CAPITA, 1975

State	Current	Investment	Total
Transkei	38	20	58
Ciskei	92	44	136
KwaZulu	40	19	59
Bophuthatswana	41	27	68
Lebowa	43	25	68
Venda	48	24	72
Gazankulu	46	36	82
KaNgwane	52	51	103
QwaQwa	54	44	98
South Africa	164	169	333

SOURCE: *South African Statistics, 1978,* Report 09.17.03 *National Accounts of the Bantu Homelands, Statistical Survey of Black Development,* BENSO 1979.

From the data in Table 9.9 it does seem that the size of the population of the Black States affects the public sector investment rate. The per capita levels in government current spending are much more similar than those of public investment per head, suggesting that these current needs receive priority, at least up to some basic minimum. The large States, in population terms, do seem to be at a disadvantage. Transkei and KwaZulu both have populations that are approximately twice as large as the next largest, Lebowa. The average per capita government expenditure in the four smallest Black States, Venda, Gazankulu, KaNgwane and QwaQwa was 1,5 times greater than that of the two largest.

It is the difference in government investment expenditure per head that is the more significant from the long term viewpoint, because of the crucial role that an adequate level of infrastructural investment plays in the development process. In this respect the gap in economic development potential between the Black States and the rest of South Africa still appears to be widening, despite the recent increases in expenditure in the homelands.

DEVELOPMENT OVER THE PERIOD 1960–75

It was pointed out earlier that the present levels of economic development in the Black States are low. This does not, however, mean that no progress has been made. Table 9.10 shows the average yearly percentage growth rates in the real values of the output of particular sectors of the economies for four of the States, for which data is available for the period 1960–75.

If one uses the average rate of growth in Gross Domestic Product as a yardstick for measuring development performance, the Black states show up as having made good progress. Even in Transkei which had the lowest average growth rate in the real value of its production, total output grew over the period more than twice as fast as population. Migrant and commuter earnings in all four states also grew rapidly in real terms over the period. On average, therefore, living standards in these regions rose significantly during this time. It is, however, essential to bear two factors in mind – firstly, that average living standards in the Black States were still very low in 1975. Indeed with the exception of KwaZulu and Gazankulu the averages were below the internationally accepted poverty cut-off level of $200 per year. Secondly, as we saw earlier, a large proportion of the increases that took place over the period from 1970–75, reflect an increased participation in the migrant labour system, with all its attendant social costs.

Table 9.10

GROWTH IN SELECTED SECTORS FOR THE PERIOD 1960–75

Average Annual Growth in Real Terms for the Period 1960–1975	Transkei	Ciskei	KwaZulu	Bophuthatswana
Gross Domestic Product	6,5	9,2	8,1	15,0
Subsistence Production	4,3	3,3	3,8	1,7
Mining, Manufacturing and Construction	10,0	1,9	8,5	15,3
Finance and Trade	5,0	12,1	12,4	11,8
Community and Personal Service	3,8	6,7	5,8	3,2
Migrant and Commuter Earnings	10,0	8,6	14,9	10,9
Government Investment	18,0	20,3	19,8	19,9

SOURCE: *Black Development.* (BENSO 1976) 09.17.03 and 09.17.01. *National Accounts of the Bantu Homelands 1971–1975 and 1969–1970 to 1973–1974.* Transkei 1975 data kindly supplied by Transkei Government.

Some people assess development in the Black States by comparing progress in living conditions in these areas with those African countries beyond South Africa's borders, that are at a similar level of development. The data in Table 9.11 show that in these terms, the economic performance of these four Black States has been good.

One can however, question the relevance of comparisons of this type, since the Black States are in actuality both geographically and economically integrated into the wealthy South African economy. A more meaningful comparison would be that between the Black States and the other regions within South Africa itself. There is not sufficient data available to enable one to undertake such an exercise in detail, but it is interesting to note, in this respect, that the South African economy as a whole grew in real terms at 5,2 per cent per annum over the 15 year period 1960–75, very much more slowly than the average for the four Black States. Nevertheless, the gap between the value of Real Gross Domestic Product per head in the Black States and in the economy as a whole widened from R344 in 1960, to R478 in 1975. (1970 prices)

Table 9.11

A COMPARISON OF ECONOMIC PERFORMANCES

Countries	Average Yearly Growth Rate in Gross Domestic Product (Money Terms) 1965–1975 (Per Cent)	Black States	Average Yearly Growth Rate in Gross Domestic Product (Money Terms) 1960–1975 (Per Cent)
Tanzania	5,3	Transkei	11,7
Malawi	6,2	Ciskei	14,6
Burundi	3,5	Bophuthatswana	20,6
Botswana	12,3	KwaZulu	13,4

SOURCE: International Data from *World Bank Tables 1976,* John Hopkins Press 1976, Black States from the same sources as Table 9.10.

The other aspect one needs to question is the source of the growth in output in the Black States. From the data in Table 9.10 it seems that this growth has originated almost entirely in the public sector. Not only did public sector spending account for a very substantial proportion of the Gross Domestic Product in these areas, but it increased very rapidly in real terms over the 15 years 1960–75. The other source of growth was the Finance and Trade Sector. Manufacturing, the cornerstone of the industrialization process, is still largely insignificant in the Black States.

Growth rates in the output of the subsistence sector have been low, barely higher than the rates of population growth. When one links this relatively poor performance with the fact that by far the major proportion of the population live in the rural areas and are dependent on the subsistence sector for their support, it is not surprising that a growing percentage of the working adults continues to join the flow of migrant workers.

When one talks about economic development in a region, one is in fact interested in increasing the standards of living of the people in the area. One of the major ways of achieving this in underdeveloped areas is to offer people productive employment. Progress in the field of employment creation in the Black States has also not been good. Table 9.12 below contains an estimate of the average increase in work seekers and in the number of jobs created over the period 1973–75.

Table 9.12

THE AVERAGE ANNUAL GROWTH IN JOBS AND JOB SEEKERS IN THE HOMELAND AREAS FOR THE PERIOD 1973–75

| | Increase in the Workforce | Jobs Created | | Difference between Job Seekers and Jobs Created |
		in Homeland	Within Commute Distance	
Transkei	25 430	3 870	60	21 500
Ciskei	7 970	z 978	3 503	1 489
KwaZulu	29 930	7 410	18 143	4 377
Bophuthatswana	12 200	3 970	10 485	– 2 255
Lebowa	14 870	5 920	2 601	6 349
Venda	3 100	1 700	50	1 350
KaNgwane	1 670	1 440	1 070	– 840
Gazankulu	3 730	730	856	2 144
QwaQwa	1 200	410	90	700
	100 100	28 428	36 858	34 814

SOURCE: *Black Development in South Africa, 1976.*

According to these estimates, the outcome of an average year's development activity within the Homelands was the creation of employment opportunities for only 28 per cent of the annual increase in work seekers from these regions. A further 37 per cent of these new work seekers were able to find jobs in the centre economy within commuting distance from their homes, whilst the remaining 35 per cent were faced with the necessity of either joining the migrant workforce, or of becoming part of the disguised unemployment backing up in these peripheral economies. The present lack of what could perhaps be termed 'real development' in the 'Black States' is underlined by the fact that, of the 28 400 jobs created per year over the period 1973–75, approximately 21 900, or 77 per cent, were created in the public sector.

The Impact of Economic Development on Rising Standards of Living

One frequently observed characteristic of the process of economic development through the capitalist mode of production is that it is accompanied, during the early stages at least, by an increasingly unequal distribution of income. (Kuznets: 1965, Chenery and Syrquin: 1975). The major division between the 'haves' and the 'have nots' in a developing area often has a substantial rural-urban overlay, with the urban dwellers benefitting from the development process to a greater extent than the rural people. (Lipton: 1975)

Although in general urbanization levels are low in the Black States, there is evidence that this rural-urban gap is beginning to emerge. The urban areas in the Black States are either concentrated on the boundaries of the White economy, serving as dormitory towns for Black commuters, or have grown up around the administration process and so contain a high proportion of civil servants. Civil servants in the Black States comprise, as they do in most developing countries, the core of a new élite class and command wages well above those paid to their fellow countryman employed in other sectors of the economy. Commuters are also relatively favoured members of the community, as not only does the breadwinner enjoy modern sector wage levels, but frequently the second earner in the family is also able to obtain a job in the high productivity economy, boosting family incomes well above those of a migrant's family, whose second worker is, in general, employed in subsistence agriculture at very much lower earning levels.

There is not sufficient data to enable one to undertake a thorough assessment of the distribution of income within the Black States. There is, however, some relevant evidence relating to one of them, KwaZulu, which suggests that there may be quite a significant degree of inequality present, both between the rural and urban areas and within the areas themselves. A conservative estimate of the shares of the net area income accruing to urban and rural dwellers in KwaZulu in 1975 suggests that urban average incomes were 2,5 times greater than those in rural areas. (Nattrass: 1978a)

Although the major split may be a rural-urban one, incomes within both areas also tend to become more unequally distributed during the early phases of economic growth. In the urban area of Umlazi in KwaZulu for example, the average income in 1973 of an

African retailer was R3 552 per annum, whilst the average wage paid by these businesses over the same period was only R408. (Lenta: 1977). The value added per man also varies quite significantly between the major sectors contributing to output. Not only will these variations affect the distribution of income, but in addition, their impact will be intensified by differences that occur within the sectors between firms of different sizes and levels of efficiency. Further, the average wage paid in the public sector was considerably higher than that in commerce, whilst those in personal service and the informal sector are likely to be well below. All these factors will contribute to growing inequality levels within the urban areas.

In the rural areas there is also evidence of the existence of substantial income differentials. Lenta estimated the average output per worker in agriculture in KwaZulu in 1973 at R65 per year and pointed out that the average income of the Zulu sugar planters in the same year was R582; nine times greater. (Lenta: 1977). Other studies undertaken in the Nongoma and Nkandla districts by the Bureau for Market Research, yielded average annual subsistence earnings per family of 5,8 and 6,8 persons respectively of R25 and R18; well below the average estimated per subsistence worker for the sector as a whole. Incomes in the rural areas are significantly affected by the remittances from migrant labourers. Families without a migrant worker remitting income on a regular basis, and forced to survive on the income from subsistence farming activities alone, may well be virtually 'destitute', whereas a family with one migrant worker supporting them, could have an average income per head three times higher.

Not only does there seem to be an apparent urban-rural gap in living standards emerging in the Black States, but it seems that this gap may well widen in the immediate future. The rates of growth in subsistence agricultural output have failed to cover the increases in the population and any improvements in the rural living standards have come almost exclusively from the increased participation in and earnings from the migrant labour system.

Earnings of migrants and commuters from the Black States grew very rapidly over the 15 year period 1960–75, averaging 19,5 per cent in real terms throughout the period in the four states discussed in Table 9.10. This massive rate of increase has two components; firstly, a rapid rate of growth in the number of people entering the migrant workforce and, secondly, the very substantial increases in Black earnings that took place, particularly over the period 1972–75. It does seem at present that this momentum is unlikely to be maintained and that this source of income growth for people in the rural areas of the Black States may well dry up.

The economy was extremely buoyant in the early part of the 1970s, but started to enter a recessionary phase towards the end of 1975 from which it is only now (1980) beginning to emerge. This will have undoubtedly slowed down both the rate of employment growth amongst migrants and the rate of increase in average Black wage rates.

In addition the implementation of the recommendations of the Riekiert Commission seems likely to give preference, in the employment field, to Blacks with domicile rights in urban areas in White regions. This will have the side effect of making it more difficult for would-be migrants from the rural areas in the Black States to enter the modern workforce. Unemployment is likely to start building up in these rural communities and this will depress living standards there. (R.P.32/1979)

One mitigating factor will be the growing number of jobs outside subsistence agriculture. As development proceeds in the Black States a growing number of people should be able to find work in the high productivity modern sector and, as people leave the subsistence sector for the high wage jobs, inequality levels in the Black States as a whole will be reduced, even though the rural-urban income gap may still be widening.

THE BLACK STATES AS DEPENDENT ECONOMIES

Dos Santos describes economic dependence as follows:

> The relation of interdependence between two or more economies . . . assumes the form of dependence, when some countries (the dominant ones) can expand and can be selfsustaining while other countries (the dependent ones) can do this only as a reflection of that expansion which can have either a positive or a negative effect on their immediate development. (Dos Santos p. 23)

In terms of this definition it seems that the relationship that exists between the South African centre economy and the Black States is one of economic dependency. The nature of this dependency has a number of distinct aspects to it; employment, production and consumption, fiscal and finally capital inflows and investment.

The Employment Aspect of Dependency

At their present levels of economic development the Black States are unable to provide sufficient jobs for their economically active citizens. In 1970 more than half of the economically active men aged between 14 and 65, who were normally resident in the Black States, were away from their homes working as migrant labourers in the centre economy. We saw earlier how important the earnings and contributions sent home by these migrants are to the maintenance of the existing living levels of the inhabitants of the Black States. On average the national income of the Black States in 1975 was more than three times greater than the value of the goods and services produced in these areas. The value of the remittances sent home by the migrants was nearly one and a half times greater than that of agricultural output and was the equivalent of 86 per cent of the subsistence sector output in the same year. In these terms it is obvious that the living standards in the rural areas of the Black States are being substantially supported by the work provided in the centre economy.

The Production and Consumption Aspects of Dependency

The Black States are also heavily dependent upon the South African economy for the supply of basic inputs into production and for the major proportion of both manufactures consumed and investment goods. In an area in which in 1975 the estimated net national income was three times greater than Gross Domestic Product and six times greater than domestic production, excluding government services, it is obvious that imported products will be of considerably greater significance than domestically produced commodities. Even in agriculture the domestic production is not sufficient to provide for the food needs of the people living in the region.

The Fiscal Aspects of Dependency

Although the independent and selfgoverning Black States are responsible for their own budgets, the major source of government finance for the Black States remains the South African Government. In the fiscal year 1975/76, of the total expenditure by the Governments of the Black States, only 20 per cent came from the local sources, the balance being provided by the central government.

In addition, in the same year, although total government expenditure in the Black States (i.e. the sum of expenditure by the Black governments, the central government and the para state institutions such as the Development Corporations and the South African Bantu Trust) was R653 million, the Black Governments had control over the allocation of only 58 per cent of these funds.

There is no doubt that the actions of the Black governments are circumscribed by the overall policy objectives of the government of the Republic since the latter is effectively 'paying the piper'. From the development viewpoint this could well be a limiting factor, since it is quite possible that at sometime the development objectives of the Black governments could well be in conflict with the overall strategy of the central government.

A STRATEGY FOR THE FUTURE

Poverty, Inequality and Economic Development[1]

'It is now almost universally accepted that the existence of widespread poverty constrains both economic growth and economic development in all instances other than the case in which growth takes place solely in an export oriented enclave. Poverty impedes growth and development through the impact that it has on the accumulation of human capital, on the level of domestic saving, on the size and rate of growth of the local market for goods and services and on average levels and rates of growth in labour productivity.

'The case as to whether economic inequality encourages or hinders growth is not so clear cut. In the 1950s Kuznets hypothesised that, whereas in the early stages of growth, increasing income inequality

1. Reprinted with permission from Nattrass 1979b.

was likely to be functional to the growth process through the impact that it exerted upon domestic savings levels and capital accumulation; in the later stages continuing high rates of inequality would ultimately impede growth because they would restrict the rate of growth of the domestic market and so hinder profitability. (Kuznets: 1955)

'This view of the economic growth process led planning strategists, such as Galenson and Leibenstein (1955) and Sen (1960), to advocate that developing economies adopt capital intensive growth paths, in the belief that this would enable such countries to maximize, with a given level of resources, both the rate of economic growth and the rate of reinvestment, thereby ensuring that wealth would be rapidly, if unequally, accumulated. These strategists argued that once a reasonable level of economic activity had been achieved through growth with inequality, measures could be instituted to redistribute income and that these measures, in their turn, would further fuel the engine of economic growth, whilst at the same time ensuring a better distribution of welfare.

'At present this view of the relationship between income inequality and economic growth is out of fashion amongst development planning strategists, largely because, firstly, patterns of economic growth actually experienced by many developing countries during the first development decade suggested that this type of economic growth in no way leads to economic development in the wider sense. Secondly, experience also showed that many of the recipients of the high incomes, far from saving and investing substantial proportions of their income, in fact indulged in luxury consumption, lowering the rate of capital accumulation, distorting the patterns of production in these countries away from the provision of the necessities of life, and increasing import levels to the point where balance of payments problems resulted. Finally, increasing income inequality has proved to be a politically destabilizing influence in developing countries, particularly in those countries which initially started down the development road clad in the trappings of capitalism and democracy.

'Current planning theory favours a strategy that incorporates measures to redistribute wealth to the poorer members of the community early on in the development process. (Fiqueroa: 1975, Foxley: 1975). This view is based upon the belief that one of the major reasons that the high growth strategies failed was because they ran into constraining factors, other than a shortage of capital, such as a lack of needed foreign exchange, or the lack of adequately trained manpower to run the sophisticated factories that were built. It is now argued that a strategy incorporating both growth and redistribution measures may succeed in avoiding these other constraints. The redistribution aspects of the strategy mean that the bulk of the increase in the domestic market will come from the increased demand from the poorer levels of society and be manifested mainly in an increased demand for food, clothing and basic housing requirements. These commodities are ones for which production is suited to labour intensive techniques and which have low import coefficients. As a result, the growth process will incorporate more people into it from an early stage, as employment levels will rise fairly rapidly. Further, because of the low import coefficients, the process is unlikely to run up against an inhibiting foreign exchange constraint and so will continue for a longer period of time.' (Nattrass: 1979b)

Development Strategies for the Black States

The economy of the Southern African region is dominated by the productive capacity of the South African economy and as we have seen in this chapter, apart from some highly profitable mining centres, the economic activity in the remainder of the region is largely limited to subsistence agricultural pursuits and to relatively small scale manufacturing for the local markets. A large proportion of the communities outside the modern South African core economy supplement their domestically generated income with the proceeds earned from the export of labour to the economic core. Average standards of living in the areas outside the economic centre are low and in many regions are maintained only as a result of the continued participation by the local residents in the migrant labour system.

'In Southern Africa poverty and inequality manifest themselves in the form of unproductive agriculture, over population, poor average educational levels, poor housing standards, low levels of nutrition, low levels of saving and investment and participation in the migrant labour system.' (Nattrass: 1979b)

Consequently a successful development strategy will be one that includes within its framework policies that will alleviate these conditions as quickly as possible, whilst at the same time providing an overall foundation for a healthy economic future.

Transkei and KwaZulu have both attempted to formulate a total approach to the problem of generating economic development within their region. The two approaches differ very significantly and as a result, it is interesting to compare them. Two quotations from the publications introducing the strategies highlight these differences. Transkei planners state: 'The cornerstone of the economic restructuring of Transkei must be the development of its agricultural potential, if the labour force is to be gainfully employed at even its present income levels (by the year 2000) and if the basic needs of the people are to be met'. (Transkei: 1978, p. 46)

The strategy followed by KwaZulu planners on the other hand is well summarized in the following quotation that has been taken from the initial planning document.

'The plan takes as its starting point the assumption that the process (of modernization and westernization) is irreversible and that the necessary growth climate will be created . . . High among the priorities is the need to reduce the rural population and promote urbanization and industry which will stimulate internal development.' (Thorrington-Smith, Rosenberg and McCrystal: 1978, p. 3)

Both planning periods start in 1975 and at this stage the economies of the two Black States were similar in terms of the sizes of their populations, the extent of their dependence on subsistence production; the average educational attainments of their people, the overriding importance of government activity in the economy and the level of infrastructural capital available. They differed from one another in terms of the degree and nature of the spatial dislocation in the economy; KwaZulu being fragmented to a greater extent than Transkei, but enjoying better physical access to the existing centres of economic development in South Africa.

Table 9.13 contains data comparing the structures of the two economies in terms of the sectoral contributions to output and employment at the start of the planning period and that estimataed for the year 2000. The KwaZulu planning document covers the period 1975–90. The estimates for the year 2000 have been made by assuming that the trends over the planning period continue to hold over the decade 1990–2000.

It seems that despite the differences in emphasis in the two

Table 9.13

A COMPARISON OF THE PROJECTIONS FOR THE FUTURE MADE FOR TRANSKEI AND KWAZULU

Sector	Percentage Contribution to Total							
	Employment				Gross Domestic Product			
	1975		2000		1975		2000	
	Transkei	KwaZulu	Transkei	KwaZulu	Transkei	KwaZulu	Transkei	KwaZulu
Agriculture	43,9	49,1	30,3	30,4	43,3	28,6	18,2	8,7
Mining	,1	,1	1,5	,4	–	,4	4,1	3,5
Manufacturing and Construction	1,5	1,6	15,8	5,6	12,4	17,5	31,7	46,3
Electricity and Transport	,4	2,9	4,5	2,4	4,2	4,0	18,5	4,6
Commerce, Finance, Business Service and Tourism	1,1	5,9	10,3	4,5	13,1	15,6	11,4	20,2
Community and Personal Service (including Government)	7,8	2,7	12,6	6,6	27,0	33,9	16,1	16,7
Unemployment			2,6	3,8				
Migrants and Commuters	45,2	37,7	22,4	46,3				

SOURCE: *A Development Strategy for Transkei.* Transkei Government, Umtata, 1978. Thorrington-Smith, Rosenberg and McCrystal: 1978. Benso: 1979.

development strategies, by the turn of the century in both economies 30 per cent of the total workforce will be employed in the agricultural sector. However, whereas in Transkei it is estimated that this workforce will generate 19 per cent of the total output, in KwaZulu this percentage will only be 9 per cent. The extent of the projected structural change in KwaZulu is, therefore, very much greater than that for Transkei.

The other major difference relates to the planning approach to the development of the modern manufacturing and construction sectors. The KwaZulu planners estimate that these two sectors will provide one-third of the total output by the year 1990. If the planned development patterns continue through to the end of the century, these sectors will provide nearly half of the Gross Domestic Product, which is clearly an unrealistic expectation. In Transkei these two sectors are expected to develop, over the remainder of this century, to the point at which they will provide approximately one-third of the total output. When one remembers that even in the relatively well developed and modern South African economy, the contributions of manufacturing and construction in 1977, were only 26,1 per cent of the output, it is obvious that both plans are somewhat over optimistic in this respect.

The differences in the planning strategies are clearly revealed in a comparison of the projected changes in the structure of employment and in labour productivity levels. It was estimated by the Transkei planners that by the year 2000, 16 per cent of the Transkeian workforce would be employed in manufacturing and construction and that the average output per man would be only R1 000 (1975 prices) which is low by modern standards. In KwaZulu on the other hand, the planners believe that, notwithstanding the fact that these two sectors are expected to provide well over one-third of the state's output by the year 2000, they will employ only 6 per cent of the workforce. Average output per man in the sector is correspondingly higher and is estimated at approximately R4 000, four times greater than that projected for Transkei.

The most important single determinant of the level of labour productivity is the quantity of capital that is combined with the labour in the production process, and it is the different emphasis laid upon the allocation of development funds that underlies the differences in the sectoral projections for the economies of the two states. Transkei places the emphasis on agriculture and small-scale, low productivity manufacturing, whilst KwaZulu planners emphasize the need to create an export base and rely on large scale agriculture and modern manufacturing to achieve this. Table 9.14 contains the relevant data.

Table 9.14

PROJECTED PRODUCTIVITY LEVELS FOR TRANSKEI AND KWAZULU IN THE YEARS 2000 AND 1990 RESPECTIVELY

	Estimated Average Output Per Man (1975 Rands)	
Sector	Transkei 2000	KwaZulu 1990
Agriculture	299	171
Mining	1 250	2 750
Manufacturing	1 000	3 440
Construction	1 000	4 500
Government	1 000	1 862
Average for Economy	640	817
Gap between average and highest	610	3 683
Gap between average and lowest	341	646

SOURCE: *Towards a Development Plan for KwaZulu.* Thorrington-Smith, Rosenberg and McCrystal. KwaZulu Government 1978. *A Development Strategy for Transkei,* Transkei Government White Paper 1979.

In terms of the two development strategies if the projections made by the planners are realized, it seems on the basis of the data in Table 9.14 that firstly, average per capita output levels will be higher in KwaZulu than they will be in Transkei at the end of the planning period, and secondly, in view of the significant differences in the average productivities of the highest and lowest productivity sectors in KwaZulu that the distribution of income projected will be considerably more unequal in KwaZulu than in Transkei.

Development planning is a very difficult process and in the case of the Black States it is made even more so by the absence of an adequate data base. Consequently, the probability of either of the tentative projections being realized, is in fact low. Nevertheless the exercise we have just been through, serves to illustrate the importance of obtaining a reasonable solution to the famous planning dilemma, namely whether to plan for the generation of economic growth or to plan for development.

The strategy put forward for KwaZulu goes for growth and may well have the side effect of increasing poverty levels. The strategy proposed for Transkei seems likely to raise the standards of living of the poorest segments of the community significantly. However, if adequate government measures are not taken to ensure a reasonable level of domestic capital accumulation, the Transkeian strategy may founder on the rocks of economic growth. Widespread income growth from low levels tends to generate consumption rather than saving and this tendency is exacerbated if the increased income is spent on imported goods.

An Alternative Strategy

One thing is certain; the ultimate upgrading of the regions of South Africa that presently constitute the Black States, will require a massive transfer of resources from the developed areas into these less favoured regions. One of the major reasons for the rejection of the policy of separate development by the international community is the fact that no real effort has yet been made by the central government to provide 'the separate but equal facilities' that are the cornerstone of the policy. The policy has instead to date been limited to the implementation of racial separation, giving credence to the alternate view advanced; namely, that it is politically impossible to create separate but equal facilities.

The analysis of the conditions within the Black States and the identification of the constraints on their development that have been undertaken in this chapter, have been done within the present government policy of the separate development of the African homelands, on the basis of the land allocation established by the Bantu Land Act of 1913 and the Bantu Trust and Land Act of 1936, and within the limits imposed by the constraints on Black population movements in South Africa. An alternative solution could be sought through the removal of the present framework itself and the establishment in its place of a political system that is acceptable to all South Africans.

The acceptance of a common society, whether it be within a federal system, a confederal system or a system based on one man one vote in a single political unit, would remove the political need to establish viable Black nation states; and the problems that are presently posed to such states by the dependency relationship between the centre economy and the peripheral Black States would become largely irrelevant.

The problems of poverty and regional underdevelopment would, however, remain. The solutions to these problems are also subject to the presupposed framework. A change in government policy concerning African population movements would do a great deal to alleviate poverty as it would allow people to leave the poorer areas altogether. Similarly, the removal of the group area reservations on land holdings, or the redrawing of the boundaries of the Black States to incorporate significant increases in the land area, would also substantially alter the situation.

At present there are two factors that make it virtually impossible to draw any firm conclusions regarding the short-term prospects for development within the Black States. Firstly, towards the end of 1980, largely as a result of a pessimistic assessment by the parastatal institution BENSO, of the prospects for the creation of economically viable, independent Black States, the government repudiated its previous policy in favour of one that was based upon regional development. Little detail has been given to date, but the new emphasis does appear to rest upon the creation of regional development, on the basis of dispersed 'growth nodes'. It is hoped by these means to raise the living standards of all the race groups within the various regions and it appears that the regions will be built up from both the modern economy and the less developed areas, including the Black States.

Secondly, a commission of enquiry into the consolidation of the Black States, the Van der Walt Commission, completed its work and handed its report to the State President towards the end of 1980. Up to now (December 1980) the report has not been tabled in Parliament, nor have its contents been revealed. It is, however, likely that this report too contains a number of wide ranging recommendations, which, if accepted and implemented by government, may affect the development prospects of the Black States and the living conditions of the people within them quite significantly.

TEN

The Role of the State

INTRODUCTION

It must by now be very obvious to the reader that economic conditions react to the social and legal environment in which they exist, as well as to the outcomes of past decisions that have been made in the economic field itself. Satisfactory economic progress will only take place if the existing social, legal and economic infrastructures are favourable to it. The government (or the State) can play a crucial role in determining the nature and rate of economic growth, through its ability to influence and mould these underlying aspects of economic development.

The dynamic, driving the operation of a private enterprise economy, is the ability of an individual to accumulate wealth in his personal capacity. This dynamic depends on the legal structure which, if it is to be functional to economic progress, must encourage wealth accumulation, through such things as the provision of an adequate and easily enforceable law of contract and some means of identifying, transferring and enforcing ownership rights. There is also no doubt that the creation of the legal entity 'a company', as a legal persona with limited liability rights for its owners, has been a force in the economic growth of modern capitalist market economies, and this again requires the co-operation and backing of the State.

The social environment also influences economic progress. Whilst the best known example is the relationship between the spread of the 'protestant ethic' and the growth of the western industrial economies, the opposite, negative relationship between the social institutions and economic development has also occurred. Many developing countries of today are severely hampered on the economic front by the fact that their social environment fails to value highly enough the amassing of personal wealth, or, alternatively, bases access to social power on such things as age, family relationships and service to society, rather than upon an individual's economic abilities. The State can often play a major role in generating social attitudes, as in most countries the government controls education and the national broadcasting network, both of which are powerful weapons in this field.

Private enterprise thrives in a socio-political climate that offers prospects for economic expansion and government policy can go a long way towards creating such an environment. The key invisible elements in this process are social stability and business optimism, but there are also certain minimum levels of physical development that have to be provided before privately-owned business can flourish. An adequate transport system is one such essential prere-quisite, as is the availability of a reliable source of power, a communication system and a minimum level of social services, including such things as the provision of health care and education facilities. In this area too, due largely to the nature of the infrastructure, the State usually plays the major role.

In addition, economic growth is more easily maintained in an economy that has a well developed financial infrastructure. Al-though growth itself is ultimately measured in terms of an increase in the flow of goods and services, the existence of a well developed financial structure 'oils the wheels' of the economy and greatly facilitates the generation of the needed increases in output. An adequate financial infrastructure makes it easier for businesses to obtain the funds that they need for expansion, and provides a simple link between the people in the economy who are saving and those needing the investment funds. Further, a well developed monetary system provides the State with a significant increase of the weaponry in its armoury for use in the fight against economic instability, which, in its turn, also helps to create the stable economic environment conducive to progress.

Finally, there is a strong relationship between the development of the political system and the growth of the economy. This relationship is extremely complex, as these systems interact both positively and negatively with one another. At the simple level in South Africa, the relationship is reasonably straightforward, as social and political unrest appears to be negatively related to economic progress, in the short term at least, as is shown by the sharp economic downturns which followed on from the social upheavals which took place in 1960 and 1976.

Economic development is a process of change and one of the most important economic roles of the government is to stage-manage this change. It is essential that law and order prevail, but they will do so only if the rising aspirations of the groups who are improving their position as a result of the change, are met. If instead these aspirations are frustrated, the continued maintenance of law and order will probably require the introduction of increasingly repressive control measures and it is highly likely that progress will be interrupted by outbursts of social unrest, which will have a depressing effect on further economic progress. Once again, it is the government which bears the responsibility for overseeing the introduction of the necessary social and political reforms which will meet the aspirations of the groups who are gaining economic power. (Nattrass: 1978b)

Another aspect of economic growth is that it takes place in an uneven manner with respect to people, time and space. This unevenness also opens up a role for government. Wealth accumulates in cycles; it accrues to particular people or institutions and in certain geographic regions. The development process, largely as a result of its uneven character, both creates and destroys economic opportunities, and since, broadly speaking, poverty is connected with the lack of economic opportunity, economic development is a force that tends both to create and alleviate poverty. People that are well placed to be able to benefit from the impact of economic development are those capable of adapting to changing life patterns, particularly the young and the better educated. The older members of the community, and the people who are already relatively deprived in terms of their control over economic resources, are less likely to benefit. These people will probably lose ground in relative terms and in some instances may become poorer in an absolute sense. One of the roles of the government is to minimize the degree of such deprivation that accompanies economic growth.

In some instances, there may be a direct political dimension to economic inequality. It is possible for the political system to be harnessed to the cause of defending the interests of particular groups, and consequently it may be used either to generate, or to alleviate poverty. For example, in areas in which urban interests are politically powerful and urban living standards are threatened by a continuous influx of people from the poorer rural areas, it may be possible for these interests to force through legislation limiting the population inflow. Such legislation would, by limiting access to the areas of greater economic opportunity, effectively condemn the would-be immigrants to a life of continuing poverty. Similarly, strong rural political influences often lie behind the successful implementation of rural development schemes. Under such conditions, the State may find that far from ameliorating the effects of economic growth, it is itself acting as the instrument that is intensifying inequality.

In most modern societies it is generally accepted that the State has a positive and direct role to play in the field of income distribution. This role is generally referred to as the distributive function of government. The precise nature of this role varies between communities and reflects the combined influences of the existing level of wealth in the society, the nature of the dominant social ideology and the strength of the State commitment to that ideology. As a result, even amongst market economies, one finds government policies for redistribution that range from those that are limited to the payment of poor relief and the provision of basic services financed from a mildly progressive taxation system, to policies that are strongly redistributive and which include direct affirmative action programmes to redress existing imbalances between groups or regions within the society.

The Economic Role of the State

Although the economic role of government is clearly interlinked with the legal and political roles, which are also its responsibility, it is conventional for economists to divorce these issues and to discuss the economic aspects separately. The economic responsibilities of the government of a society, whose economic relationships are organized on the basis of private enterprise, all relate to the inability of the market system to handle specific areas adequately. The economic responsibilities of the State in such a society are usually summarized into three groups: those relating to the need to ensure an efficient allocation of resources, those relating to the need to stabilize the path of economic progress, and those relating to the distribution of income and wealth.

The allocative economic function of the State involves the

government in action in a number of separate, but related, fields. The first is in the production of what are called by economists 'public goods'. These are goods and services whose costs of production are not related in any economically meaningful way to the stream of benefits that flows from their production. As a result of this lack of a link between costs and benefits, it is impossible for the market mechanism to price the output of these goods satisfactorily. In the absence of price signals the private enterprise system cannot respond adequately. The creation of a public park is a favourite example of such a commodity, as the benefits to the community in whose neighbourhood the park is situated, are related to the number of people who are able to make use of the facility and to its environmental impact, rather than to the costs incurred in its construction.

The second role for the State in the allocative field relates to its duty to encourage or control the production of goods and services which are not public goods, but are, nevertheless, products whose market price, for some other reason, does not truly reflect their social value. These are usually products which have a wider impact on the community than is reflected by the flows of information within the market system. Education, health care, sanitation and refuse removal are all examples of products which are under-valued by the market, because of the external benefits that they provide to the community as a whole. On the other hand, products that are produced at the cost of pollution are usually over-valued by the market in terms of their net social benefits.

The third State role in this area relates to its obligation to provide for the production of goods and services which, although they are needed by the community, require an initial level of resource input that is beyond the current capability of private sector business. The role of the State as a supplier of power and communications networks is usually justified on these grounds.

The economic role of the State in the area of stabilization is more directly related to its political and social objectives than are the allocative roles. Fluctuations in the level of economic activity are a concomitant of the private enterprise system. Unfortunately the cost of such fluctuations is significant and is not borne equally by all members of the community. Those who become unemployed in a recession clearly carry a greater economic and social burden than those who do not. If it is considered socially undesirable or politically inexpedient that some groups should suffer more than others, then it is the State that is charged with the responsiblity for redressing the situation. In addition, severe economic fluctuations make forward planning difficult, and tend, as a result, to affect economic progress adversely in the community in which they take place. Here, too, if one of the major communal goals is the maintenance of economic growth, the State will be charged with the responsibility of minimizing such fluctuations.

The final area of State economic responsibility is in the field of income distribution. Here again, the nature and intensity of the role that will be played by government will be related to its social and political objectives to a greater extent than to its economic aims. It is certainly no accident that poverty relief programmes are notable for their absence amongst the politically powerless communities in societies other than those which strongly espouse human rights and a fair measure of egalitarianism.

The government can attempt to achieve its overall economic objectives through action in a number of related spheres. Firstly, it can use the political system to obtain direct control over certain areas of the economic system that it considers to be crucial. Secondly, it can influence the economic system indirectly through its fiscal and monetary policies, and finally it can exert a direct influence through the impact of its own economic activities undertaken in the pursuance of its goals. The exact nature and interrelationship of these influences will reflect the structure of the particular economy into which they are introduced, the nature of the State's economic objectives and its overall ideology, and consequently will be peculiar to the economy itself. In the remainder of this chapter we will examine the nature of the economic role that has been played by the South African government and attempt to assess the impact that this has on the standards of living of South Africans.

THE STATE AND THE SOUTH AFRICAN ECONOMY

Although the government has played an active role in the development of the South African economy since the early days of the growth of the mining industry, the passage of time has seen a significant alteration in the nature of this role. In the early days of the emergence of the modern South African economy, the major role played by the government was in the creation of the necessary underlying network of physical infrastructure for the infant economy. Apart from the role it played in the labour market in assisting the mines in establishing an adequate supply of low cost labour, the State interfered very little in the workings of the market mechanism. Prior to 1924, the dominant economic ideology was that of economic liberalism and the emphasis was on the need to minimize government interference, in order to allow both national and international economic forces to influence the economy through the market mechanism.

As we saw earlier in Chapter Four the transference of political power to the PACT Alliance in 1924, produced a dramatic change in government attitudes towards the economy, and in the way in which the State perceived its own economic role. This government was the result of an alliance between White labour interests, those of the infant Afrikaner business sector and the White rural areas. Quite naturally, in view of its constituent members, this ruling party placed strong emphasis on the need for the South African economy to develop in its own right and on a broader basis than that of the mining industry alone. It also placed a high value on South African economic independence and sought to build up the country to a point where it would emerge as something more than a peripheral area in the British Commonwealth.

The ideology brought in by the PACT government was destined to live on long after the alliance itself and the 56 years from 1924–80 saw a continuous growth in the extent of the economic activity undertaken by the South African State. Not only did the size of the public sector's economic contribution expand significantly, but this period also saw the introduction of a network of legal and economic measures that were designed to encourage industrialization, to ensure economic stability as far as was possible and to upgrade conditions in the White farming sector. The outcome was, however, not only the development of a modern industrial State but also the entrenchment of the preferential position of White South Africans and the creation of the policy of racial separation known as 'apartheid', or separate development.

1978 appears to have heralded the commencement of a movement away from continued State economic interference, and government spokesmen started to emphasize the need for and advantages of a move towards the establishment of a 'free market' in South Africa. Up to the end of 1980, however, the exact nature of the proposed reforms remained somewhat tenuous and the concept was largely limited to the field of rhetoric, rather than being revealed in determined action.

The Growth in the Size of the Public Sector

A significant proportion of the total economic activity in South Africa rests directly in government hands. Throughout the period after 1946, the public sector's contribution to Gross Domestic Product averaged between 28 and 29 per cent of the total. Estimates of the national fixed capital suggest that the State's overall direct economic control may be even greater, as the public sector's share of this capital rose from 49 per cent to 58 per cent of the total during this time.

The relative economic size of the public sector is not so surprising when one remembers that, in South Africa, the government is responsible for the maintenance of law and order, national defence, education at all levels, the major proportion of health care, the payment of social pensions, the postal and telecommunications network, the road networks, the railways, the harbours, the airways and for the generation of power. In addition, the South African State is heavily involved in the industrial sector through the large public corporations and it produces iron and steel, chemicals, fertilizers, oil from coal and enriched uranium through this medium. Table 10.1 contains data relating to government expenditure over the period 1946–79.

The period covered in the table shows a rising trend in the importance of the State's share in economic activity. Of even greater interest, however, is the way in which the structure of the government spending has changed over this time period. Government investment activity rose steadily to reach 11,5 per cent of the gross domestic product by 1975; government investment also increased as a percentage of total investment over this period and, together with investment by the public corporations, on average accounted for a massive 53 per cent in the years 1978 and 1979.

The other interesting aspect of the changing structure of govern-

Table 10.1

THE GROWTH IN PUBLIC EXPENDITURE, 1946–79

	Years					
	1946	1950	1960	1970	1975	1979
Current Government Expenditure (R Millions)	268	328	655	1 993	3 782	6 204
Percentage of Gross Domestic Product	*16,4*	*12,9*	*13,2*	*16,8*	*15,3*	*13,9*
Government Investment Expenditure (R Millions)	97	138	350	1 067	2 713	3 285
Percentage of Gross Domestic Product	*5,9*	*5,4*	*7,0*	*9,0*	*11,0*	*7,4*
Total Public Sector Spending (R Millions)	365	466	1 005	3 060	6 495	9 489
Percentage of Gross Domestic Product	*22,3*	*18,3*	*20,2*	*25,8*	*26,3*	*21,3*
Public Corporations (R Millions)	20	38	159	433	1 081	3 038
Percentage of Gross Domestic Product	*1,2*	*1,5*	*3,2*	*3,7*	*4,4*	*6,8*
Total State Economic Activity (R Millions)	385	504	1 164	3 493	7 576	12 527
Percentage of Gross Domestic Product	*23,5*	*19,8*	*23,4*	*29,5*	*30,7*	*28,1*

SOURCE: South African Reserve Bank *Quarterly Bulletins* for selected years.

ment spending is the increasingly important role that is being played by the public corporations. It is largely through this medium that the South African State provides the products that it believes are of strategic economic or political importance, and the massive increase in State expenditure in this area largely reflects an increasing State commitment to self-sufficiency in the fields of fuel and power and the production of military hardware. Whilst the recent government statements on the need for less State economic participation in the economy should be reflected in future reductions in the relative importance of government current and investment expenditures, the change in economic ideology is probably unlikely to be reflected in the behaviour of government spending through the public corporations, unless a decision is taken to sell off part of the State's capital holdings in certain of these corporations, such as ISCOR, in much the same manner as the recent offer of some SASOL shares to the public. The overall economic importance of these activities, however, seems likely to continue to grow, particularly in the fields of the provision of power and fuel, as these will reflect not only the continued growth of the economy, but also the upgrading of services in the African urban areas and the rising living standards of black South Africans from all groups.

Ideally, if one wanted to look at the changing contribution that the State is making to economic activity as a whole, one would like to have data relating to the output levels of the public and private sectors in the different spheres of the economy. Unfortunately such data are not available for South Africa and one has to use investment shares as a surrogate. Table 10.2 shows data relating to the public sector's share of total investment by sector and (in parentheses) the share that this investment forms of total public sector capital for the period 1946–72.

Table 10.2

PUBLIC SECTOR SHARE OF FIXED CAPITAL BY SECTOR, 1946–72

Sector	Percentage of Total				
	1946	1950	1960	1970	1972
Manufacturing	8 (1)	16 (3)	20 (3)	23 (4)	25 (5)
Electricity, Gas and water	100 (11)	100 (12)	100 (14)	98 (13)	96 (12)
Transport, Storage & Communication	99 (49)	99 (46)	98 (44)	97 (36)	97 (34)
Finance, Assurance, Real Estate & Business Service	8 (3)	10 (5)	9 (4)	12 (5)	12 (5)
Community, Social & Personal Service	95 (36)	93 (34)	93 (35)	95 (42)	95 (44)
Other	1	1	1	1	1

SOURCE: South African Reserve Bank *Quarterly Bulletins,* June 1973 and December 1974.

One can see from the data in Table 10.2 how the public sector has moved increasingly into the industrial sector over this period. With the massive expansions of SASOL, ESCOM, ISCOR and

ARMSCOR, that have taken place since 1972, this trend is likely to have intensified up to 1980. One gets quite a sobering indication of the potential power of the State from the data in Table 10.2. In 1972, although the public sector owned one quarter of South Africa's manufacturing capital, in terms of the State's total capital holdings, this only consisted of 5 per cent.

The predominance of the government in the electricity, gas and water, and transport and storage sectors reflects the continued commitment of successive South African governments to their role as the major source of infrastructural investment. The State's predominance in the service sector reflects a similar role as provider of the social infrastructure. In the latter instance, it is interesting to note the growing relative importance of investment expenditure on social overhead capital in terms of total State investment. In 1946 social capital made up 36 per cent of total public sector capital, but by 1972 this proportion had increased to 44 per cent and the total investment of the State in this sector grew at an annual average rate of 6,8 per cent over the period. With the recent emphasis on the need to upgrade Black education and on the development of the Black States, this trend is also likely to have been maintained through to 1980.

Public sector expenditure in South Africa takes place on four levels; through the central adminstration itself, through the public corporations and other parastatal institutions, through the provincial administrations and 'Black States', and through the local authorities. In general, the public corporations are the medium through which the South African State undertakes its direct contribution to the production of goods, whilst the other three levels of government activity largely handle the services that are provided.

Local authorities represent the lowest tier of government and are responsible for local administration, traffic control, community health, sanitation, roads and the reticulation of power, light and water within their own communities. They are largely financially self-sufficient through property taxes. The next level up is occupied by the provincial authorities and the governments of the self-governing Black States. The provincial administrations are responsible for the maintenance of roads within the province, the provision of education for White children up to the end of secondary school (excluding those who attend technical high schools which are administered by the central government) and for the provision of subsidized health care. Provincial administrations are financed on the basis of a grant from the general tax collected by the central government.

The central government itself is directly responsible for the maintenance of law and order, justice, defence, tertiary education, for the education of Coloured and Indian children and of Black children living outside the 'Black States', for foreign affairs, for the establishment and overall development of the Black States and the Indian and Coloured Communities, and for the collection and adminstration of taxes.

The responsibilities of the governments of the Black States fall somewhere between those of the provincial administrations and those of the central government, any one State's precise position being dependent upon its current level of 'political evolution'. The three States that the South African government regards as being fully independent, Transkei, Bophuthatswana and Venda are fully responsible for the administration of all their affairs, but at the same time their freedom of action is somewhat curtailed by the fact that the major proportion of their funds is provided from the budget of the South African Central Government. The self-governing Black States have control over the administration of most of their affairs, excluding foreign affairs and defence, but here again their freedom of action is circumscribed by the extent of their financial dependence upon Pretoria.

The Allocation of Government Current Expenditure

As a result of the different levels of government administration, it is extremely difficult to trace through the accounts of the various branches of government in South Africa to obtain any reasonable idea of the final allocation of the funds spent through the State. McGrath has made one such estimate for government current expenditure for certain selected years and his results are given in Table 10.3.

In a developing country like South Africa, which has a number of regions (housing over one-third of the total population) which are deprived in terms of access to State social services, one would expect that expenditure on items such as health care, education and other

State social services would grow faster than total public expenditure, as efforts are made to extend these services into the deprived areas. Unfortunately one finds, when one looks at the changing structure of government expenditure in South Africa, given in Table 10.3, that this has not been the case, at least over the period covered by the data in the table. Expenditure on education did manage to keep pace with total State expenditure, but expenditure on health care and other services grew very much more slowly than total expenditure and declined in relative importance. Government spending on justice, police, prisons and defence, on the other hand, grew very much faster than the average and increased in relative importance from 11 per cent of the total in 1949/50 to 25 per cent in the years 1975/76.

Table 10.3

THE COMPARISON OF GOVERNMENT CURRENT EXPENDITURES FOR SELECTED YEARS

Category of Expenditure	Fiscal Year			
	1949/ 1950	1959/ 1960	1969/ 1970	1975/ 1976
Justice, police, prisons & defence	11	12	21	25
Education (all races)	18	19	19	19
Health and hospitals	13	13	8	7
Agricultural services & subsidies	6	7	7	6
Income generating services	12	11	12	16
Other services	23	18	19	14
Transfer payments	8	10	7	7
Other	9	10	7	6

SOURCE: McGrath 1979b.

Table 10.4 shows the changes that have taken place in the size and relative importance of selected individual departmental votes over the period 1960–1979 and confirms some of the findings illustrated in Table 10.3.

One might be tempted to comment that the data in Table 10.4 show little other than the rising costs of maintaining the system of 'apartheid'. This would, however, not be entirely true, although it clearly has some validity. The increases in the votes to the Departments of Co-operation and Development, Coloured Affairs and

Indian Affairs in particular contain finance for measures other than the administration of separate development. They also include amounts designed to upgrade the living standards of the non-White sections of the South African population. For example, it is through the Co-operation and Development vote that Black pensions are paid and funds are allocated to the various Development Corporations operating within the 'Black States'. A large proportion of this expenditure would still be required regardless of the political system in operation, simply in an attempt to upgrade what have now become very poor areas of the country. In the fiscal year 1977/78 only roughly 4 per cent of this vote was spent directly upon population movement control and the allocation of labour, i.e. directly upon the maintenance of 'apartheid'. There is, however, little doubt that the same could not be said regarding a substantial proportion of the country's massive defence budget.

Table 10.4

THE CHANGING RELATIVE IMPORTANCE OF SELECTED VOTES IN THE CENTRAL GOVERNMENT BUDGET

Vote	Percentage of Total Budget			Average Annual growth rate %		
	1960	1970	1979	1960/ 1970	1970/ 1979	1960/ 1979
Defence	6	15	15	21	22	21,5
Law & Order	8	8	4	10	12	10,9
Black Education	3	2	3	7	25	15,0
Co-operation & Development	3	3	8	13	31	21,0
Indian Affairs	—	1	1	—	19	—
Coloured Affairs	—	4	3	—	18	—
National Education	4	3	3	10	22	15,5
Agriculture	8	7	3	9	11	9,7
Social Welfare	12	8	4	7	14	10,2
Total	44	51	44	11	21,9	16,0

SOURCE: South African Statistics, 1964, 1974 and R.P. 85/1979.

Financing Government Activities

Modern day governments finance their activities mainly through two sources – taxation and borrowing. Although one might argue that since loans have to be repaid, the major source of long-term revenue is taxation – this is at present not the case. State loans are often repaid through refinancing and the long-term tendency is for the government's debt (the public debt) to rise, thus being a source of finance in its own right. Both taxation and State loan financing involve a transfer of resources from the private sector to the public sector. The major difference between the two sources is that taxation payments are usually mandatory and earn no revenue for the person paying them, whereas with the loan capital an element of choice is present and the State normally pays some reward for the sacrifice, in the form of interest.

Table 10.5 shows the amounts and relative importance of these sources of funds to the South African government over the period 1950–79.

Table 10.5
SOURCES OF GOVERNMENT FINANCE, 1950–79

Period	Taxation		Other		Increased Debt	
	Amount (R m)	% of Total	Amount (R m)	% of Total	Amount (R m)	% of Total
1950–59	5 967	79	694	9	938	12
1960–69	13 199	72	2 251	12	2 942	16
1970–79	52 316	74	3 863	5	15 000	21

SOURCE: *Quarterly Bulletin of the Reserve Bank,* various issues.

One can see clearly from the table the dominant role that has been played by taxation in government financing throughout the period. In general, it has been the policy of the South African government to finance only capital expenditure items from loan sources and, indeed, not even those are fully financed in this manner, as the surplus on the government current account was applied to the funding of State investment projects throughout this period. It is, however, interesting to note that despite this relatively conservative financial policy, the national debt still increased at an annual average rate of 11 per cent from 1960–79 and debt financing grew in importance as a source of funds for the State over the 30 year period covered in the table.

Both of the major methods used by the government to raise funds to finance its planned activities can affect the economic environment to a far greater degree than the mere size of the funds would suggest. The nature and direction of this impact does, however, depend on the manner in which the government implements its financial policies, i.e., it will depend on the structure of the taxation system and the sources from which the government raises its loan capital.

Taxation Policies

Most governments, when forming their taxation policies, aim not only to raise the requisite quantity of funds in the most efficient (cheapest) manner, but also seek to use the fiscal system as a means of achieving some of their other social and economic goals, such as a degree of income redistribution, the stimulation of economic activity, the development of backward areas or groups of people and even, in some instances, the control of inflation.

Most tax systems comprise a mixture of direct and indirect taxes. Direct taxation, as its name implies, is levied directly upon the income of the individual or firm and the rate of tax is often also related to the level of the income being taxed. Indirect taxation, on the other hand, is not levied directly on income nor is the amount that one pays necessarily linked to one's overall position in the income hierachy. This taxation is usually levied on products or activities rather than people.

Most taxation systems are designed to be 'progressive' in nature, that is, they are designed so that the tax rate on the richer members of the community is higher than that on people with lower incomes. There are two reasons why a degree of progression is usually built into a taxation structure. The first is related to the basic assumption used in consumer theory, namely that of diminishing marginal utility. This axiom states that the more you have of anything, including income, the less likely you are to want still more of it. On this basis the 'cost' of losing a rand in taxation to a rich man is less than it is to a poor man and this being so, if the government aims to raise its taxation revenue in the least costly manner, or to attempt to equalize the sacrifice made by each person when paying tax, it follows that the rich should bear a larger tax burden than the poor.

The second reason for building in a degree of progression is related to the fact that most modern governments accept, as one of their social responsibilities, the need to reduce the size of the income gap between the rich and poor strata of society. A progressive taxation system, coupled with social relief schemes, is one of the means by which the government can seek to achieve some measure of income redistribution within the community.

A hidden advantage to the government of a progressive income tax system is that in times of inflation, government receipts increase almost automatically. As people's money incomes rise to keep pace with the rising prices, so they enter income ranges with higher taxation rates and pay a large proportion of their income in taxation. If the tax structure is steeply progressive this process can prove to be troublesome, as government revenues may rise faster than is necessary to compensate for the increased cost of government services. Concomitantly, the burden of taxation on individuals becomes too great.

Historically, direct taxation, with its two major subcomponents, a progressive income tax and a proportionate tax on company profits, was, and indeed still is, the major source of tax revenue for the South African government. This meant that the tax base of the country was relatively narrow, as the major proportion of all tax receipts came from a small number of wealthy taxpayers. Over the past decade, following on from the recommendations of the Franzen Commission, a serious attempt has been made by government to broaden the tax base; firstly by the introduction in 1969 of a selective sales duty and then by its replacement with a general sales tax of 4 per cent, which was levied for the first time in 1978. Table 10.6 shows the distribution of tax revenue in terms of whether or not it was directly levied on income for selected years between 1950 and 1978.

Table 10.6

THE PROPORTION OF TAXATION THAT IS DIRECTLY LEVIED ON INCOME

	1950	1960	1970	1978
Direct Taxation	58	54	57	57
Indirect Taxation	42	46	43	43

SOURCE: Browne in Lombard, Table 7 for 1950–1970. R.P. 85/1979 for 1978.

As the General Sales Tax was only levied for part of 1978 and, indeed, replaced the sales duty previously levied, its introduction made no noticeable impact on the structure of taxation revenue in 1978.

There is a significant difference between a set of selective sales duties and a general sales tax. The former is seldom applied to essential commodities, such as basic foodstuffs, whereas the latter is applied across the board and is levied on all products sold to final consumers. This means that the impact of the new General Sales Tax is likely to be more regressive than that of selective sales duties, as a higher proportion of it will be paid by low income earners. However, notwithstanding the recent increased emphasis on indirect taxation, direct taxes seem virtually certain to remain the major contributor to the State's coffers for the foreseeable future.

The basis on which taxes are assessed can also be used by government as a tool in the implementation of their overall policies and there are a number of examples of this type of fiscal policy in South Africa; for example, the additional deductions from taxable income for new plant and machinery installed during the year acts as an incentive to businessmen to invest further. Similarly, the deductions allowed for expenditure incurred on training encourage entrepeneurs to institute training schemes for their labour force. Finally, the taxation allowances that are related to industries that are sited in 'border areas' and 'Black States' are designed to encourage the decentralization of economic activity to the less developed regions of South Africa.

Although taxation can be a useful long-term policy instrument, its short-term usefulness is somewhat limited. The taxation rates are set when parliament passes the annual budget and although the Minister of Finance now has the right to vary the tax rates between budgets to a limited extent, this does not in practice introduce a great deal more flexibility into the system. This is because of the manner in which the tax is collected and the length of time that it takes to re-adjust the taxation rates. Most South Africans pay their taxes through deductions made from their earnings at source on a 'pay as you earn' basis, but individuals who earn substantial income from investments are 'provisional tax payers', and are required to pay their tax quarterly. Companies, partnerships and sole proprietors pay their tax annually and it is levied on the results of the year's trading activities.

One of the present anomalies of the South African tax system is the fact that the rates of tax and the taxation structures that are applied to White, Asian and Coloured taxpayers differ from those applied to Black South Africans. This difference adversely affects the Black group, who are the group least able to face up to any additional hardship. The government did improve the situation in the 1980 budget and has pledged to remove the differences as soon as is practically possible.

Loan Financing

As was shown by the data in Table 10.5, loan financing has been an important source of revenue to the South African government. Loan finance has been used to fund large scale public sector investment projects, as well as the expansion of the public corporations. The South African government raises loans from both foreign and local sources, and particularly with regard to the funds raised locally the manner in which the loan is raised can have quite a substantial effect on the level of economic activity. At the end of March, 1979, of the R16 154 million debt owed by the South African government, 97 per cent had been raised within South Africa. 37 per cent of the locally raised debt was held by the Public Debt Commissioners, who are responsible for the investment of government pension and provident funds, social security funds, the state sinking fund and the investable funds of the Railways and the Post Offices. 18 per cent was held by the banking sector and 10 per cent by individuals and companies in the form of loan levies whilst the balance was held by insurance companies, building societies, pension funds and individuals and comprised both short and long-term government paper.

The government can manipulate both the level and the composition of its debt finance and this ability is an important weapon in its armoury to control the overall level of economic activity. At the direct level, should the government wish to stimulate the economy by injecting purchasing power, one of the easiest ways in which it can achieve this is by the re-payment of loans, particularly loans such as the 'loan levy', which are predominantly held by individuals. On the other hand, an increase in the quantity of public debt held by individuals and non-banking institutions will act to reduce the money supply. Government stock held by the banking sector, however, poses more complex problems, since in some instances, it can form the basis for a further increase in the money supply through the medium of an increase in bank credit. This aspect will be picked up again later in this chapter.

Government Activity and the Racial Distribution of Income

In view of the significant racial overtones to the unequal distribution of income in South Africa, if government is to improve the overall allocation of income it will have to approach the problem on the basis of race, as any improvement will require a distribution of income (at the margin at the very least) from White South Africans to the other population groups. Since the State is a major employer in its own right, one of the ways this can be achieved is through its own employment practices, whilst further improvements can be sought through the application of various government policies.

Historically, the South African State is one of the few that can look back upon a series of policies that were successfully implemented, eliminating a serious poverty problem. The pressing social problem of the first quarter of the twentieth century in South Africa was growing White indigence – a problem that had been totally eliminated thirty years later, as a result of a determined, well co-ordinated government-orchestrated attack upon it. The problem of poverty amongst the White, mainly Afrikaner, community was eliminated by the introduction of preferential employment policies, particularly in the government service, by a substantial effort to upgrade the rural areas, by a number of measures designed to foster the growth of a local captalist class and by the activities of the Afrikaner community itself, in its attempt to preserve 'volkseenheid' and obtain both economic and political power through institutions such as the Broederbond.

Obviously the elimination of black poverty and racial inequality will not be as simply achieved. Firstly, the scale of the problem is many times larger and secondly, at present, political and economic power are both strongly concentrated in the hands of the Whites. Nevertheless, if the government is serious in its stated intentions to reduce black poverty and the degree of racial inequality, one would expect that one of the first places that this would be reflected would be in the policies of the State in general, and particularly in government employment practices. Table 10.7 contains data show-ing aspects of the central government's racial employment policies over the period 1960–77. It is apparent from the data that there has, indeed, been a very significant swing in government employment policies since 1970, away from the maintenance of White privilege, with respect to both the percentage of employment and the wage rate.

Table 10.7

CENTRAL GOVERNMENT RACIAL EMPLOYMENT POLICIES

	Year		
	1960	1970	1977
Total Employment	219 736	272 827	431 932
Percentage African	48	50	58
Asian	–	3	2
Coloured	5	11	12
White	47	36	28
Total Wage Bill (R 000)	210 056	450 884	1 190 221
Percentage African	18	16	31
Asian	–	3	4
Coloured	3	9	10
White	79	72	55
Average Real Wage (1970 Prices) (Rands)			
African	475	566	764
Asian	1 044	1 745	2 293
Coloured	709	1 349	1 230
White	2 093	3 268	2 767
Average Real Wage Gap (Rands)			
White : African	1 618	2 702	2 003
White : Asian	1 049	1 523	474
White : Coloured	1 384	1 919	1 537

SOURCE: *South African Statistics 1964 and 1978.*

In 1960 Whites filled 47 per cent of central government jobs and received a massive 79 per cent of the State's wage bill. By 1970 Black South Africans had made some inroads on the employment side; Asians and Coloureds filled 14 per cent of the jobs as compared with 5 per cent in 1960 and the African share had risen to 50 per cent. Whites, however, notwithstanding the fact that they then filled only 36 per cent of the jobs, still obtained 72 per cent of the wage bill.

Only seven years later a significant change had occurred, reflecting both the government's intention to close the wage gap and the growing development effort in the Black States. The White share of total employment had declined to 28 per cent and of the wage bill to

55 per cent. White average wages paid by government fell in real terms over this period from R3 268 in 1970 to R2 767 and the racial wage gap also narrowed.

When it comes to assessing the racial impact of overall government economic activity, the problem is more complicated. It is extremely difficult to isolate the people who ultimately benefit from government expenditure and to quantify the extent of such benefits. It is also difficult to establish exactly how the burden of taxation is borne throughout the community. Over the years a number of economists have tried to estimate the burdens and benefits of the State expenditure on a racial basis. The most recent and most thorough-going are the estimates made by McGrath. He only covers government current expenditure and makes estimates for three fiscal years, covering the period 1950–76. His estimates are made on three different bases and his middle estimates are given in Table 10.8 below.

Table 10.8

RACIAL INCOME REDISTRIBUTION THROUGH GOVERNMENT

	Percentage Change in Average Per Capita Income			
	1949/50	1959/60	1969/70	1975/76
Africans	11,9	9,5	9,5	10,6
Asians	2,8	7,8	13,2	3,4
Coloureds	9,7	15,2	13,3	19,2
Whites	–5,0	–5,1	–5,4	–6,9

SOURCE: McGrath 1979 (b), Table 15.

The data in Table 10.8 show that there is some racial redistribution of income on a per capita basis through the government, although the percentage is not high. The degree of redistribution has also risen slightly from 1970 to 1976.

However, in view of the present racial differences in average living standards and the low absolute income levels of the majority of the African group, it is clear that the State needs to make a much greater effort regarding the redistribution of income between the race groups in all the sectors of the economy over which it is able to exert some influence. This is particularly true in the area of government expenditure and the way in which this is financed. The recent attempts by the government to widen the tax base, through the introduction of a general sales tax, will act to reduce the rate of racial redistribution through government, unless the potentially regressive effects of these changes in taxation are offset by changes in the patterns of government expenditure in favour of the black groups.

Inflationary methods of financing State expenditure will also be regressive and act to negate government efforts to redistribute income between the race groups, unless they too are offset by deliberate switches in government spending in favour of the poorer groups in the community.

To some extent the very poor elements in South Africa, the rural African groups, are protected against these influences, since in so far as they operate in the non-monetized sector of the economy, these groups are able to avoid both the payment of indirect taxes and the immediate effects of domestic inflation. One cannot, however, place too great an emphasis on the protection that the subsistence economy gives to the rural poor, because, as we saw earlier, the capacity of this sector in terms of its ability to support its resident population has declined continuously in recent times.

Radical theorists of the State argue that its major role lies in the protection of the economic system that gave it birth. In the South African case that system was capitalism. South African capitalism is becoming increasingly threatened by the persistence of both racial inequality and absolute poverty on a wide scale. If the present economic system is to be maintained, these characteristics will have to be eliminated and the government will have to play a far more positive and determined role in the upgrading of both the backward regions of the economy and those communities whose present quality of life is far from adequate.

THE STATE AND THE FINANCIAL INFRASTRUCTURE

Simple economic systems can operate quite effectively on the principle of direct exchange or barter. However, as soon as any degree of complexity develops, the system will only continue to expand freely if it develops an acceptable method of indirect exchange. This has, as a prerequisite, the acceptance of money, a commodity that can be used as a common denominator in the valuation process, so too as a store of value, and a commodity that is acceptable to all who participate in the economic system.

Because of the nature of money, it is essential that its integrity in value terms is maintained. Like any other commodity, the relative price of money, in terms of other goods, is related to the quantity demanded and supplied at a particular point in time. This means that if the value of money is to remain reasonably constant, the conditions relating to its supply have to be carefully controlled in terms of the changing demand conditions, which are a feature of a growing economy. It is accepted that one of the functions of the government of a capitalist market economy is to manage the money supply in such a way as to ensure the integrity of the currency, both within and beyond the country's borders, as well as to foster continued economic progress.

In a modern sophisticated economy, although the currency unit is easy to identify, money comes in a number of different forms and the process of controlling the overall money supply is not simple. (McCarthy: 1977). Neither is it easy to set up and manage a monetary system that is conducive to economic growth. Here again, the more sophisticated the economy, the more sophisticated must the financial infrastructure be. The structure must be able to handle the changing flows of both short and long-term capital in the economy in a manner that will cause the least possible disruption to the economic system as a whole. The responsibility for ensuring adequate evolution of the financial infrastructure of a developing country is also usually accepted by the government.

The present South African financial system is essentially modelled on that of the United Kingdom. The system is controlled by a central bank, the South African Reserve Bank, which was established in 1920 and has a monopoly over the right to issue currency. The Reserve Bank is also the banker to the government itself, handles all South Africa's foreign exchange transactions, is responsible for marketing the country's gold output and is the vehicle through which the government attempts to control the financial sector of the economy.

The financial sector itself falls into two parts, one of which consists of the institutions handling long-term capital requirements, whilst the other comprises those that are concentrated mainly in the market for short-term funds. Inevitably there is some overlap between the two. The institutions involved in providing a smooth flow of medium to long-term capital are the Johannesburg Stock Exchange, the government through the Public Debt Commissioners, who are responsible for the investment of civil service pension funds and other government trust funds and who hold the major proportion of the public sector long-term paper, building societies specializing in private mortgage bonds, property companies, and some specialized banking institutions such as the State-owned Land Bank, which provides both long and short-term agricultural credit, and the hire purchase banks.

The short-term market comprises the commercial banks (who also do some de facto long-term financing), the National Finance Corporation, the Discount Houses and the Acceptance Banks. In general, in South Africa, this side of the financial sector is not as well developed as its counterpart handling long-term capital and the commercial banks are by far the most important institutions in the short-term market.

Commercial banking in South Africa dates back as far as 1792, the year that saw the foundation of the government-owned Lombard Bank in the Cape Colony. The first privately-owned bank was the Cape of Good Hope Bank, founded in 1837. This marked the start of an era of financial expansion and by 1862 there were 28 private banks operating. The 1860s also saw the foundation of the South African branches of two imperial banks and they, particularly the Standard Bank, set out to centralize banking to a greater degree. They were so successful in their efforts, notwithstanding opposition, that by the time of the formation of the Union of South Africa, only seven separate commercial banks remained.

In 1917 the Union Parliament passed legislation aimed at forcing some uniformity in banking practices and by this stage the number of commercial banks had dwindled still further to five:

The African Banking Corporation,
The National Bank of South Africa,
The Netherlands Bank of South Africa,
The Standard Bank of South Africa,
The Stellenbosch District Bank.

In 1920 legislation was enacted which established the South African Reserve Bank as the country's central bank and the core of the present financial structure was created.

The dominant position held by the two major foreign-owned banks resulted in a situation in which it was relatively commonplace for the liabilities of the banking sector to the South African public to exceed the assets held by them within South Africa. This lack of a covered local position caused some worry to the authorities and in 1942 comprehensive legislation was passed that was designed to improve their control over the activities of the commercial banking sector as a whole. The 1942 Act stipulated that commercial banks must fully cover their South African liabilities with locally held assets and introduced a requirement that such banks must maintain 'liquid assets' up to 30 per cent of their total South African liabilities, in addition to the legal cash reserve requirements. The effect of the legislation was a significant improvement in the supply of funds to finance local expansion.

The introduction of the liquid assets provision highlighted a significant shortcoming of the financial system as it then existed, namely, the lack of a short-term money market. In 1949 legislation was passed establishing the State-owned National Finance Corporation, which was an institution empowered to accept large deposits from the public, on call or short notice. This was the first step towards the creation of a money market and it was followed in the 1950s by the establishment of a specialized Discount House and an Acceptance Bank. In the following thirty-year period both the long and the short-term sides of the capital market continued to develop and De Kock was able to comment in 1978:

> South Africa has a remarkably sophisticated monetary and banking system for a country in its stage of economic development. This sophistication is potentially of great benefit to the country. (De Kock: 1978)

By the beginning of 1979 there were 50 registered banking institutions in South Africa, 11 commercial banks, 10 merchant banks, 3 discount houses, 18 general banks, 2 hire purchase banks and 6 savings banks. Table 10.9 shows the growth and changing structure of the assets of the banking sector over the period 1948–79.

As the financial infrastructure of the economy developed, so the

Table 10.9
THE CHANGING STRUCTURE OF SOUTH AFRICA'S BANKING SECTOR, 1948–79

Year	Total Value of Assets Held by (R Millions)						
	Monetary Banking Sector	Commercial Banks	South African Reserve Bank	National Finance Corporation	Discount Houses	Merchant Banks	Hire Purchase and General Banks
1948	1 020	815	381	130	74	76	
1960	1 814	1 298	473	215	363	347	1 792
1970	6 150	3 826	1 234	608	1 019	1 272	5 518
1979	24 226	13 368	5 617				
Annual Average Growth Rate 1960–1979	14,6	13,1	13,9	8,5	14,8	16,0	13,3*

*1970–1979

SOURCE: Various South African Reserve Bank *Quarterly Bulletins*.

nature of the money supply also changed, since a greater degree of availability of easily convertible short-term paper significantly enlarged the range of financial assets that could perform the functions of money or 'near money' (close substitutes for money). This, in its turn, enlarged the range of institutions over which the government had to try to exert an influence in its attempts to maintain the integrity or value of the South African currency.

The State and Monetary Policy

As Professor Lombard points out, monetary policy is only one aspect of total government policy and, as a result, over the long term it must be applied in a manner that will contribute to the achievement of the government's overall economic objectives. (Lombard: 1973). He goes on to argue that the maintenance of a stable currency value will, in the long run, be the policy most suitable for an economy interested in long-term growth and employment generation. Certainly in South Africa the authorities have always maintained a relatively conservative approach to the monetary aspects of the economy and, in general, they have given preference to monetary measures that were designed to foster price stability over those directly aimed at fostering economic growth. This has been largely because, until the increases in the gold price that took place in the 1970s, the profitability of the South African gold mining industry was particularly vulnerable to the ravages of rising costs of production resulting from internal price inflation.

Although one can argue that in general the South African monetary authorities have acted conservatively, this does not mean that they have not used an expansionary approach when it has been necessary to counter cyclical downturns in the level of domestic expansion. What it does mean, however, is that they have been fairly quick to shut down on expansionary phases that have shown any tendency towards overheating, and in their policy formation have placed a high relative value on the maintenance of domestic price stability.

Table 10.10 shows the movements that have taken place in the consumer price index and the yearly rates of inflation that these reflect for selected periods from 1935 to 1979. The data show that whilst the South African monetary authorities were reasonably successful in maintaining the domestic value of the currency right through to the end of the 1960s, they have been far less successful in their efforts over the past ten years. The annual rate of inflation in 1979 was nearly four times higher than that in 1970.

As we said earlier, the relative value (price) of money, like that of any other commodity, can only fall if the supply grows faster than the demand, i.e. faster than the supply of all other commodities in the economy. There are two elements in the supply of money; firstly, the actual quantity that is created by the financial institutions that are in a position to do so, and secondly, the rate at which the stock of money changes hands. It is fashionable today amongst many monetary economists to argue that the latter element, the velocity of circulation, is likely to remain fairly constant over time, and that consequently any reductions in the value of money are the result of an over supply of money itself.

Table 10.10

THE CHANGING VALUE OF THE RAND AND THE RATE OF INFLATION, 1935–79

Year	Consumer Price Index 1970 = 100	The Value of One 1970 Rand in Cents	The Average Annual Inflation Rate
1935	31,9	313	–
1945	44,9	223	3,5
1950	54,1	185	3,8
1960	76,4	131	3,5
1965	85,0	118	2,2
1970	100,0	100	3,3
1975	157,2	64	9,5
1979	247,8	40	12,1

SOURCE: *South African Statistics 1978* and Statistical News Releases.

What Comprises the Money Supply?

Prior to the development of the money market, the money supply in South Africa was defined by the authorities to consist of the quantity of notes and coins in circulation, and the total of the demand deposits with the commercial banking sector. However, as the market for short-term finance developed, so it became apparent that some other financial institutions were also in a position to offer credit to the public in excess of the amounts on deposit with them and so were able to affect the money supply. Consequently, the monetary authorities slowly amended their definition of the banking sector until, by 1965, it included the National Finance Corporation, the discount houses and the short-term activities of the Land Bank.

1965 brought into effect a new Banks Act, which sought to control the credit creating ability of the banking sector on a much wider front. The definition of an institution that was to be classified as a bank was significantly widened, and substantial changes were made to the definition as to what comprised the liquid assets, acceptable as part of the 'liquid assets reserve ratios', that banking institutions were required to maintain against their liabilities to the public. This, once again, changed the emphasis that the monetary authorities placed on the roles played by the various money market institutions in the creation of money, and led to a further widening of the class of financial assets considered as money. The definition of money, introduced in 1966, is still in current use by the authorities and defines money as

> being broadened to include, in addition to coin and bank notes outside the banking sector, all demand or call deposits held by the private sector (including the Railways and Harbours and Local Authorities) with institutions in the newly defined monetary banking sector, which includes the South African Reserve Bank, commercial banks, merchant banks, the National Finance Corporation, discount houses, the short-term business of the Land Bank and all other registered banking institutions with monthly deposit liabilities of R1 million or more. (De Kock: 1966)

Near money was also re-defined on a somewhat more arbitrary basis as

> all short-term deposits, other than demand deposits and all medium-term deposits (between 30 days' and 6 months' duration), including savings deposits held by the private sector with the re-defined monetary banking sector. (De Kock: 1966)

At the same time, the Reserve Bank also commenced the publication of ex post data showing the major sources of increases in the money supply. These are shown in Table 10.11 for selected years from 1965 to 1979. (Van Staden: 1966)

Table 10.11

CAUSES OF CHANGES IN THE SUPPLY OF MONEY AND NEAR MONEY IN SOUTH AFRICA, 1965–79 (R MILLIONS)

Year	Total Money and Near Money at End of Period	Change Over Period		Causes of Changes				
		Amount	Percentage	Net Foreign Exchange and Gold Holdings	Net Claims on Government	Claims on Private Sector	Long-Term Private Deposits	Other Net Assets
1965	2 470							
1966	2 623	153	6	115	66	104	− 172	40
1967	2 832	209	8	2	− 16	275	− 49	− 3
1968	3 421	589	21	471	− 204	280	12	30
1969	3 774	353	10	− 52	42	488	− 91	− 34
1970	3 983	209	5	− 282	157	362	− 6	− 22
1971	4 276	293	7	− 250	318	244	− 35	16
1972	4 863	587	14	464	85	448	− 375	− 35
1973	5 983	1 120	23	− 103	120	1 536	− 362	− 71
1974	7 317	1 334	22	− 206	405	1 102	− 119	152
1975	8 591	1 275	17	− 463	719	1 409	− 602	212
1976	9 368	777	9	− 912	896	556	6	231
1977	10 012	644	7	60	212	526	− 423	269
1978	11 277	1 265	13	489	− 253	1 367	− 825	487
1979	12 778	1 501	13	426	213	1 684	− 672	150

SOURCE: Various *Quarterly Bulletins of South African Reserve Bank.*

The data in Table 10.11 show that the total money supply, as defined by the Reserve Bank, increased substantially over the 15 year period and was actually five times greater in 1979 that it was in 1965. In the majority of years the most important source of the increases was the expansion of credit to the private sector, the exceptions being 1971 and 1976, years in which government deficit financing was the major cause. However, in view of the link between government, domestic, short-term loan financing and the ability of the commercial banks to create credit (which operates through the liquid assets reserve ratio), in the years in which there was not a ceiling imposed on bank credit to the private sector, the impact of government spending on the money supply was greater than is suggested by the data in the table.

The other interesting aspect of the data is the role that has been played by the foreign trade sector. In general, in the past, this sector either acted to decrease the supply of money within the country, or was relatively neutral. In only four of the fifteen years was the increase in gold and foreign exchange holdings a major contributor to increases in the money supply. However, there are signs that this situation is currently changing. The very high gold price that was maintained on international markets throughout 1980 resulted in a massive increase in both South Africa's foreign exchange and gold holdings and the domestic money supply, and caused the authorities some concern.

The Money Supply and Domestic Price Levels

There is a link between changes in the money supply and changes in the domestic price level, although the exact nature of the link is not clear. In general terms one can say that providing the money supply is being utilized more or less fully, in the sense that there are not significant quantities being held in idle balances that can be put back into circulation, the economy will not be able to expand with a stable price level unless the quantity of money in circulation also expands. If the money supply grows more slowly than average real output, prices in general will start to decline and alternatively if it grows more rapidly than output, prices will start to inflate.

It is this loose overall relationship that exists between the money supply and price level changes, coupled with a belief that economic progress is more easily achieved and maintained with stable price levels, that leads to the monetary authorities establishing policies through which they endeavour to control the money supply.

Table 10.12 contains data that show the relationship between the changes in the money supply, the price level and the level of economic activity in South Africa for the period from 1965 to 1979. The data show very clearly that there is, in fact, no *direct* causal relationship between changes in the money supply (as defined by the authorities) over and above the needs of an expanding economy, and changes in the general price level. This apparent divergence between economic theory and the real world creates problems for the monetary authorities and has its roots in a number of different causes.

Table 10.12

THE RELATIVE RATES OF CHANGE IN THE MONEY SUPPLY, GROSS DOMESTIC PRODUCT AND PRICES IN SOUTH AFRICA 1965–79

Year	Percentage Change in			Movements in Total Index 1970 = 100		
	Money Supply	Gross Domestic Product	Prices*	Money	Gross Domestic Product	Prices
1965–66	6	5	4	66	80	88
1966–67	8	8	3	71	86	91
1967–68	21	4	2	86	90	93
1968–69	10	7	2	95	95	95
1969–70	5	5	5	100	100	100
1970–71	7	4	6	107	104	106
1971–72	14	3	7	122	107	113
1972–73	23	4	10	150	111	124
1973–74	22	8	12	184	119	139
1974–75	17	2	13	216	121	157
1975–76	9	1	11	235	123	175
1976–77	7	1	11	251	124	194
1977–78	13		10	283		214
1978–79	13		16	321		248

*The Consumer Price Index has been used as an indicator.

SOURCE: Various *Quarterly Bulletins of the South African Reserve Bank* and *South African Statistics 1978.*

Firstly, there is a problem in correctly identifying the components of the money supply itself. As we saw earlier, the authorities' views on the constituents of the money supply have altered over time and will undoubtedly continue to do so, but even with this degree of flexibility there is no certainty that the current definition, whatever it may be, includes all the assets in the economy that are presently actually fulfilling the functions of money. It is possible that the de facto money supply may be very different in both quantity and constituent from that defined by the authorities. The recent growth in credit card purchasing power might be seen as an example of this type of divergence, as is the growth of the so-called 'Grey Market' for short-term funds operating in the corporate sector.

Secondly, the rate at which the money is used in the economy is actually not constant through time, as people and firms change their views on how great a proportion of their funds should be held in the form of assets, constituting the money supply. Individuals and businesses hold money for three reasons: to enable them to finance their day to day transactions, to ensure that they are in a position to take advantage of any profitable opportunities that may present themselves and as a precaution against any unexpected, but essential, outlay.

The strength of these factors underlying the demand for money alters from time to time. When one considers the significant reductions in the money supply (shown in Table 10.11) that individuals and firms switching from monetary assets to longer term financial assets, it becomes obvious that any decisions to reverse the flow of funds could equally well substantially increase the supply of money in the economy.

In a developed, expanding economy, in which average living levels are rising, both the transactions demand for money and the precautionary demand are likely to increase with the growth in output. This is firstly because people and firms have to be able to finance the larger volumes of current expenditure that accompany higher levels of output, and, secondly, because as their incomes rise, they are in a better position to be able to provide for the unexpected. The speculative demand for money is more volatile, and responds to changes in expectations, rather than to actual changes in output. As a result, the speculative demand for money is likely to fluctuate ahead of fluctuations in output levels.

In a developing country like South Africa the demand for money will probably grow faster than the economy as a whole. This is because these economies usually have a significant proportion, the subsistence sector, that operates outside the monetized area. As development takes place, people in the subsistence sector gradually move into the money economy and as this happens the demand for money increases. The exact nature of the influence that such changes will have on the money supply is difficult to predict, as it will depend upon the circumstances of the time. For example, the bad drought that occurred in KwaZulu, Transkei and Ciskei in the 1979/1980 growing season had the effect of forcing subsistence farmers to buy their food from trading stores, and by doing so temporarily increased the demand for money. Similarly, in many unsophisticated communities there is a tendency to hoard currency and if this is the case, then the supply of money can increase to the extent of the increased hoarding before it will have any influence on the price level through increased spending.

The third factor that can break the link between increases in the money supply and increases in domestic price levels is the cause of the increase in the money supply itself. Taking the major contributors illustrated in Table 10.11 as an example, increases in the money supply that reflect increased credit to either the public or the private sector are likely to have a greater impact on domestic price levels than increases that are the result of a favourable international trade situation. This is because the latter cause is backed up by an increase in the country's gold and foreign exchange holdings, which could be used to finance increased imports, which in their turn will help to ease the pressure of demand on the local markets.

One cannot state, however, that inflows of funds from abroad will not be inflationary; they may well be and the extent of their impact on the domestic price level will be determined by whether or not the increased domestic demand, resulting from these inflows, can be satisfied through the medium of increased imports.

Finally, increases in the money supply can only have an impact on the general price level through the relationship between aggregate demand and supply in the economy. If the increase is not translated into increased domestic expenditure, it will not affect the price levels. Further, if there is excess productive capacity present in the economy at the time of the increase in the money supply, and the excess is taken up and output levels rise, then, providing the increase in output is adequate, prices will not increase, even if the increased money supply is translated into increased domestic expenditure.

Notwithstanding the lack of a direct link between the money supply and domestic price levels, it remains true that prices cannot rise in the absence of a signficant increase in the money supply and, conversely, that such increases raise the distinct likelihood of concomitant increases in prices. When there is excessive liquidity present in an economy, there is always the danger that money that is lying relatively dormant is moved into active use. If this happens, the de facto money supply can increase substantially over a very short period of time. It may be very difficult for the 'real sector' of the economy to respond to this change with an increase in real output and under these circumstances, prices may rise sharply.

Monetary Policy in South Africa

When the government seeks to intervene in any market, it has the choice as to whether to concentrate its efforts on influencing the demand side of the market, the supply side of the market, or to use some combination of policies that will influence both simultaneously and hopefully in opposite directions. There is, at present, a difference of opinion amongst monetary theorists as to what constitutes the most effective approach. This difference has persisted since the 1930s and, as is inevitable, one or other of the two competing views has been the more popular throughout the period of the theoretical disagreement. Since sound theory must eventually provide the basis for effective action, the theoretical disarray amongst monetary economists over the past fifty years has posed significant problems for policy makers.

The South African monetary authorities, whilst they have shown some tendency to vacillate in sympathy with the movements in the theoretical fashions of the moment, have in general remained uncommitted to either school. Instead, in the absence of a sound, generally accepted theoretical base on which they could 'hang their policy hat', they have developed a pragmatic approach to managing the monetary side of the economy. (De Kock: 1978, Du Plessis: 1979). Although they have, in many instances, attempted to influence the demand side of both the short and long-term capital markets through fiscal policy and through movements in the interest rate, the

South African authorities have concentrated their major efforts upon influencing the supply side of the market, and they have made a particular effort to control the supply of money itself .

Operating through the central bank, the South African Reserve Bank, the authorities can make use of 'the classical instruments of monetary control'; namely, the alteration of the reserve requirements of the banking sector, the alteration of the rate at which the Reserve Bank is prepared to rediscount short-term paper for the private banking sector (the Bank Rate), the alteration of the rate of exchange between the Rand and other foreign currencies and, finally, by buying or selling government securities on the open market. (Lombard: 1973)

The Authorities, the Private Banking Sector and the Money Supply

When one looks back on the history of commercial banking in South Africa, one sees that it has in general been one of excess liquidity. This has made it difficult for the authorities to use changes in the reserve requirements of the commercial banks as an effective means of controlling the money supply. Prior to 1956 no real attempt was made to use the reserve ratios at all and they were seen largely as a means of ensuring the integrity of the banking sector. However, from 1956 onwards, right through to the present time, the major focus of the monetary authority's efforts switched from moral suasion and movements in the Bank Rate to attempts to control the money creating ability of the private banking sector. De Kock has argued that the importance of the commercial banks has been over-emphasized during this period and that, in part, this over-emphasis reflects the Reserve Bank's decision to collect data in the form of that given in Table 10.11, which certainly highlights the quantitative importance of the sector in terms of the overall changes in the money supply. (De Kock: 1978)

The period after 1956 saw the introduction of a number of changes in the banking legislation that were aimed at changing both the nature and the quantitative measures of the reserve requirements of the private banking sector. These changes, however, had little success. Despite the fact that alterations were made to the requirements in 1956, 1965 and 1972, which sought both to increase the power of the authorities to call for additional reserves and to limit the nature of short-term assets that would be acceptable as reserves, the most pressing monetary problem remained excess liquidity and a rapidly expanding money supply. The problem was compounded by the lack of a well developed money market, which severely limited the authorities' ability to use open market operations, i.e. to sell government paper to the public and the banking sector to mop up excess liquidity and by their reluctance to vary the Bank Rate very significantly, due to the adverse effect it would have on the rates on long-term loans, particularly those on mortgage bonds on private property. (De Kock: 1978)

As a result, in the late 1960s the Reserve Bank resorted to a somewhat less classical method of controlling the credit creating ability of the commercial banking sector, and imposed quantitative ceilings on the amounts these institutions were permitted to lend to the private sector. This direct control remained as the major weapon in the Reserve Bank's arsenal through to September 1980, although alterations in the ceiling and in the way in which it was applied, were made from time to time. The authorities did, however, view this direct control as something of an 'aberration'. When the Commission of Enquiry into the Monetary System and Monetary Policy in South Africa (De Kock Commission) was appointed in 1977, amongst the items which it was specifically charged to look into were 'credit ceilings, cash reserve and liquid asset requirements'. (R.P. 112/1978)

Dissatisfaction with the method of direct control over the credit creating ability of the Commercial Banks stems from three main sources. Firstly, it is felt that such controls adversely affect the position and profitability of the commercial banks *vis-à-vis* their competitors, the building societies and savings banks. Secondly, and related to the first point, it has been argued that the squeeze on profitability levels has led to unsound banking practices, which caused the recent failure of two small banks and has severely affected the integrity of the banking sector. (Du Plessis: 1979)

Thirdly, the imposition of the credit ceiling on formal short-term banking activities in South Africa has lead to the growth of a significant informal banking activity, the so-called 'Grey Market', a system in which some members of the corporate sector place short-term surplus funds 'on call' or short notice with other companies who have need of the funds. The growth of the Grey Market is unsatisfactory on a number of counts. Firstly, there is no means of ensuring the security of the funds and under some circumstances this could lead to multiple business failures. Secondly, information flows within the system are very limited and there is no guarantee that these funds are being allocated in the optimal manner. The Grey Market tends to concentrate amongst the large firms, making it even more difficult for the smaller firms to raise their short-term finance needs. (Nattrass: 1972). Thirdly, the market is only indirectly influenced by the other policy measures of the authorities and so its activities are difficult to control.

Finally, whilst the imposition of the credit ceilings did provide some means of controlling the increases in the money supply that were generated within the banking sector (endogenous increases), by their very nature they were totally unable to control the increases from the two major exogenous sources, namely, the government and the foreign sector. As we saw earlier in Table 10.11, these sources can be extremely significant at particular moments of time and in recent years the monetary authorities have increasingly tended to shift their attention away from the banking sector towards these other outside influences.

Monetary Policy and Government Finance

Over the past decade increasing attention has been paid to the effects that government deficit financing and the management of the public debt have on the monetary variables in the economy. The government appears, in recent years, to have accepted two propositions, firstly, that government expenditure should be financed in as uninflationary manner as is possible and secondly, that in times of excess liquidity, government expenditure should be held down to as low a level as is feasible.

Whilst this new emphasis will eventually produce gains in the monetary field, it could equally well generate serious problems on the political front. It was argued earlier in this chapter that the preservation of the present economic system will only be achieved if the present levels of poverty and inequality are significantly reduced and, further, that this means increased, rather than decreased, government effort.

There is a political aspect to monetary policy that is often overlooked. In a democratic economy there is a limit to how far one can push deflationary policies before one faces a political backlash. The fact that the South African government has been relatively successful in applying a conservative approach to the economy over a fairly long period of time reflects the political powerlessness of the groups who bear the brunt of the cut backs, at least as much as it does the determination and far-sightedness of the monetary authorities.

The political muscle of these groups is, however, rapidly increasing in strength, and as this process continues, it will become more and more difficult, on the political front, for the authorities either to keep down the level of State expenditure, or to implement policies that are aimed at contracting the current level of economic activity. It has been argued that in some developing countries there is a minimum economic growth rate that must be obtained if social upheavals are to be avoided and that governments in these situations choose growth even at the price of high inflation rates. (Seers: 1964). The South African government is likely to find itself in this situation to an increasing extent in the future, and as this happens monetary prudence is likely to give way to political expediency and the monetary authorities may well find themselves having to face up to the inflationary problems that are current in so many developing countries of today.

Exchange Rate Policy and the Money Supply

It is the rate of exchange, the conversion rate at which the authorities are prepared to convert South African rands into other currencies that links the foreign trade sector to the rest of the domestic economy. As a result, there is a definite link between changes in the exchange rate and changes in the supply of money in the domestic economy. Other things being equal, a reduction in the rate of exchange between, say, rands and dollars, will lower the rand value of exports sold on dollar markets and so reduce effect that the revenue earned from such sales will have on the economy. Other things are, however, seldom equal and as a result, whilst economists accept that the exchange rate links the domestic and foreign sectors of the economy, very few are prepared to commit themselves as to the exact nature of such a link.

The interim report of the De Kock Commission, which conce

trated its attention on this particular relationship, included the following statement:

> One of the first and most basic conclusions reached by the Commission in this regard is that there are few hard and fast a priori rules which can be laid down about the many different effects of exchange rate changes in South Africa. In most cases the nature and significance of the relationship between exchange rates and other economic variables depend upon circumstances. (R.P. 112/1978, p. 9)

Not only is the domestic economic outcome of a change in the exchange rate difficult to predict, but also, because the exchange rate is the link between the South African economy and the rest of the international trading community, and as changes in it are likely to affect the real trading flows between the Republic and her major trading partners, alterations in the rand exchange rate are not, in general, either a feasible or a flexible means of affecting local monetary conditions. This was particularly true before the setting up of a competitive international market for gold, for, as long as gold was sold for a fixed price, changes in the rand exchange rate directly affected the rand value of the turnover of the massive gold mining industry and this had repercussions throughout the rest of the economy.

South Africa's overall exchange rate policy has been determined by the factors that have influenced the rest of the international trading community, but within these overall limits domestic exchange rate policy has been reasonably conservative, with the authorities, in general, favouring the maintenance of a stable exchange rate.

After leaving the gold standard in 1936, South Africa signed the Bretton Woods Agreement in 1945 which established a system of relatively fixed international exchange rates. Signatory governments were expected to maintain their spot exchange rates, unless they could show that their economy had become chronically out of balance with those of its main trading partners. During the time that the Bretton Woods agreement remained in force, the South African currency was realigned only once, in 1949, when it was devalued by 30 per cent against the United States dollar.

Despite the apparent stability of the South African currency between 1945 and 1971, there was a significant change in the authorities' attitude towards the foreign sector of the economy during this period that was not reflected in the exchange rate. In 1960 there were significant social disturbances throughout South Africa and these triggered off a feeling of economic insecurity that was reflected in a massive outflow of capital. In 1961 the authorities closed the gates; they imposed a limit on the outflow of capital and tightened up on exchange control regulations. These restrictions have remained in force up to the present time (December, 1980) and have had a significant influence on the domestic monetary situation.

1968 saw the start of the end of the era of relatively fixed international exchange rates with the establishment of the two tier gold market. This failed to stabilize the international economy and in 1971 the Bretton Woods system was finally abandoned. In the readjustments that followed, the South African authorities decided to tie the rand to the dollar and to allow them to 'float' together, within limits, against the other international currencies.

The decade of the 1970s has been one of considerable instability on the international currency markets and it is virtually impossible to detail all the movements that took place over this period. The rand was, however, devalued quite significantly against the dollar in 1975 and lost ground, with the dollar, to other major currencies, such as the German mark, the Swiss franc and the Japanese yen. Throughout this period the controls on the outflow of capital were maintained, which, in effect, resulted in an overvaluing of the rand on the international market.

The build up of liquidity and the strengthening of South Africa's balance of payments situation in the latter half of the decade, however, altered the situation and generated pressure for a relaxation of the exchange controls.

The interim report of the Commission of Enquiry into Monetary Policy recommended that steps should be taken in this direction. As a first move towards freeing the rand, a dual exchange rate was introduced via the creation of the 'financial rand' at the end of 1978. This was a system which allowed foreigners wishing to export their capital to purchase financial rands which they could then sell abroad to those people (also foreigners) who wished to invest in South Africa. The financial rand is on sale at a discount *vis-à-vis* the commercial rand and the discount rate varies between 40 and 25 per cent. This system has the dual advantage in that it now makes it possible for people to move their capital out of the country, providing they are prepared to pay the premium, but at the same time it encourages capital inflows in to the country. Foreign investors currently stand to reap a substantial financial gain through bringing their funds into the country via the financial rand.

The De Kock Commission recommended the dual exchange rate system as an interim step along the road to an exchange rate policy that it saw as desirable, namely:

> a unitary exchange rate system under which an independent and flexible rand finds its own level in a well developed and competitive spot and forward foreign exchange market. (R.P. 112/1978, p. 43)

The report was favourably received and is in keeping with the tone of other government policy statements and it seems likely that further reforms in the exchange rate policy will be introduced in the near future.

THE STATE, FOREIGN TRADE AND THE BALANCE OF PAYMENTS

One of the major roles of the State is to ensure the integrity of the national currency from both the domestic and the international points of view. On the international trading scene the government can influence the situation in two ways; the first is by changing the exchange rate itself, as we discussed in the previous section. The second is by the implementation of policies that are designed to affect the behaviour of the flows of trade themselves, i.e. the imports and exports of both goods and services, and factors of production. Policies implemented in either one of these two areas will affect the other, but despite this interdependence, it is nevertheless useful to discuss them separately, as the time horizons over which the influences are felt differ. Policies designed to influence the trade flows themselves are in general long-term policies, whilst the effects of changes in the exchange rate feed through the economy quite rapidly. As we discussed South Africa's exchange rate policy in the previous section, here we will concentrate on policies affecting the real trade flows.

South Africa's Foreign Trade

The South African economy has always had a high degree of 'openness', i.e. the import and export of commodities have formed a significant proportion of the total economic activity in the region. Table 10.13 illustrates this.

Table 10.13
IMPORTS AND EXPORTS, GROSS DOMESTIC PRODUCT AND THE TERMS OF TRADE FOR SELECTED YEARS BETWEEN 1911–76

Year	As a Percentage of Gross Domestic Product				Terms of Trade	
	Imports[1]		Exports (not Gold)	Gold Exports	Total Exports	Merchandise Only	Gold and Merchandise
	(FOB)	(CIF)					
1911	23		15	21	36		
1920	33[2]		19	13	32		
1930	24		13	13	26		
1940	21		9				
1950	24	26	21	9	30	120	122
1960	22	24	18	11	29	90	94
1970	22	24	13	7	20	96	95
1976	21	23	15	8	23	99	110

1. Free on board = FOB. Cost insurance and freight = CIF.
2. 1920 is unusual. The average for the years 1919/20/21 was 24%.

SOURCE: *South African Statistics 1978.*

Over the period from 1911–76 there has been a slight tendency for the importance of the foreign sector to decline, particularly on the export side. However, this reflects the rapid growth in the domestic economy to a greater extent than it does a reversal in South Africa's international trading situation. Although the terms of trade did decline somewhat in the ten years 1950–60, apart from a fluctuation between 1972 and 1976, they have remained remarkably constant over the period since 1960.

As the quantity of exports and imports have grown with the expansion of the economy, so the nature of South Africa's foreign trade has changed. The Reynder's Commission, a commission of enquiry into South Africa's export trade, divided her export performance into three distinct phases. The first phase, from 1652–1868, the Commission labelled 'the agricultural phase'; the second period, that from 1869–1939, 'the agricultural – mining phase'; and the third period, from 1939 to the present time, the 'agricultural – mining – manufacturing' phase. (R.P. 69/72). Despite this diversification, South Africa remains heavily dependent upon the successful export of relatively few items and the composition of her exports largely reflects her natural resource endowment. Growth, in the volume of merchandise exports in general, and in the export of manufactured products in particular, has been slow throughout the period from 1950–76. Analysts have attributed this relatively poor performance to a combination of increasing domestic demand, less favourable trading conditions on the international markets, poor agricultural harvests in certain years, the slow growth in productivity in the sectors exporting manufactured products and a deterioration in South Africa's international political situation. (Reynders and Van Zyl: 1973)

The import side of the foreign trade market has also seen a significant change in its major structural components as the South African economy has developed. In the early period imports consisted mainly of consumer goods, then as the mining industry started to expand and to generate an infant manufacturing sector, capital goods were imported. This trend continued and it has been estimated that over the 20 year period from 1950–70, the proportion that capital formed of total imports rose from approximately 32 per cent to 40 per cent. A further 10 per cent comprised raw materials, which were inputs into South African industry. (Reynders and Van Zyl: 1973). The importance of imports as a source of development has been highlighted in a study that showed that over the period 1956–64, imported capital goods represented approximately 70 per cent of total fixed investment in the manufacturing sector, and 30 per cent of the country's total fixed investment. (Du Plessis: 1965)

This type of structural change is a common feature of developing countries and is often a cause for concern to the authorities. As the content of a country's imports hardens, in the sense that the proportion of consumer goods in total declines, it becomes increasingly difficult for the government to take any corrective action that might be required in the field of import restriction, without severely affecting the level of domestic economic activity. In the case of the South African economy this problem has been compounded by the fact that, in times of economic expansion, it has been coupled with a chronic tendency for imports of goods and services to exceed exports, and the concomitant development of a deficit on the current account of the Balance of Payments.

Foreign Trade Policy

If one takes a very general approach to the changes that have taken place in South Africa's foreign trade policy over the past century, it is possible to isolate three distinct phases. The first phase, which lasted up to 1925, was characterized by a liberal, 'laissez-faire' approach towards international trade. The second phase, which ran from 1925 up to the early 1970s, was a period in which the government adopted a much more 'inward looking' policy and concentrated its efforts upon encouraging the development of 'import replacing' investment. The third phase, which is still current, shows yet another switch in philosophy, this time in favour of policies designed to stimulate exports.

The liberal approach to foreign trade ended with the successful election of the PACT government, which was both nationalistically oriented and committed to the elimination of white poverty. Both these characteristics led them to favour a policy of protectionism and 1925 saw the introduction of the Customs Tariff Act. This Act gave the State extended powers to impose protective tariffs, with the stated aims of encouraging the further development of industry, that it be administered in such a way as to minimize the increases in costs to primary producers, the mining industry, and the cost of living to the consumer, and subject to the provision that industries using a high proportion of 'civilized labour', (White), should get preference over those employing black labour. (Botha: 1973)

It has been argued that this policy was successful in developing manufacturing from both the output and employment viewpoints, and that it contributed to the eventual elimination of the Poor White Problem, but that it failed in two of its other objectives. Firstly, it failed to keep down either the cost of living, or the costs of production to the gold mining industry, and, secondly, that whilst it helped to develop a manufacturing industry, it did not succeed in developing an *independent* manufacturing sector. (Lumby: 1976, 1977). As we saw in Table 7.5, even as late as 1975, the manufacturing sector was still totally dependent upon mining to finance its foreign exchange needs.

The disappointing export performance of the manufacturing sector, coupled with the belief that the long-term export prospects for the mining industry were limited, lead to a gradual evolution in government policy away from one in which the major thrust was tariff protection, towards an increased emphasis on the need to increase exports. This was further encouraged by South Africa's membership of GATT (General Agreement on Tariffs and Trade), an international organization founded in 1947, with the aim of promoting a 'free' international trading system. 1957 saw the first of a number of actions taken by the government to improve the level of exports, which, as we have seen, were largely unsuccessful in volume terms, although they did improve the income levels of South African exporters. (Meyer: 1980). 1971 saw the appointment of a Commission of Inquiry (Reynders Commission), which reported in 1973 and paved the way for a switch in government policy towards the positive promotion of exports as the only long-term solution to the provision of South Africa's future foreign exchange needs.

OTHER ASPECTS OF GOVERNMENT IN THE ECONOMY

As we have seen throughout this study, the government influences economic activity in South Africa in a number of ways apart from those we have just discussed. As most of these other influences have been dealt with in reasonable detail in other sections, they will only be referred to now in broad detail for the sake of completeness.

Over the past 70 years various administrations have brought in legislation enabling the government to influence directly the patterns of economic development in South Africa. The extent of the growth in such government control is illustrated by a study of the discussion at a conference in 1979 on free enterprise in South Africa, which showed that in those discussions delegates referred to some 492 different pieces of legislation affecting the operation of the economy in some manner. (Louw: 1980). The legislation can be categorized loosely as being one of two types; either legislation aimed at improving the functioning of the economic system, or legislation which, although aimed at implementing a particular political ideology, also has an impact on the economy.

The major area of government influence has been, and still is, in the field of labour. The government has, however, also had a significant impact upon the patterns of capital accumulation in South Africa, both from the racial and the spatial point of view. This influence has been exerted through such legislation as the Physical Planning Act, the Group Area's Act, the Land Act, the various measures that have been taken to conserve the land and to limit pollution, and the measures that control conditions in the workplace, such as the Factories Act and the Shops and Offices Act.

The latter part of the decade of the 1970s appears to have seen a change in emphasis with respect to government economic ideology. There have been numerous statements from various government representatives regarding the need to create a 'free enterprize economy'. These have been coupled with a reduction in the rate of growth of State expenditure, the incorporation of private capital into SASOL and a significant increase in the degree of consultation between private sector leaders and government. If this impetus is maintained, the next decade may see a gradual decrease in the level of government control over the economy.

It is difficult to assess what the overall effect of such a policy change will be. As we said earlier, it will become increasingly difficult to redress the racial inequalities in social services by reducing either the rate of growth, or the level of public sector expenditure, unless such a reduction is accompanied by a significant redistribution of funds within the public sector itself. As far as any removal of direct economic controls are concerned, whilst the elimination of legislation that discriminates in favour of Whites is certainly likely to improve the economic lot of the black groups, it is not possible to generalize on the effect of a wholesale reduction in government intervention. Indeed since as yet no significant concrete moves have in fact been made in this direction, it seems that one should perhaps wait to see 'the colour of the government's money' before attempting such an assessment.

Conclusion

There is no doubt that the government plays a major role in the South African economy and that this role can be a significant force in achieving particular State objectives. It was government policy that succeeded in eliminating the Poor White Problem. It was government policy that created the massive productivity differences between the Black and White agricultural sectors. It was government policy that segmented the labour force on racial grounds and it has been government policy that has led to the recent redistribution of income from Whites to blacks.

It is crucially important that the government remains aware of the magnitude of its impact on the economy and that it orders its administrative priorities so as to ensure that government activity in fact continues to influence the economic variables in the direction that will achieve its overall objectives.

ELEVEN

Growth and Change in South Africa – An Overview

In this concluding chapter we will discuss the nature of the growth path that has been followed by the South African economy as it has developed, and the relevance of this path for social, political and economic change.

Changes on the economic and socio-political fronts are closely intertwined. Economic development itself is a process of change, and consequently opens up opportunities in all fields that are not present in a static society. The precise nature of the economic growth path is also an important influence on the type of change that takes place, because on each growth path different people and groups benefit from the opportunities that emerge. These people, in some instances, find that they are able to use their new-found economic leverage to open up change in the social and political structures of the society. The relationship also works in the other direction, as change in the social and political structures often generates an environment that stimulates economic development.

Finally, the existing economic structures in many instances restrict the opportunities that are available for political and social change, and limit the real choice of political options available to a community at a particular point in its economic development.

In this chapter we will first review the arguments concerning the nature of the South African economic growth path and then ask what the implications have been for the relationship between change on the economic front and concomitant social and political change. Finally we will look at the limits that the present economic structure is likely to place upon the choice of various political and economic systems, and the implications of these for South Africa.

THEORETICAL APPROACHES TO ECONOMIC DEVELOP-MENT AND THEIR IMPLICATIONS FOR SOCIO-POLITICAL CHANGE

Any economic development path will only be maintained so long as there is a corresponding evolution in the socio-political structure of the community sufficient to meet the aspirations of the groups who are gaining economic power as a result of the economic growth process. However, different groups gain power on different growth paths and at different times on the same growth path and, as a result, there is no one to one relationship between economic and social and political evolution.

Social and Political Change on an Orthodox Development Path

The orthodox view of economic growth in an economy in which an infant capitalist sector is introduced into a traditional, subsistence-oriented economy, has been well explained in the models of Lewis and Fei and Ranis. (Lewis: 1954, Fei and Ranis: 1963). In terms of this view, the economy is divided into two major sectors, the growing modern industrial sector, and the original agricultural sector. The modern sector grows through the transfer of labour (at a constant wage) and food from the agricultural sector, in exchange for manufactured products. The flows of goods and factors of production in this type of development model are shown in Fig. 11.1.

In this type of development, the nature of the intersectoral trade flows causes a policy dilemma. Labour is supplied, from agriculture to manufacturing, at a wage which is determined by the average living standards in agriculture, together with a premium to cover the costs involved in moving. As long as living standards in agriculture do not rise, labour will be supplied at a constant wage rate; however, any increases in rural living standards will act to increase the supply price of labour to the modern sector.

The dilemma arises because the wage in manufacturing is set in terms of the real living standard in the rural areas. If the relative price of agricultural products increases, then the proportion of the modern sector output needed to buy food for the sector's workforce also increases (the wage in terms of manufactures rises even though the wage in terms of food does not), and profits are reduced. One way of preventing the terms of trade from moving against the modern sector in this way is to invest capital in agriculture, which will increase food output; however, if this increase allows standards of living to rise in the agricultural sector, it too will increase the modern sector wage.

Figure 11
THE FLOWS OF RESOURCES BETWEEN SECTORS

11.1 A TYPICAL DUAL ECONOMY

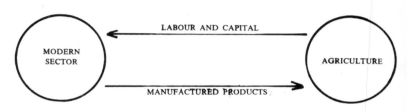

11.2 THE SOUTH AFRICAN ECONOMY

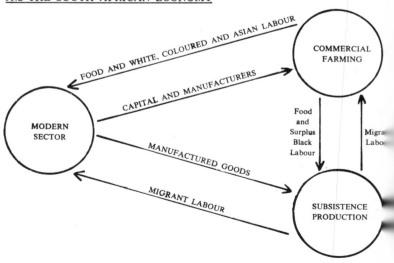

On this type of development path, economic growth continues unchanged, fuelled by the reinvestment of profits in the modern sector and the transfer of labour from agriculture, as long as modern sector wage rates do not increase. Once all the surplus labour in agriculture has been absorbed, however, the wage rate in both sectors will be forced up. It will no longer be possible to withdraw any further labour from agriculture without jeopardizing the supply of food, unless capital is transferred to replace it. The capital that is introduced into agriculture will increase labour productivity levels in the sector and wage rates will start to rise. This increase will feed through into the industrial sector, reducing profits and slowing down the rate of growth, but, at the same time, it will start to distribute output between capital and labour more evenly.

It has been argued elsewhere that economic development along a path of the Lewis or Fei and Ranis type will, in the first instance, be likely to be accompanied by a political system that is favourable towards maintaining the interests of the capitalist class. However, as development proceeds in this manner, so the economic power of labour gradually increases. It continues to do so until eventually a situation is reached whereby labour holds a sufficiently powerful economic position to be able to force through significant political and economic reforms as part of their price for continued co-operation in the process of production and capital accumulation. (Nattrass: 1978b)

However, the orthodox view of development is not the only interpretation of growth in a dual economy. An alternative and equally plausible explanation of the process is the one postulated by Frank and Arrighi; the 'underdevelopment view'. In terms of this explanation, the introduction of a capitalist core economy into a traditionally organized agricultural economy has very different implications for the development of the latter. On this growth path, the growing capitalist centre uses both the economic and political relationships in the community to entrench its economic position and to continuously undermine the position of labour through the process of underdevelopment. On this type of growth path, surplus labour, far from being gradually absorbed into the expanding modern sector, is continuously regenerated, strengthening the relative position of capital. In such an economic scenario, not only is the political system virtually certain to be controlled by the capitalist class, but there is also very little likelihood of any forces for political reform being engendered through the economic development process. Political and social reform in societies with this type of growth path are unlikely to be achieved without a radical restructuring of the political and economic systems themselves.

Proponents of the orthodox and the underdevelopment theories of economic development usually see these two growth paths as being mutually exclusive. Whilst Lewis himself did acknowledge the possibility of development ceasing before the labour surplus had been absorbed, neither Fei and Ranis, nor the underdevelopment theorists, see any possibility of the one form of development evolving into the other. However, the author has developed a model which suggests that these paths are in no way isolated from one another and consequently, a society can move from one to the other, and that the direction of such a movement will be a reflection of the nature of the development of the underlying relative economic and political power structures that accompany all economic change. (Nattrass: 1978b)

In terms of this somewhat more eclectic view of economic development, one could describe the South African modern economic development path as one which, in its early stages, approximated the underdevelopment view of economic expansion, and subsequently moved onto a path better described by the orthodox theory. One could then ascribe the changes that have taken place in the late sixties and seventies to an indication of endogenous influences within the economy, improving the relative economic strength of the Black population groups.

It appears, however, that this is too simple an explanation of growth and change in the South African economy. Certainly the first part of this view appears to be correct. In the early part of the twentieth century political power in South Africa was largely centred on interests that were concurrent with those of mining capital and, as we have seen in Chapter Four, this power was used for economic ends. Not only was it used to establish a stable and cheap labour supply for the mining industry, through the recruiting network, but it was also used in a number of attempts (ultimately unsuccessful) to break the power of the growing White union movement. However, after the 1924 elections, political power shifted away from mining interests towards those of White labour, rural capital and the infant manufacturing sector. This shift in political power altered the nature of the relationship between the growing modern sectors and agriculture and by doing so, moved the economy onto a very different growth path.

The change in political strength entrenched, over time, White agricultural interests and, in so doing, dichotomized the agricultural sector on the basis of race, and at the same time successfully separated the sources of supply of food and labour. This separation was extremely important as it offered a way out of the development dilemma, posed by the Lewis model. It enabled the economy to continue to grow, without having to face the conflict between policies designed to encourage the generation of a cheap supply of food, and those aimed at the creation of a source of supply of cheap labour. Once agriculture has been divided in this way, capital can be introduced into the food supplying sector, without fear of it causing a concomitant increase in the supply price of labour to the modern sector. (Nattrass: 1977b). In terms of this approach to South African economic development, one would have to analyse the process by means of a three-sector basic model, and the relevant intersectoral flows of goods and factors of production are illustrated in Fig. 11.2.

Once the source of food supply has been separated from the source of labour supply, living standards of those supplying food (White farmers in the South African case) can increase along with living standards in the industrial sector, without affecting living conditions in the labour reserve economy, (Black agriculture), for as long as the latter continues to supply an adequate labour force to the growing modern sector. There are two things that might change the situation.

Firstly, the demand for labour in the modern economy might start to outstrip the available supply and eventually absorb the labour surplus in the labour reserve economy. If this happens the economy will revert back to a conventional (two sector) development path.

Secondly, the type of labour being supplied by the labour reserve economy could become inadequate for the needs of the modern sector. Modern, growing economies need increasingly sophisticated labour and once the industrial sector has reached the stage whereby part of its skilled workforce has to be provided from the labour reserve sector, standards of living in that sector will have to be increased in order to enable the right type of labour to be produced and educated. In Neo-Marxian terminology, standards of living in the labour reserve sector will remain constant, or decline until the cost of reproducing the necessary workforce increases; once this happens, so the situation in the reserve economy can be expected to evolve.

An important aspect of this three-sector approach to economic development is that it enables the nature of the relationships between the sectors to differ radically from one another. In South Africa, for example, one could best describe the flows of labour, food and capital that have taken place between the industrial sector and White agriculture in terms of those in the later stages of the Lewis model, in which capital is transferred from the modern sector to agriculture, to increase productivity there.

The relationship between the modern sector and the labour reserve sector has been very different and far more closely approximates those that are set out in the underdevelopment theories, with the major engines of underdevelopment being the migrant labour system, the racially discriminatory legislation and the uneven allocation of government expenditure. As we saw in Chapters Four, Six and Nine, conditions in subsistence agriculture improved in the late nineteenth century, only to decline again in the early part of the twentieth century. Output in these areas virtually stagnated after 1924 and once the influx control laws became fully operational, living conditions started to decline and continued to do so to the point where these regions were no longer able to support their population and had to import food from White agriculture. At this stage, even though the maintenance of the labour reserve sector was no longer costless to the growing modern economy, its continued existence still exerted a downward pressure on modern sector wages, to the extent that the sector was able to provide social security in the form of homes for the young, the aged, the sick and the unemployed, which would otherwise have to have been provided by the industrial sector.

In this type of economic scenario, one would expect endogenously generated social and political change to be relatively slow and to be limited to the needs and demands of the modern industrial and White agricultural sectors. Reforms in the labour reserve areas are likely to be particularly slow and will largely reflect pressures brought to bear from outside the economic system, or take place through the linkages between the labour reserve areas and the modern sector that are the result of the migrant labour system.

Having set out a tentative theoretical framework for the analysis of economic growth and change in South Africa, let us now turn to an examination of the development of the structures of power, and its impact on social and political change in South Africa.

ECONOMIC GROWTH AND SOCIO-POLITICAL CHANGE IN SOUTH AFRICA

Introduction

An individual's position, (or a group's position) within the community hierarchy reflects the access that he has to the sources of power within that society. These sources are often wide-spread and their particular nature in any one community will reflect the rules by which its members govern the social, religious, political and economic aspects of their lives. As a result, one would expect the sources of power in a society that accept the principles of individualism and private enterprise to be very different from those in a society that is highly centralized, or from one that is run on decentralized communal lines.

These sources of power are not independent of one another and indeed, access to power in one form often significantly enhances the chance of obtaining power from one of the other sources. Consequently, in a capitalist society, economic growth, which is essentially a process that implies a change in the balance of economic forces, often generates, or is generated by, concomitant changes in the social and political structures of that society. The nature of the exact relationship between economic growth and social and political change is extremely complex and in no way unidirectional. Economic growth may equally well be the result of either liberalism, or reactionary social and political change. The exact nature and direction of the relationship between economic growth and socio-political change, at any one particular time, will be a reflection of that between the changing economic forces, the existing social and political structures and the aspirations of the current power majority.

It is extremely difficult to trace power relationships in a society, as they tend to be volatile and to change, as different cross-cutting or reinforcing alliances are made and broken. In general terms, however, in a private enterprise society, one's economic power is largely determined by the extent to which one can obtain control over the forces of production, namely, labour, capital and the environment in which they are combined together in the production process. Again, in general terms, one's access to power is usually reflected in one's status in the income hierarchy and, as a result, one can make use of changes in the distribution of income in the community, as a surrogate measure for changes in the distribution of economic power.

The sixty years that followed the formation of the Union of South Africa, saw the almost continous erosion of the political power of South Africa's Black population groups. Starting with the failure to extend the Cape franchise to blacks in the other provinces, at the time of Union itself, the process continued with the loss of the African vote and the replacement by nominated Native Representatives, the removal of the Coloured community from the voters roll, and the eventual elimination of the Native Representatives once again. This reduction in overt political power was accompanied by increased restrictions on population movements and limitations on the economic rights of these same population groups, through the introduction of measures like the Land Act, the Group Areas Act and the Bantu Urban Areas Act. It is not surprising, therefore, that this 60 year period was one that saw relatively little improvement in the average absolute standards of living of black South Africans, and no improvement at all in their relative economic position. (McGrath 1977)

The period from 1970 onwards, however, appears to have different characteristics. As we saw in Chapter Two, on the economic side the period up to 1975 saw a redistribution of income from the White group to the black. On the political and social fronts this was accompanied by some measures designed to eliminate 'hurtful or petty apartheid', by increased state expenditure on both black education and black housing, as well as on the development of the Black States; by the removal of statutory job reservation; by the opening of apprentice training to Africans and, probably most significantly, by the extension of the right of freedom of association to the African workforce and the legal recognition of the African labour unions. On the basis of these indicators, it would certainly appear that the relative power of black South Africans has increased to the point where it is starting to be reflected in both the economic and social structures of South Africa.

Small though this change in the racial distribution of power may be, it raises some very interesting questions; what the cause of the change was; whether it originated from economic or political factors, or perhaps some combination of the two; whether the change will be maintained and, if so, what directions these new changes will be likely to take.

SOME FACTORS AFFECTING THE DISTRIBUTION OF POWER POTENTIALS

Although economic and political sources of power are ultimately intertwined, in the sense that power from one of these sources can be used both to counteract, or reinforce, that flowing from the other, and on its own, it is useful, from an analytical point of view, to consider the sources and their influences separately; particularly in view of the fact that the characteristics of economic and political power differ from one another. However, when one is involved in such a 'separate analysis', it is important that one does not lose sight of the fact that the final outcome of change, flowing from either source, will be largely dependent upon the ability of those who become more powerful, as a result of the change, to link up successfully with the alternate power structures.

It is also important to remember that when one is discussing power in an academic sense, one is talking only of the potential to exercise power. It is quite possible, at any one moment, for the distribution of the sources of power actually being exercised, to differ quite significantly from the distribution of the power potentials. The actual exercise of power depends to a large extent upon social and psychological factors, which vary through time and are related to perceptions, aspirations and group coherence.

The Sources of Political Power Potential

In any community one can divide political power sources into those that are overtly connected with the existing political structures, and those that are covert, in the sense that their power is derived from the cost to the existing system of the introduction of an alternative political framework, together with the extent of any particular group's determination and actual ability to effect such changes.

Within these two general categories the situation is complicated still further by the possibilities that arise for the formation of alliances. Such alliances can be either of short or long-term duration and can cut across, or reinforce, the existing power network. In the political arena, South Africa has seen a number of such alliances. Of the overt alliances, certainly the most spectacular and, in terms of its long-term effects, probably the most effective was the one formed between White labour, White rural and Afrikaner business interests which resulted in the election of the PACT government in 1924. The present 'Black Alliance' is another example, and particularly interesting, because it not only cuts across the formal overt power network, but also acts to reinforce the covert power system.

Sources of political power are more volatile than those that arise in the economic or social systems. Not only is it a reasonably simple process to form new political alliances but, as can be seen from the wide variety of political alternatives currently being presented to South Africans, it is relatively easy to reorganize the format of the political system itself, together with its underlying power network. However, such a reorganization will not be without cost. In certain instances the immediate cost, both social and economic, that is involved in the reorganization of the polity in a particular direction may be extremely high. This would be the case, for example, if such reorganization necessitated a violent revolution.

The Sources of Economic Power

It was argued earlier that, in general terms, economic power comes from control over the factors of production and the environment within which they operate. This control can also be exercised both directly and indirectly. In a private enterprise economy direct control flows from the actual ownership of part of the accumulated wealth of the various communities, (including education and training, or the creation of special skills), whilst indirect control can be obtained through the corporate management system, the public service sector, by means of controlling part of the markets for goods, or for the factors of production themselves, and even, in some instances, by means of political manipulation.

In a private enterprise economy there is another source of potential economic power, derived from a person's, or group's, ability to disrupt the process of profit generation. The workforce can exercise this power by means of strike action, as indeed can groups that are prepared to create social unrest and economic disruption as a means of furthering their objectives.

The Racial Distribution of Power Potential in South Africa

It is apparent from the discussion above that when one tries to identify the network of power potentials in an actual society, one will have little hope of doing anything more than isolating some of the major indicators. Table 11.1 contains some such indicators of the racial power networks in South Africa for the years 1960, 1970 and 1977. These indicators are very limited in their usefulness and should be treated with caution. Within these limitations, however, they do illustrate firstly the extent to which power remains concentrated in the hands of the White group, and secondly, that there has been some shift in favour of the black groups over the period covered in the table, particularly in regard to the indirect sources of power.

The data show no overt political change over this period, although black political leverage did increase slightly. The most significant political influences are, however, not represented by the indicators in the table; namely, the increased levels of domestic social unrest, which are centered around the black groups and the increased foreign pressure for change, which is concentrated upon obtaining an improvement in 'the quality of life' of black South Africans. Finally, also not included amongst the indicators in the table is anything related to the increased military threat, which is also a significant force for change. Ultimately the maintenance of South Africa's territorial and political integrity will require the co-operation of all her population groups, and this is unlikely to be forthcoming unless sincere attempts have been, or are being, made to reduce the present disparities in political and economic rights between the race groups. (Giliomee: 1980)

From the economic viewpoint, the situation is very similar. The major share of economic power is still under White control, but here again there are indications of change, particularly over the period after 1970. The black share in the total workforce has increased, as

Table 11.1
INDICATORS OF CHANGES IN THE STRUCTURE OF POLITICAL AND ECONOMIC POWER IN SOUTH AFRICA

Nature of Indicator	White Group			All Black Groups		
	1960	1970	1977	1960	1970	1977
Political Power						
Overt						
Percentage Control of Seats in the House of Assembly	100	100	100	0	0	0
Covert						
Percentage of Total Population	19	17	17	81	83	83
Percentage Urban	84	87		38	40	
Economic Power						
Through Capital						
Share of Personal Income	74	74	68	26	26	32
Share of Managerial Jobs	97	97	97	3	3	3
Share of Public Sector Jobs	47	36	28	53	64	72
Share of Industrial Jobs	28	24	21	72	76	79
Through Labour						
Actual						
Percentage of Top Jobs	80	75	73	20	25	27
Percentage in Top Jobs	41	47	43	2	4	5
Potential						
Percentage of Economically Active Population	20	18	17	80	82	83
Percentage of Matriculation Passes	94	88	80	6	12	20

SOURCE: Nattrass (1977a). Nattrass (1980a). Malherbe (1977). 1970 Population Census, Various Reports.

has their share of the unionized workforce, of public sector employment, of industrial employment and of the number of children who successfully completed the final year of a full school education.

One factor, however, not included in the table, that one would expect to undermine growing black economic power, is the increase in the number of blacks who are unemployed or underemployed. There are indications that, at least from the middle of the 1960s onwards, the modern sector of the South African economy has been increasingly unable to absorb the expanding workforce. (Simkins: 1978, Loots: 1980)

Also omitted from the economic indicators is the increased moral pressure for improved working conditions for the black labour force that has been brought to bear on employers, particularly multinational corporations, from both inside and outside South Africa's borders.

When we analysed the growth of the major sectors of the economy earlier and attempted to assess to what extent they had contributed to the behaviour of the racial differential in living standards, we concluded that, whilst it was difficult to assess the exact role that the agricultural sector had played, on balance the likelihood was that the sector had contributed to the widening of the gap. However, we also concluded that the expansion of the other major sectors, mining, manufacturing and government, had certainly influenced narrowing racial differences in living conditions, particularly over the period after 1970. These earlier conclusions are reflected in the changes in the racial distribution of income shown in Table 11.1.

There is also evidence, however, that suggests that, within the black community, there are at present significant differences between the power potentials of different black groups. Amongst the African population this growing power potential appears to be very largely concentrated amongst those living and working in the urban areas of South Africa and, as a result, the relative living conditions of Africans in the rural areas seem to have worsened. Table 11.2 contains data relating to the economic profiles of South Africa's population groups for 1975, distinguishing between Africans who are *legally* permanently settled in urban areas and those whose *legal* homes remain in the rural areas.

The education levels, the average earnings and the occupational positions differ significantly between the population groups shown in Table 11.2, with the White group being in the most favoured position. It is interesting to note, however, that the gap, in terms both of years of formal education and of average earning capacity, was greater between the urban and the rural African group at 6,7 years: 0 and R8,3: 1, than between the White group and the urban African group; these ratios being 1,4 years: 1 and R5,6: 1. The former education gap was also greater in absolute terms, but the earnings gap in absolute terms was smaller.

Table 11.2

ECONOMIC PROFILES OF SELECTED SOUTH AFRICAN POPULATION GROUPS, 1975

Indicator	Africans		Asian	Coloured	White
	Rural	Urban			
Average Income per Head 1975 (Rands)	100	381	560	430	2 500
Average Earnings per Worker (Rands)	160	1 335	3 866	1 846	7 500
Median Level of Education of Economically Active	Nil	6,7 years	7,3 years	5,4 years	9,7 years
Percentage in Top Jobs	2	5	23	7	47
Percentage in Low Level Jobs	69	28	11	30	7

SOURCE: Adapted from Tables 1 and 4 in Nattrass, 1980b.

The Future Outlook

It is obviously impossible to push this type of analysis too far into the future since, by its very nature, it is confined to South Africa's present economic and political structures. Within this framework, however, it seems likely that the recent trends, evident within the network of potential power, will be maintained – at least through the decade of the eighties. It also appears that the major sources of increased black economic power stem from the labour market.

In numerical terms, black South Africans not only dominate the labour scene, but are also increasing at a faster rate than White workers. The African population group not only provided 71 per cent of the workforce, but also grew at an average of 4 per cent per year over the period from 1960–75, as against a growth rate for the White workforce of just over 2 per cent per annum. The potential power of the black workforce was well illustrated by the significant influence that the wide-spread strike action, by Black workers in 1973, had upon both black working conditions and employer attitudes towards their black labour force.

In addition, the economic position of the black workforce will be improved still further, in the immediate future, by the increasing inability of the White group to provide sufficient people to fill the skilled labour positions. There is a growing shortage of semi-skilled, skilled and management personnel and members of the black workforce will have to be trained in increasing numbers to fill these positions. It has been estimated that, with present trends, by the mid 1980s the number of black children in the twelfth and final year of school will be greater than that of White and it is by these people that the labour needs must be met. (Lombard, *et al* 1980)

Both the recent and the proposed changes in labour legislation, which have followed from the recommendations of the Wiehahn and the Riekert Commissions of Inquiry into various matters related to the effective operation of the labour market, also seem likely to increase the power potential of the black workforce, but to do so in an uneven manner.

The labour reform proposals that are most likely to affect the power structures in the labour market are:[1]

'(1) The extension of the right of freedom of association to South African Blacks, including those who come to work in the Republic from the now independent Black States of Transkei, Bophuthatswana and Venda (Wiehahn).

(2) The extenstion of the system of apprentice training to Blacks (Wiehahn) and the improvement in training facilities for Blacks in general (Riekert).

(3) The removal of the practice of reserving jobs for particular race groups (Whites in the main) (Wiehahn).

---

1. This section ending at the top of p. 296 has been reprinted from Nattrass (1980a) with the permission of the South African Foundation.

(4) The streamlining of the registration procedures for Black workers and the recommendations for the improved mobility of urban Blacks in White areas (Riekert).

(5) The labour market preference to be given to Blacks with permanent residence rights in White areas (Riekert).'

The extension of the right of 'freedom of association' in the labour market to Blacks should improve the group's bargaining position. Prior to these reforms Blacks were not permitted to join registered trade unions and although a number of unregistered Black unions operated, the lack of official recognition signficantly undermined their bargaining position *vis-à-vis* that of both the employer groups and the registered unions.

The growth of a strongly unionized Black workforce may well ensure growth in the average level of real wages earned by its members. The Black group will not, however, find it as easy to achieve this as the White unions have done, as the potential strength of the Black union movement will be undermined by the high levels of unemployment and underemployment present in the Black community, which seem likely to persist for at least the next decade. Also, the White unions succeeded in raising the earnings of their members partly by depressing the rate of increase of black wages – an avenue which is not open to the Black unions. Black unions may, however, be able to make some economic gains at the expense of the non-unionized sector of the workforce.

The proposals to remove job reservation and to improve Black training facilities will help those members of the Black group who benefit to obtain a higher level of marketable labour skills, which will also improve their economic position in the labour market. However, too much emphasis should not be put on the removal of the job reservation clauses from the legislation, since not only did these clauses affect very few workers, but they were also never the key element in the maintenance of the dominant position of the White workers. Far more important were the 'closed shop' agreements negotiated by the exclusively White trade unions.

The Riekert recommendations regarding the streamlining of the registration procedures should also improve the relative position of the Black workforce through their impact on the costs of hiring. The recommendations regarding the need to improve the mobility of urban Blacks in White areas will have the same effect, but will operate through increased labour productivity levels.

Whilst the labour reforms that are proposed will certainly redistribute some economic power from the Whites as a group to Blacks as a group, over time they may also act as a divisive force within the Black community. Both the training recommendations and the removal of job reservation will clearly benefit those Blacks who already have some education, to a far greater degree than they will those who do not. Urban Blacks are on average better educated than those who come from the rural areas and so are better placed to capitalize on the changes. Education in the Black rural areas is hampered by a lack of facilities and by poverty, and urban Blacks will continue to enjoy their advantage until these obstacles to rural education are overcome.

The recommendations regarding influx control will also place urban Blacks in White areas in a preferential position. Migrant workers will only be allowed into controlled areas if it can be shown that there is no 'suitable local labour'. The recommendations regarding the imposition of more severe penalties for employing illegal migrants will also favour the settled workforce.

At present only a relatively small proportion of the Black workforce is unionized and the overall impact of the union movement will be limited. However, as Black unions grow in strength, so their influence on the Black workforce may also be divisive. Strong trade unions can drive a wedge between their members and the non-unionized workforce, and by so doing achieve a better deal for the unionized sector. However, union membership is based on the possession of a job and it is through this coincidence that the impact of the Riekert reforms may widen the scope of the division between unionized and non-unionized workers, to the point where it will also reflect an urban-rural split.

At present over one-third of South Africa's modern sector Black labour force comes from the rural areas. The unionization of Blacks, therefore, will mean that the unions will have to cater for the special needs and interests of the rural-urban migrant if they want the support of this significant section of the workforce. The recommendations of the Riekert Commission, giving urban Blacks preferential access to jobs, will ensure that the bulk of the growing burden of Black unemployment will be carried by the rural areas, particularly those in the newly created Black States. As this happens, the relative importance of the rural influence on the union movement will decline and the unions will reflect the needs of the urban workforce to an increasing extent. Through this process the unions themselves may become an agent fostering the division between the urban and rural areas of South Africa.

The educational differences between the urban and the migrant workforces may become skill differentials through the relationships that exist between education and training. This may also spill over into the union movement. Divisions between and within unions tend to take place at the interest levels, and a significant force for differences in interests is the difference in job classification. Skilled and unskilled workers may have very different needs and aspirations as may technicians, craftsmen in the different trades and workers in disparate industries. Union movements may split along these lines either formally through the creation of separate unions, or informally through the practical administration decisions taken within the movement itself.

If unionization amongst the Black workforce is predominantly based on craft or occupational divisions, the movement will probably be an influence increasing the Black income disparity. The more highly trained sections of the labour force will be in a stronger economic position *vis-à-vis* the employers than the others. Consequently, divisions on the basis of skills enable the skilled sector to carve for itself a larger slice of the economic pie at the expense of the less skilled sector. General Black unions, however, are not likely to be as divisive.

There are, however, two factors that may undermine the strength of the infant African union movement. The first of these is the persistence of growing surplus labour amongst the African work force. As a result of an increase in the population growth rate, the African labour force grew at an annual average rate of 4 per cent over the period from 1960–75. Although this growth rate can be expected to drop as the population growth rates stabilize once more, nevertheless presents a serious and immediate challenge in the field of employment creation. Economic growth has been the engine of job creation in South Africa and it is essential that the momentum for growth is maintained. It will be extremely difficult for the Black union movement to realize its full potential in times of economic recession, particularly in view of the fact that history has shown the White workforce to be considerably more adept at protecting their position under such conditions, largely at the expense of the Black workers.

The second factor, that will hinder the African union movement, is growing government control over its activities and the continued harassment of much of its leadership. Unionism is a crucial element in the successful evolution to a mature capitalistic economy and government moves, which have the effect of stifling the development of such a movement, will, in the long run, turn out to be an extremely short-sighted policy.

There is a further dimension to the reforms that were mooted by the Riekert Commission, which relates to the improvement of the economic position of the African group, with respect to the extent of its control over capital and capital accumulation.

The Commission made a number of recommendations relating to the improvement of the Black business environment, the most important being:

(1) The removal of the present restriction on Black businessmen, which, amongst other things, prevent them from employing members of any other race group and limit them to operating as many premises as they *personally* can supervise.
(2) The creation of 'international zones' in White controlled areas. These would be regions in central business districts, at present limited to whites, which would be open to ownership and occupation by all race groups.
(3) The proposals for the general upgrading of the Black urban areas in White controlled regions, which would greatly improve the general environment in these areas.

The growth of a Black capitalist class is a crucial element in the redistribution of power within a private enterprise system. These reforms, particularly if they are backed up with increased financial assistance, may well significantly strengthen the economic power of the Black community.

However, here again, since economic activity and urbanization are closely related, these reforms will work to the advantage of urban Blacks and will tend to increase the power gap between urban Blacks and those living in the rural areas.

The Impact of the Reforms on South African Economic Growth

The three constraints on South African economic growth that are most frequently referred to are a shortage of capital, a shortage of adequately trained labour and the size of the domestic market. The reforms will affect these constraints in a number of ways. The improvement in urban Black living standards, which seems to be a certain outcome from the reforms, should increase the size of the domestic market significantly. Increases from low income levels are almost certain to be consumed and so should feed rapidly through to the domestic market.

The effect that the changes will have on capital accumulation are not so clear cut. The improved labour dispensation is likely to encourage foreign capital into South Africa and in doing so will act as a positive force for economic growth.

On the other hand, the reforms may increase labour costs per unit of output and by so doing reduce profit levels and the rate of re-investment in the private sector. This could be offset by lower tax rates on profits or by subsidizing employment. There is, however, no certainty that the reforms will increase labour costs per unit of output. Rising Black urban wages could be offset by reductions in migrant earnings, or by increased labour productivity. Further, the higher earnings will increase the size of the domestic market and economies of scale may result in cost savings.

Turning to the labour constraint, the training recommendations in both the Wiehahn and the Riekert Commissions should improve the supply of skilled and semi-skilled Black labour and so generate a higher rate of economic growth, particularly when coupled with the recommendations for the removal of statutory job reservation. However, this positive effect could be severely limited, should the White trade unions succeed in limiting Black access to skilled jobs through the use of closed shop agreements. In this respect the Government's final attitude towards the continued use of the principle of closed shop will be very important.

The recommendations of another Commission of Inquiry, the De Kock Commission, are also likely to be positive force capital accumulation. The eventual creation of a market for the rand that can respond to a greater extent to normal economic pressures will both encourage private investors and provide the authorities with a additional means of countering cyclical fluctuations. The increased stability should further encourage capital accumulation and economic growth. The transition phase, which has seen the establishment of a dual exchange rate for the rand through the financial rand, allows foreign investors to bring funds into South Africa at a substantial premium. This should also encourage capital formation.

The proposed withdrawal of the public sector and the greater emphasis on the private enterprise system should also encourage growth. Despite the many shortcomings of the market system, the one thing that almost all who analyse its operation agree on, is the system's undoubted economic efficiency. Increased efficiency is an important component in raising the rate of economic growth. A more rapid rate of implementation of the De Kock proposals would increase this influence.

However, the most important component of growth in a private enterprise economy is business optimism; without that, all else fails. The labour reforms and the De Kock Commission's recommendations have generated a very optimistic attitude in the private sector, particularly as they have been coupled with a number of other very promising reform moves, such as the appointment of Commissions to reconsider the consolidation of the Black States and to examine the Black citizenship question. So long as this momentum for change is maintained, the future economic prospects for South Africa should be good.

There are, unfortunately, also a number of negative influences on the horizon. Chief amongst these is the growing threat of political and military upheaval. The Government has advanced the view that the formation and implementation of a total strategy is the only way to counteract this threat. The labour reforms are an integral part of this. The success of the strategy will depend upon its ability to carve out a meaningful place for all South Africans within the present economic system.

This must include the Blacks in the rural areas, who form more than half of the Black population. Not only are they the poorest strata of the South African community, but, in many instances, are living in areas that are highly vulnerable from the military point of view. The parts of the new strategy that have been specified to date have failed to come to grips with the rural aspect and, indeed, as was argued earlier in this chapter, the labour reforms seem set to make the economic conditions in many of the rural areas worse rather than better. If economic conditions do deteriorate in these areas, they may become the new focus for social unrest and could generate instability of sufficient magnitude to offset the potential gains emanating from the present package of reforms.*

*(Reprinted from Nattrass (1980a) with the permission of the South African Formation.)

ALTERNATIVE ECONOMIC AND POLITICAL SYSTEMS FOR SOUTH AFRICA

In this concluding section we will examine the extent to which the present South African economic structure limits the range of the real alternatives regarding economic and political organization.

The major ideologies in arguments over alternative economic systems for South Africa can be loosely described as capitalism and socialism. These terms have been used in discussion to cover a wide variety of very different power configurations and the consequent lack of rigour that has developed in the debate, lead to it becoming, on occasions, overheated and extremely confused.

Somewhat ironically, in view of the degree of their mutual dislike the ultimate distributions of power that are sought by the extreme versions of these two ideologies, ideal communism and the perfectly competitive version of capitalism, are, in fact, very similar. Both of these ideologies essentially seek to set up conditions that will prevent the exploitation of man by man through the use of economic or political means. The ideologists arguing for the ideal form of capitalism see this as being achieved on the economic front through atomized competition in the market place (the free market) and on the political side through a decentralized democratic process, based on 'one man one vote'. The 'pure' or socialist ideologies, on the other hand, see the elimination of private ownership of the means of production and its replacement by a system of decentralized common ownership, as a prerequisite for the elimination of the unequal accumulation of economic power. On the political front the solution is largely seen to lie in the process of decentralized consensus politics.

Although these ideologies offer very different alternative scenarios, they both believe that poverty, inequality and exploitation have their roots in the unequal accumulation of power and it is the analysis of the power situation that has lead them to their conclusions.

One of the dangers in using simple idealistic models in a discussion of a solution for an actual socio-economic situation is that there is a significant difference between the theoretical discussion and the practical implementation. When one comes to apply such solutions, one actually has to do so in a situation in which there already is an existing network of economic, social and political relationships, which underlies and reinforces the lines of power in the community. The ideal solutions imply that these networks can be easily broken down and replaced by a more desirable form of organization. In practice this may well prove to be difficult, if not virtually impossible. Economic power is particularly difficult to redistribute, as it has its foundations in the structure of the economy itself, including its physical attributes, and if this is centralized or concentrated, then one cannot effectively decentralize the power flowing from it without first decentralizing the structure itself.

Figure 11.3
ALTERNATIVE POLITICAL AND ECONOMIC POWER CONFIGURATIONS

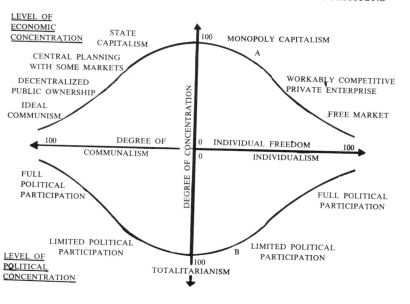

Figure 11.3 illustrates the possibilities for power distribution on the economic and political fronts. The y axis shows the degree of concentration possible, whilst the x axis illustrates the area of possibility under two forms of socio-economic organization, one based essentially on the institution of the private ownership of property (loosely termed capitalism) and the other on communal ownership of one sort or another (loosely termed socialism). On the theoretical level at least, both systems offer political and economic power concentrations that could run from 0 to 100 per cent.

Using such an approach, it is possible to rank any particular economic and political formation in terms of the degree of power concentration that it has, and the range over which it could be placed would then run from 0 to 200. Some of the more common forms of politico-economic organization would then be ordinally ranked on this scale, roughly, as follows, shown by the data in Table 11.3.

Table 11.3
ALTERNATIVE POWER STRUCTURES WITH CAPITALISM AND SOCIALISM

Capitalism	Degree of Concentration	Socialism
The ideal free market and democracy	0	Ideal communism
Mixed market economy Low level of concentration and democracy		Decentralized public ownership, some central control, democracy
Mixed market economy Strong concentration democracy		Public ownership centralized planning democracy
Mixed market economy Strong concentration and limited democracy		Public ownership centralized planning limited democracy
Monopoly capitalism with totalitarianism	200	State Capitalism strong centralized planning no democracy

Such a formalization, whilst it is obviously limited, has some usefulness; firstly, if one plots an actual power configuration on the profile in Figure 11.3, one can obtain some idea of the path that lies between the present politico-economic structure and the one being advocated. For example, it is clear that the path from a situation of concentration under capitalism to one of ideal socialism must lead through the domain of state capitalism, or nationalization and centralization.

To take this path, one would have to face the physical planning problems that would accompany attempts that are made to decentralize an already centralized economic activity. The problem may be further complicated by the fact that the centralized phase of socialism, which would inevitably follow as socialists endeavour to transform a capitalist economy to the ground rules of socialism, offers such gains to those who wield the power at this stage that they may well be tempted to linger and perhaps even to stray into either or both of the political quicksands of increasing totalitarianism, or the economic quicksands of excessive bureaucratic planning.

Equally, one must face the fact that one cannot leap from a capitalist structure that is highly centralized and unequal to one that is decentralized, competitive and open to all, simply by decree or by a reduction in the degree of state interference. A free, decentralized market will not generate an acceptable level of freedom for everyone, unless all people are in a position to enter the market on reasonably equal terms.

The market operates on the basis of money votes and does so objectively, automatically and efficiently. The problems arise when one asks, 'Who gets to exercise those money votes?' If this question is answered honestly, it becomes obvious that it is those who enter the system with the money who will exercise the majority vote and it will be their wants and needs which will be efficiently satisfied. The free market solution can only be an optimal solution if the distribution of wealth present in the community during its operation is judged, by that community, to be in some sense 'just or optimal'.

Those who genuinely seek to introduce the free market solution into a situation in which economic power is heavily concentrated, may well find that the needed redistribution of wealth can only be achieved at the expense of a significant period of concentration of political power and a loss in economic efficiency. In other words increasing totalitarianism and lower average living levels may well also turn out to be the price that has to be paid in a capitalist system to obtain conditions under which the distribution of economic power can be made to be more equal.

A further major problem that confronts any group seeking to change the ground rules governing social organization is the length of time involved. Changes in the economic structure pose special problems, as not only are they difficult to implement, but the cost of the implementation is often extremely high. The situation is complicated further, because, whilst the costs are felt almost immediately, the full value of the benefits that may ultimately accrue, could take as long as a generation to manifest themselves completely. The fact that it is the present generation that bears the costs of the re-organization, whilst a later one stands to reap the benefits, may create significant problems of political and social control for the ruling group, which may again result in their recourse to increasing political repression.

Alternatively, if the system itself is threatened by the costs of the necessary changes, the ruling party may settle for a solution that is not the ideal one. A group seeking to establish true socialism from a situation of monopoly capitalism may, for example, settle for state capitalism, at least as an interim measure. Alternatively, the route to perfect capitalism may end with some form of social democracy, as rulers substitute a system of counterveiling power for a true redistribution of economic power, rather than face the political problems that might be engendered by a determined policy of redistribution.

Alternative Systems for South Africa

As we have seen in our earlier analysis, in present day South Africa the sources of both political and economic power are strongly concentrated. Not only are they both concentrated in the hand of Whites, but they also exhibit evidence of a significant degree of geographic concentration.

The two most famous alternative scenarios proposed for South Africa are those known as the revisionist solution and the reform solution, perhaps better described loosely as the socialist solution and that of social democracy. However, the last few years have also seen the resurgence of a group arguing for a free market solution. In the section that follows, we will discuss these three separately, ignoring the question as to whether or not they will be adopted, or even be acceptable to the majority of South Africans.

Before turning to these aspects, however, it may be useful to summarize, once again, some of the major characteristics of the distributions of economic and political power that we found in our analysis, which may influence the decisions made by the ruling group:

(1) Both economic and political power are highly concentrated.
(2) The concentration has racial and spatial overtones.
(3) The quality of life of those without power is, on average, very poor.
(4) The State has in general, until recently, been an agent that has widened, rather than narrowed, the racial economic and political disparities in South Africa.
(5) The present disparities have emerged, and more importantly, are perceived as having emerged under an economic system organized along capitalist lines.
(6) White supremacy and the capitalist system are, historically linked together.

The Present Economic Power Structures and the Socialist Option in South Africa

A government coming to power on a socialist ticket would do so in the face of the existing structure of economic power. Since this is strongly concentrated, a ruling group seeking to change the rules of social organization to a set more suited to its particular brand of socialism would have no alternative but to keep the sources of political power as equally strongly concentrated. Unless the new ruling élite succeeds in building a state presence that is strong enough to enable it to overcome the economic power structures built up under the capitalist regime, it will have no hope of dismantling the existing economic structures.

The usual course followed by a government seeking to transform a relatively advanced capitalist economy into a socialist mode of production, in the transitionary phase, includes the adoption of such measures as the introduction of compulsory State ownership in private corporations, nationalization and in some instances, even the confiscation of property. These actions will have the immediate effect of further increasing the concentration of economic power in the hands of the State. It seems inevitable that, with whichever brand of socialism the new party comes into power, any attempts to actually implement socialist principles must bring with them an increase in the degree of concentration of political and economic power.

In addition, one must also ask to what extent the new ruling group will, in fact, be prepared to decentralize economic power. It was argued earlier that the costs incurred in the decentralization of the economy are likely to be very substantial. When a large segment of the population is already living under very poor conditions, it becomes politically difficult for any government, no matter what its ideology, to embark upon a set of policies that might well lower these living levels even further.

Whilst it is possible for a socialist movement in theory to overcome the motivational costs that result from any attempt to redistribute personal wealth, by providing alternative, non-economic, motivating forces, in practice this often proves to be difficult and to involve quite a significant delay. The costs involved in the spatial reorganization of the economy are even more problematic and likely to be so large that the concept of spatial reorganization may well be abandoned, in favour of a long-term development policy designed to eliminate the spatial disparities over time.

In short, in countries which have a well developed economic core and an unequal distribution of economic power, the costs of eliminating the latter in terms of either actual damage to the former, or simply the resulting lower production levels, may be too large in the short-term for even a socialist ruling group to face. If this is the case, then, as the ruling group seeks to maintain output levels but at the same time to come to grips with some aspects of the unequal distribution of income and wealth, the true socialist or communist cause may degenerate into one that is closer to a social democracy.

Following this line of reasoning, the present distribution of economic power in South Africa may in fact rule out any possibility of the establishment of a true 'peoples republic' and limit the range of options available to a socialist group coming to power to those of State capitalism on the one hand, and social democracy, or reform capitalism, on the other.

The Present Power Structures in South Africa and the Free Market Option

The free market option couples the philosophy of economic libertarianism with a system of decentralized democracy. The most developed exposition by a member of this school is that of Professor Jan Lombard. He bases his thesis on two fundamental axioms; firstly, that the élites in all groups in South Africa are more interested in evolutionary, than revolutionary change and secondly, that all South Africans would accept the goals of increased individual freedom and improved material welfare. (Lombard: 1978)

However, he sees three fundamental prerequisites for the overall acceptance of a liberal ideology, namely, the need to narrow the differences in living standards of South Africans; education on a wide scale in what he terms the 'ethics of personal responsibility in a free society'; and the institution of a rule of law that is free from racial discrimination.

Lombard argues against the introduction of measures designed to redistribute income or wealth and in favour of measures to open up 'opportunities for all'. Unfortunately, without some redistribution, a call for the opening up of opportunities becomes merely rhetorical. The simple removal of entry barriers will not enable the less privileged to compete with their more favoured fellow citizens on an equal footing. With the present degree of inequality in South Africa, some measure of redistribution, even if it is limited to the introduction of a positive action programme, will be a prerequisite for the creation of an equal opportunity society in South Africa.

The spatially unequal distribution of power in South Africa also poses problems for this solution.

Lombard argues for the spatial decentralization of political power to the point where one will obtain groups of people with common ideas and ambitions. Because of the emphasis that he places upon the need for a more even distribution of wealth and the requirement of individual freedom, he sees the decentralization of political power as a feature of the future. It will, in fact, only be introduced when the measures taken to free the economic system have generated a more equal distribution of economic activity through geographical separation.

However, a significant leap of faith is needed if one is to assume that freedom in the market will necessarily reduce the concentration of economic power. It is equally possible that a reduction in the level of state interference could result in increased power concentrations.

An even greater practical problem which arises with this approach is that, even if measures introduced to free the market process do successfully engender forces that will ultimately decentralize and redistribute economic power, the time horizon required for these forces to produce the situation envisaged as a prerequisite for political decentralization may be too far into the future to represent a political reality.

The Reform Option

The characteristic that distinguishes the reform option from that proposed by the revisionists is the fact that reform is built squarely upon the existing capitalist structures of production. Reformists seek to minimize the costs that are involved in any needed social transformation, but at the same time to achieve meaningful levels of real social change. Reform solutions start from the existing social, economic and political structures and seek to introduce improvements through compromise.

As a result of the nature of the reform solutions, the precise content of the packages of reforms that are proposed are not usually spelled out. Instead, the proponents of this approach argue that the actual elements in the packages should emerge through a process of ongoing negotiation. Again, because of the compromise nature of the reform solution, its supporters usually see the solution as being based upon the creation of counterveiling power blocks, rather than upon the redistribution of power itself; although some redistribution measures may well be included in the final packages. The ultimate aim of the creation of counterveiling power is both the eventual redistribution of economic power on a more equitable basis, and the decentralization of political power into mutually non-dominating sectors. (Van Zyl Slabbert and Welsh: 1979)

Essentially, reform solutions seek to move South Africa from her present position in Figure 11.3 towards the free market solution, but they usually have, as their ultimate aim, the creation of some type of social democracy, rather than the institution of economic libertarianism.

The major advantage of the reform option for South Africa is that it seeks to introduce meaningful change into the existing power structures, with as little reorganization as is possible, and this, in its turn, may well prove to be the option's most serious disadvantage. The low political profile of many of the reform measures will mak them extremely difficult to sell – particularly to those South Africans at present excluded from the existing power structures, virtually all of whom are black.

It has been argued that conditions in South Africa are not conducive to the emergence of a strong, cohesive working class and that such an emergence is a prerequisite for the true expression of the views of the people. (De Kadt: 1979). Schlemmer has also argued that preconditions for the expression of the full range of views in South Africa have not been met, and isolated the cause of this deficiency as being the non-existence of a strong, tough, well-motivated class of merchants and small traders, who are capable of articulating their views and of developing a truly South African economic and social philosophy. (Schlemmer: 1980). A further problem is that, at present, there also appear to be no social mechanisms emerging that would allow the meaningful expression of the views of the very large numbers of poverty-stricken rural dwellers, who may or may not have interests in common with those of the existing black working class.

The lack of a level of social and political coherence sufficient to permit the emergence of different group opinions, means that it becomes virtually certain that any reforms that are instituted will be largely of the 'top down' variety. They will inevitably reflect the views and needs of the élites of the groups that are participating in the negotiating process, rather than those of the people themselves. This is seen by the more radically inclined supporters of the revisionist school as being an insurmountable barrier to the introduction of true or meaningful change by means of the reform option.

Is this really so? Do the views of the people exist *per se?* It is highly likely that, in fact, the so-called 'people' comprise a number of heterogenous sub-groups, with very different opinions and interests. This being so, providing the net is cast widely enough when the negotiating process is initially set up and, further, that the process itself is sufficiently flexible to allow for the introduction of new opinions and for the formation of cross-cutting short-term alliances, the fact that the reforms are essentially introduced from the top will not necessarily preclude them from being true reforms. If the negotiating process is sufficiently widely based, there is a high probability that the views and interests of most of the sub-groups will be closely allied with at least some of those of the élites participating in the negotiations and consequently will not, in fact, be excluded from consideration.

This is not, however, to say either that the views of all the people will, of necessity, be represented, or that the views that are present will be weighted in the bargaining process in the same way as they are weighted in the wider community. These remain serious problems. It is, however, to say that it is not sufficient to argue that reform is not true reform, simply because it has been introduced into the community from the top. To make a meaningful analysis of the relevance of 'élite introduced' reform, one needs to consider the problem in a great deal more depth.

Reform capitalism has the major advantage of being a relatively low cost option. The reforms, based as they are on the concept of counterveiling power, are likely to improve the drive for economic efficiency that is present in the private enterprise system. Reform capitalism would not seek to dismantle the existing economic system, but to redirect it from both the spatial and individual aspects. The concomitant disadvantage is, however, that the reform process may be slow and there is a real danger that the changes introduced may be of cosmetic value only and that they may fail altogether to feed through to the underlying power networks.

What are South Africa's True Options?

Here we are in the realms of speculation and we can do little more than highlight some of the aspects of the present structures that seem likely to have some bearing on the final outcome.

Firstly, in terms of the arguments that have been advanced, it is obvious that one must dismiss, as being of theoretical interest only, both the options of 'free market democracy' and 'true or ideal socialism'. The present size and structure of the economy alone is sufficient to prevent either of those options from emerging as a realistic solution to South Africa's present problems. South Africa's true options lie between a range on Figure 11.3, which runs from State Capitalism to Reform Capitalism. A failure to keep the discussion of the options within these limits leads it into the realms of fantasy and illusion. Realms which, whilst they are essential in childhood to the development of a healthy adult, then become dangerous if visited too frequently, as they cause one to lose touch with reality!

Two possible options lying to the left of South Africa's present position on Figure 11.3 are those of State Capitalism, following on either from a successful full scale, socialist-based revolution or from Du Toit's suggested 'military option'; an option which uses South Africa's military machine to maintain both capitalism and the existing economic power structure, at the cost of maintaining even the present levels of social and political freedom. (Du Toit: 1980). Both of these options are possibilities, but the second appears to be more likely to occur than the first. Both use increasing political totalitarianism as a means for the introduction of economic reforms, but the nature of the reforms that will be introduced will differ.

In the case of a socialist, centralized state the reforms are likely to be oriented towards the generation of a more egalitarian distribution of wealth, than towards improving the level of economic efficiency. In the case of a totalitarian, capitalist state, the reverse is likely to be true. Both options entail increased levels of power concentrations on the political and economic fronts, but, whereas state action to nationalize economic activity will be the cause of increased economic concentration in the socialist state, increased economic efficiency and the tendency of capitalism towards monopoly, rather than competition, will be the cause in the capitalist totalitarian state.

Neither of these options are likely to offer anything of substance to those excluded from the very narrowly based power structure, who are, in fact, likely to form an ever increasing majority in the population. If possible, both these options should be avoided in South Africa. Neither hold out much possibility for genuine reform. The social cost of the revolution that would probably be required to introduce state capitalism would be immense and the introduction of a totalitarian capitalist state, far from avoiding these costs, would increase the likelihood of such a revolution eventually taking place.

The other option that is genuinely open to South Africans is that of reform capitalism (which may initially be introduced in the guise of either capitalism or socialism). Historically, capitalism has been linked in South Africa with both the present unequal distribution of wealth and White supremacy. This linkage will make it impossible to sell a reform package to black South Africans, unless it includes power sharing on the political level. If all South African groups are not genuinely included in the machinery set up to develop the reform package, reform capitalism will be stillborn – if it too is not aborted by revolution.

It was stated earlier that the reform solution is a low cost solution, but one that runs the risk of being no solution at all. The costs of the other proposals, in terms of the losses of South African lives, individual freedom of action and economic output are, however, too high to make either a reasonable alternative. The reform solution has to be tried and, if it is to have a fair chance of success, the package that is introduced must represent genuine social change. The challenge to South Africans will be to make this solution work, to face up to the tough compromises that will have to be made by all parties and to plot a course that can be navigated between the Scylla of dictatorship and the Charybdis of revolution.

AVERAGE WAGE RATES AND WAGE BILLS IN THE MANUFACTURING SUB-SECTORS

	Sector as a Whole	Food Beverages and Tobacco	Clothing and Textiles	Wood and Furniture	Paper and Paper Products	Chemicals	Non-Metallic Minerals	Base Metals	Metal Products	Machinery Non-Electrical	Machinery Electrical	Transport
Real Average White Wage												
1919	1 392	1 244	807	1 350	1 663	1 835	1 532	1 849	1 223	1 340	1 519	1 113
1936	1 290	1 100	719	1 383	1 720	1 601	1 570	1 866	1 386	1 713	1 582	1 062
1951	2 179	1 958	1 728	2 105	2 402	2 444	2 349	2 626	2 398	2 376	2 012	1 683
1970	3 348	3 122	3 225	3 326	3 277	3 436	3 320	3 396	3 533	3 400	3 186	3 159
1976	4 100	3 485	3 776	3 579	3 777	5 021	3 712	4 240	4 121	4 155	3 654	3 670
Annual Growth Rate	1,9	1,8	2,7	1,7	1,5	1,8	1,6	1,5	2,2	2,0	1,6	2,1
Real Average Black Wage												
1919	313	289	357	399	419	296	254	330	406	516	N/A	402
1936	290	284	436	411	564	287	237	246	346	411	336	365
1951	599	507	708	531	915	527	421	474	517	486	529	498
1970	683	548	632	704	911	729	535	716	737	776	706	722
1976	843	726	655	662	1 202	902	683	986	1 025	1 127	1 050	1 041
Annual Growth Rate	1,8	1,6	1,1	0,9	1,9	2,0	1,8	1,9	1,6	2,0	1,6	1,7
Black Wage Bill												
1919	23 460	7 155	2 247	2 402	1 110	2 096	2 790	2 296	646	10	357	1 636
1936	37 642	8 813	6 134	4 190	2 199	2 408	6 168	5 517	1 620	16	439	2 361
1951	204 052	36 291	45 657	18 019	11 181	11 210	18 410	7 545	20 581	6 529	5 324	12 943
1970	569 976	71 585	121 896	38 218	33 722	30 123	34 598	32 275	62 694	31 723	19 185	38 969
1976	904 592	123 572	154 291	51 357	57 441	57 515	55 446	62 289	110 561	56 505	50 015	74 480
Annual Growth Rate	6,6	5,1	7,7	5,5	7,2	6,0	5,4	6,0	9,4	16,4	9,1	6,9
White Wage Bill												
1919	62 536	9 416	4 973	4 471	7 113	4 351	2 175	19 804	1 069	79	1 178	5 660
1936	114 742	15 449	16 477	9 514	14 090	6 380	5 215	20 947	2 919	205	3 097	11 393
1951	347 962	39 233	44 286	21 159	31 100	21 819	15 629	26 379	41 047	26 829	18 495	40 788
1970	872 324	76 996	62 896	27 965	78 666	65 118	38 759	102 350	102 276	102 478	52 166	92 117
1976	1 185 824	107 844	70 873	34 068	106 242	117 202	50 112	167 563	81 025	127 736	82 970	122 449
Annual Growth Rate	5,3	4,4	4,8	3,6	4,9	5,9	5,7	3,8	7,9	13,8	7,7	5,5

SOURCE: Estimated from various Industrial Census Reports.

Bibliography

ADELMAN, I.: 'An Economic Analysis of Population Growth'. *American Economic Review,* American Economic Association, Nashville, June, 1963.

ADELMAN, I. and THORBECKE, E. (Eds.): *The Theory and Design of Economic Development.* Johns Hopkins, Baltimore, 1966.

ADLER, T. (Ed.): *Perspectives on South Africa.* African Studies Institute, University of the Witwatersrand, Johannesburg 1977.

ARRIGHI, G.: 'Labour Supplies in Historical Perspective: A Study of the Proletarianisation of the African Peasantry in Rhodesia'. *Journal of Development Studies,* Vol. 3, April, 1970, pp. 197–234. Frank Cass, London.

BELL, R. T.: 'Some Aspects of Industrial Decentralisation in South Africa'. *South African Journal of Economics,* Vol. 41, No. 4, December, 1973, pp. 401–431.

BENSO: *Black Development in South Africa.* Buro van Ekonomiese Navorsing, Saamwerking en Ontwikkeling, Pretoria, 1976.

BENSO: *Statistical Survey of Black Development 1979.* Buro van Ekonomiese Navorsing, Saamwerking en Ontwikkeling, Pretoria, 1979.

BENYON, JOHN A. (Ed.): *Constitutional Change in South Africa.* Natal University Press, Pietermaritzburg, 1978.

BOTHA, D. J. J.: On Tariff Policy: The Formative Years. *South African Journal of Economics,* Vol. 41, No. 4, December, 1973. Economics Society, Braamfontein.

BRAND, S. S.: 'The Contribution of Agriculture to the Economic Development of South Africa since 1910'. Unpublished D.Sc. Thesis, University of Pretoria, 1969.

BREYTENBACH, W. (Ed.): *Job Advancement in South Africa.* South Africa Foundation, Johannesburg, 1980.

BROOKES, E. H. and HURWITZ, N.: *The Native Reserves of Natal.* Natal Regional Survey, Vol. 7, Oxford Press, Cape Town, 1957.

BROWN, R. P. C.: 'Capital Intensity in South African Manufacturing'. Unpublished Masters' Thesis, University of Natal, Durban, 1976.

BROWNE, G. W. G.: 'Fiscal Policy in South Africa' in J. A. Lombard (Ed.). *Economic Policy in South Africa,* (selected essays), HAUM, Cape Town, 1973.

BUNDY, COLIN: 'The Emergence and Decline of South African Peasantry'. *African Affairs,* Vol. 71, No. 285, October, 1972, pp. 369–387. Royal African Society, London.

BUREAU OF MARKET RESEARCH: *Personal Income, Population and Gross Geographic Product of the Growth Areas of South Africa.* University of South Africa, Pretoria, 1977.

BUREAU OF MARKET RESEARCH: *Income and Expenditure Surveys Nos. 27.1, 27.4, 27.7 and 27.10.* University of South Africa, Pretoria, 1975.

BUREAU OF MARKET RESEARCH: *Urban Incomes, Average Income per Head of Multiple Bantu Households in Urban Areas, Report No. 19.5.* University of South Africa, Pretoria, 1975.

CHAMBER OF MINES: *Chamber of Mines 88th Annual Report 1977.* Chamber of Mines, 1977.

CHAMBER OF MINES: *Chamber of Mines 89th Annual Report 1978.* Chamber of Mines, 1978.

CHAMBER OF MINES: *Chamber of Mines 90th Annual Report, 1979.* Chamber of Mines, 1979.

CHENERY, HOLLIS AND SYRQUIN, MOISES: *Patterns of Development 1950–1970.* World Bank by Oxford University Press, 1975.

CLARKE, LIZ AND NGOBESE, JANE: *Women without Men.* Institute for Black Research, Durban, 1975.

DAVENPORT, T. R. H.: *South Africa – A Modern History.* Macmillan Press Ltd., London, 1977.

DAVIES, R.: 'The Political Economy of White Labour in South Africa' in T. Adler (Ed.). *Perspectives on South Africa.* African Studies Institute, University of the Witwatersrand, Johannesburg, 1977.

DE JAGER, B. L.: 'The Fixed Capital Stock and Capital Output Ratio of South Africa, 1946 to 1972'. *The South African Reserve Bank Quarterly Bulletin,* June, 1973. The Reserve Bank, Pretoria.

DE KADT, R.: *Does Social Democracy Constitute a Realistic Political Alternative to South Africa?* Unpublished Mimeograph, 1979.

DE KIEWIET, C.W.: *A History of South Africa – Social and Economic.* Oxford University Press, London, 1972.

DE KOCK, G.: 'Money, Near Money and the Monetary Banking Sector'. *South African Reserve Bank Quarterly Bulletin,* pp. 11–16. March, 1966.

DE KOCK, G.: 'Central Banking and Financial Markets in South Africa'. *South African Journal of Economics,* Vol. 46, No. 3, September, 1978. Economics Society, Braamfontein.

DENOON, DONALD: *South Africa Since 1800.* Praeger, New York, 1972.

DOS SANTOS, T.: 'The Structure of Dependence'. *The American Economic Review,* Papers and Proceedings, 1969, pp. 231–236. American Economic Association, Nashville.

DU TOIT, A.: *'Afrikaner Strategies'.* Presented at Platform 80, Crisis and Response, University of Natal, Durban, May, 1980. Unpublished.

DU PLESSIS, F. J.: 'Investment and the Balance of Payments'. *South African Journal of Economics,* Vol. 33, No. 4, December, 1965. Economics Society, Braamfontein.

DU PLESSIS, F. J.: 'Monetary Policy in South Africa'. *South African Journal of Economics,* Vol. 47, No. 4, December, 1979. Economics Society, Braamfontein.

ERWIN, A. and WEBSTER, E.: 'Ideology and Capitalism in South Africa' in Lawrence Schlemmer and Eddie Webster. *Change, Reform and Economic Growth in South Africa,* Ravan Press, Johannesburg, 1977.

FEI, J. C. and RANIS, G.: 'A Theory of Economic Development'. *American Economic Review,* Vol. 51, September 1961, pp. 533–565. American Economic Association, Nashville.

FEI, J. C. and RANIS, G.: 'Agrarianism, Dualism and Economic Development' in Adelman, I. and Thorbecke, E. (Eds.). *Theory and Design of Economic Development,* John Hopkins Press, Baltimore, 1966.

FIQUEROA, ADOLFO: 'Income Distribution, Demand Structure and Employment – The Case of Peru'. *Journal of Development Studies,* Vol. 12, No. 2, January, 1975, pp. 20–31. Frank Cass, London.

FOXLEY, ALEJANDRO: 'Redistribution of Consumption'. *Journal of Development Studies,* Vol. 12, No. 3, January, 1976, pp. 171–190. Frank Cass, London.

FRANK, A.G.: *Capitalism and Underdevelopment in Latin America.* Pelican Penguin Press, New York, 1969.

FRANKEL, S. H.: 'Capital Investment in Africa — Its Course and Effects'. Oxford University Press, London, 1938.

FREEMAN, C.: 'Research and Development: A Comparison Between British and American Industry'. *National Institute Economic Review,* 1962. National Institute of Economics and Social Research, London.

GALENSON, W. and LEIBENSTEIN, H.: Investment Criteria, Productivity and Economic Development. *Quarterly Journal of Economics,* Vol. LXXII, No. 3, August, 1961. Harvard University Department of Economics, Wiley/Interscience, New York.

GILIOMEE, H.: 'A Message from Zimbabwe'. *Unit for Futures Research Newsletter,* April, 1980.

HOBART HOUGHTON, D.: *The South African Economy.* Ist Impression, Oxford University Press, Cape Town, 1964.

HOBART HOUGHTON, D.: 'Economic Development 1865–1965' in Wilson, M. and Thompson, L. (Eds.). *The Oxford History of South Africa, Vol. II,* Oxford University Press, Cape Town, 1971.

HOBART HOUGHTON, D. and DAGUT, JENIFER: *Source Material on the South African Economy 1860–1970, Vols. 1, 2, 3.* Oxford University Press, Cape Town, 1972.

HORNER, D and KOOY, ALIDE: 'Conflict on South African Mines 1972–1979'. S.A.L.D.R.U. Working Paper No. 29, University of Cape Town, 1980.

HORWITZ, R.: *The Political Economy of South Africa.* Wiedenfeld and Nicholson, 1968.

HUTT, W.: *'The Economics of the Colour Bar'.* Macmillan, 1964.

INNES, D.: 'The Mining Industry in the Context of South Africa's Economic Development, 1910–1940'. *Collected Seminar Papers No. 21, The Societies of Southern Africa in 19th and 20th Centuries,* Vol. 7. Institute of Commonwealth Studies, London, 1977.

INSKEEP, R. R.: 'The Archaeological Background' in Monica Wilson and Leonard Thompson (Eds.). *The Oxford History of South Africa, Vol. 1.* Oxford University Press, Cape Town, 1969.

JEEVES, ALAN: 'The Control of Migratory Labour on the South African Gold Mines in the Era of Kruger and Milner'. *Journal of Southern African Studies,* Vol. 2, No. 1, October, 1975, pp. 3–29. Oxford University Press, London.

JOHNSTONE, FREDERICK, A.: 'Class, Race and Gold'. Routledge and Keegan Paul, London, 1976.

KALLAWAY, P.: 'Tribesman, Trader, Peasant and Proletarian: The Process of Transition from a Pre-Capitalist "Natural" Economy to a Capitalist Mode of Production in the Hinterland of the Kimberley Diamond Field during 19th Century'. *African Perspective,* Vol. 10, April, 1979. Afrika Studie Centrum, Leiden.

KAPLAN, D.: *Capitalist Development in South Africa: Class Conflict and State.* Institute of Development Studies, Working Paper 20, University of Sussex, September, 1974.

KATZ, ELAINE. N.: *A Trade Union Aristocracy.* African Studies Institute, University of the Witwatersrand, Johannesburg, 1976.

KIRKWOOD, M.: 'The Mineworkers' Struggle'. *South African Labour Bulletin,* Vol. 1, No. 8, January–February, 1975, pp. 29–41. Institute for Industrial Education, Durban.

KNIGHT, J.: 'Labour Supply in South African Economy and Its Implications for Agriculture' in Wilson, F. et al (Ed.). *Farm Labour in South Africa.* David Philip, Cape Town, 1977.

KNIGHT, J. B. and LENTA, G.: 'Has Capitalism Underdeveloped the Labour Reserves of South Africa?' *Oxford Bulletin of Economics and Statistics,* Vol. 42, No. 3, August 1980, pp. 157–203.

KUZNETS, S.: 'Economic Growth and Income Inequality'. *American Economic Review,* Vol. 45, No. 1, March, 1955, pp. 1–28. American Economic Association, Nashville.

KUZNETS, S.: *Economic Growth and Structure.* Heinemann, London, 1965.

LEGASSICK, M.: 'South Africa: Capital Accumulation and Violence'. *Economy and Society,* Vol. 3, No. 3, 1974, pp. 253–291. Routledge and Kegan Paul, London.

LEFTWICH, A.: *South African Growth and Political Change.* Allison and Basby, London, 1974.

LENTA, G.: *The Economic Structure of KwaZulu, A South African Homeland.* Unpublished Ph.D. Thesis, Department of Economics, University of Natal, Durban, 1976.

LEWIS, W. ARTHUR: 'Economic Development with Unlimited Supplies of Labour'. *Manchester School of Economic and Social Studies,* Vol. 20, pp. 139–192, May, 1954.

LIPTON, MERLE: 'South Africa: Two Agricultures?' in Francis Wilson et al (Ed.). *Farm Labour in South Africa.* David Philip, Cape Town, 1977.

LIPTON, MICHAEL: *Why Poor People Stay Poor.* Macmillan, London, 1977.

LOMBARD, J. A.: *Freedom, Welfare and Order.* BENSO, Pretoria, 1978.

LOMBARD, J. A. (Ed.): *Economic Policy in South Africa (Selected Essays).* HAUM, Cape Town, 1973.

LOMBARD, J. A., STADLER, J. J. and VAN DER MERWE, P.J. (Compilers.): *Die Ekonomie en die Mense.* Fokus op Ekonomiese Kernvrae, No. 23, Junie 1979.

LOOTS, LIEB: 'Unemployment' in W. Breytenbach (Ed.). *Job Advancement in South Africa,* South Africa Foundation, Johannesburg, 1980.

LOUW, L.: 'A Summary of Laws Restricting Free Enterprise in the Republic of South Africa' in Syncome. *Free Enterprise and the Individual,* Syncom and the 1920 Settlers National Monument Foundation, Johannesburg, 1980.

LUMBY, A. B.: 'Tariffs and Gold in South Africa'. *South African Journal of Economics*, Vol. 44, No. 2, June, 1976, pp. 139-157. Economics Society, Braamfontein.

LUMBY, A. B.: 'Tariffs and the Printing Industry in South Africa 1906-1939'. *South African Journal of Economics*, Vol. 45, No. 2, June, 1977, pp. 129-146. Economics Society, Braamfontein.

MALHERBE, E. G.: *Education in South Africa: A Critical Survey of the Development of Educational Administration in the Cape, Natal, Transvaal and the Orange Free State.* Juta, Cape Town, 1975.

MANSFIELD, E.: *Industrial Research and Technological Innovation: An Econometric Analysis.* W. Norton and Company, New York, 1968.

MATTHEWS, J.W.: *Incawdi Yami, or Twenty Years Personal Experience of South Africa.* Sampson Low and Co., 1887.

McCARTHY, C. L.: 'A Reconsideration of the Definition of Money'. *South African Journal of Economics*, Vol. 45, No. 2, June, 1977, pp. 190-200. Economics Society, Braamfontein.

McGRATH, M. D.: *Racial Income Distribution in South Africa.* Black/White Income Gap, Interim Research Report No. 2, Department of Economics, University of Natal, Durban, 1977.

McGRATH, M. D.: 'Health Expenditure in South Africa' in Gill Westcott and Francis Wilson. *Economics of Health in South Africa, Vol. 1, Perspectives on the Health System,* Ravan Press, Johannesburg, 1979.

McGRATH, M. D.: *The Racial Distribution of Taxes and State Expenditures.* Black/White Income Gap Research, Final Report No. 2, Department of Economics, University of Natal, Durban, 1979.

MEYER, W. N.: *The Role of Export Trade In South Africa's Economic Development Since Achieving Republican Status in 1961.* Paper presented at the 1st Economic History Conference, Durban, 1980 (unpublished Mimeograph).

NATTRASS, JILL: 'The Effect of Size on the Financing of Business'. *South African Journal of Economics*, Vol. 40, No. 1, March, 1972, pp. 84-93. Economics Society, Braamfontein.

NATTRASS, JILL (a): *Migrant Labour and South African Economic Development 1936-1970.* Unpublished Ph.D. Thesis, University of Natal, 1976.

NATTRASS, JILL (b): 'Migrant Labour and South African Economic Development'. *South African Journal of Economics*, Vol. 44, No. 1, March, 1976, pp. 68-83. Economics Society, Braamfontein.

NATTRASS, JILL (a): 'The Narrowing of Wage Differentials in South Africa'. *South African Journal of Economics*, Vol. 45, No. 4, December, 1977, pp. 408-430. Economics Society, Braamfontein.

NATTRASS, JILL (b): 'Migration Flows In and Out of Capitalist Agriculture', in Francis Wilson, Alide Kooy and Delia Hendrie (Eds.). *Farm Labour in South Africa,* David Philip, Cape Town, 1977.

NATTRASS, JILL (c): *Migrant Labour and Underdevelopment: The Case of KwaZulu.* Black/White Income Gap Research Report No. 2, Department of Economics, University of Natal, Durban, 1977.

NATTRASS, JILL (a): '*Economic Development Problems in KwaZulu*'. Paper presented to Human Sciences Research Council Conference of Economists and Business Economists, Bloemfontein, December, 1978, (unpublished).

NATTRASS, JILL (b): 'Economic Development and Social and Political Change' in L. Schlemmer and E. Webster (Eds.). *Change, Reform and Economic Growth in South Africa,* Ravan Press, Johannesburg, 1978.

NATTRASS, JILL (a): 'Constitutional Alternatives, Economic Growth and Equity: Preliminary Case Study of South Africa' in J. A. Benyon (Ed.). *Constitutional Change in South Africa,* Natal University Press, Pietermaritzburg, 1979.

NATTRASS, JILL (b): 'Southern African Economic Development and the Basic Needs Strategy'. *Development Studies, Southern Africa,* Vol. 2, No. 1, October, 1979, pp. 58–66. BENSO, Pretoria.

NATTRASS, JILL (c): 'The Impact of the Riekert Commission's Recommendations on the "Black States"'. *South African Labour Bulletin,* Vol. 5, No. 4, November, 1979, pp. 75–86. Institute for Industrial Education, Durban.

NATTRASS, JILL (d): 'Decision-Making and Optimality in the Provision of Health Care' in Gill Westcott and Francis Wilson (Eds.). *Economics of Health in South Africa Vol. 1, Perspectives on the Health Service,* Ravan Press, Johannesburg, 1979.

NATTRASS, JILL (e): *Economic Development in South Africa: Some Spatial Aspects and Their Major Determinants.* Paper presented at the Biennial Conference of the Economic Society of South Africa, Cape Town, 1979 (unpublished).

NATTRASS, JILL (a): 'Towards Racial Justice – What Can the Private Sector Do?' in David Thomas, (Ed.) *Resolving Racial Conflict,* South African Institute of Race Relations, Johannesburg, 1980.

NATTRASS, JILL and BROWN, R. P. C.: '*Capital Intensity in South African Manufacturing'.* Black/White Income Gap Project, Interim Research Report No. 4, Department of Economics, University of Natal, Durban, 1977.

O'DOWD, M.: 'The Stages of Economic Growth and the Future of South Africa' in Adrian Leftwich (Ed.). *South African Growth and Political Change,* Allison and Basby, London, 1974.

O'DOWD, M.: 'The Stages of Economic Growth and the Future of South Africa' in Lawrence Schlemmer and Eddie Webster (Eds.). *Change, Reform and Economic Growth in South Africa,* Ravan Press, 1978.

PARSONS, J. A.: Personal correspondence, October, 1980.

PENROSE, EDITH: 'The Theory of the Growth of the Firm'. Basil Blackwell, Oxford, 1959.

REX, JOHN: 'The Essential Institutions of South African Labour Exploitation'. *South African Labour Bulletin,* Vol. 1, No. 4, July, 1974, pp. 4–18. Institute for Industrial Education, Durban.

REYNDERS, H. J. J. and VAN ZYL, J. C.: 'Foreign Trade Policy' in J. A. Lombard (Ed.), *Economic Policy in South Africa,* HAUM, Cape Town, 1973.

ROUX, EDWARD: '*Time Longer than Rope'.* University of Wisconsin Press, 2nd Edition, Madison, 1964.

SADIE, J. L.: 'Population and Economic Development in South Africa'. *South African Journal of Economics,* Vol. 39, No. 3, September, 1971, pp. 205–222. Economics Society, Braamfontein.

SCHLEMMER, L. and WEBSTER, E. (Eds.): '*Change, Reform and Economic Growth in South Africa'.* Ravan Press, Johannesburg, 1978.

SCHLEMMER, L.: *Toadstools at War: Aspects of the Conflict of Ideology in South Africa*, presented at Platform 80, Crisis and Response. University of Natal, Durban, August, 1980, (unpublished).

SEN, A. K.: *Choice of Techniques*. Basil Blackwell, Oxford, 1960.

SEERS, D.: 'A Theory of Inflation and Growth in Underdeveloped Economies based on Experience in Latin America'. *Oxford Economic Papers,* Vol. 14, No. 2, June, 1962. Oxford University Press, London.

SILVER, S. W. and Co.: *S. W. Silver and Company's Handbook to South Africa*. London, 1884.

SIMKINS, C.: 'Measuring and Predicting Unemployment in Southern Africa' in Simkins, C. and Clarke, D. *Structural Unemployment in Southern Africa,* University of Natal Press, Pietermaritzburg, 1978.

SIMKINS, C.: *Agricultural Production in African Reserves 1918–1969*. D.S.R.G. working paper, University of Natal, Pietermaritzburg, 1980.

SIMKINS, C. and CLARKE, DUNCAN: *Structural Unemployment in Southern Africa*. University of Natal Press, Pietermaritzburg, 1978.

SLABBERT, F. VAN ZYL and WELSH, D.: *South Africa's Options Strategies for Sharing Power*. David Philip, Cape Town and Rex Collings, London, 1979.

SOUTH AFRICAN INSTITUTE OF RACE RELATIONS: *A Survey of Race Relations in South Africa 1973*. Compiled by M. Horrell and D. Horner, South African Institute of Race Relations, Johannesburg, January, 1974.

SOUTH AFRICAN INSTITUTE OF RACE RELATIONS: *A Survey of Race Relations in South Africa 1975*. Compiled by M. Horrell and T. Hodgson, South African Institute of Race Relations, Johannesburg, January, 1976.

SOUTH AFRICAN INSTITUTE OF RACE RELATIONS: *A Survey of Race Relations in South Africa 1976*. Compiled by M. Horrell, T. Hodgson, S. Blignaut, S. Moroney, South African Institute of Race Relations, Johannesburg, 1977.

SOUTH AFRICAN INSTITUTE OF RACE RELATIONS: *A Survey of Race Relations in South Africa 1977*. Compiled by L. Gordon, S. Blignaut, S. Moroney, C. Cooper, South African Institute of Race Relations, Johannesburg, February, 1978.

SOUTH AFRICAN INSTITUTE OF RACE RELATIONS: *A Survey of Race Relations in South Africa 1978*. Compiled by L. Gordon, S. Blignaut, C. Cooper, L. Ensor, South African Institute of Race Relations, Johannesburg, March, 1979.

SOUTH AFRICAN INSTITUTE OF RACE RELATIONS: *A Survey of Race Relations in South Africa 1979*. L. Gordon (Ed.), South African Institute of Race Relations, Johannesburg, March, 1980.

SOUTH AFRICAN RESERVE BANK: *Balance of Payments 1956–1975*. South African Reserve Bank, Pretoria, 1977.

SOUTH AFRICAN RESERVE BANK: various *Quarterly Bulletins for 1946, 1948, 1950, 1960 and 1965–80,* South African Reserve Bank, Pretoria.

THOMPSON, L.: 'Co-operation and Conflict: The Highveld in M. Wilson and L. (Eds.). *The Oxford History of South Africa, Vol. I,* Oxford University Press, Oxford, 1969.

THORRINGTON-SMITH, ROSENBERG and McCRYSTAL: *Towards a Development Plan for KwaZulu*. KwaZulu government, 1978.

TRAPIDO, S.: 'The South African Republic: Class Formation and the State 1850–1900'. *Commonwealth Studies,* Vol. III, 1973.

VAN DER HORST, S. T.: *Native Labour in South Africa.* Frank Cass, London, 1971.

VAN DER MERWE, P. J.: Black Employment Problems. *Finance and Trade Review,* Vol XII, No. 2, December, 1976.

VAN STADEN, B.: 'A New Monetary Analysis for South Africa'. *South African Reserve Bank Quarterly Bulletin,* March, 1966, pp. 17–23. The Reserve Bank, Pretoria.

VAN ZYL, J. C. and REYNDERS, H. J. J.: Foreign Trade Policy in South Africa in J. A. Lombard (Ed.). *Economic Policy in South Africa,* HAUM, Cape Town 1973.

WESTCOTT, G.: 'Obstacles to Agricultural Development in the Transkei' in F. Wilson et al (Ed.). *Farm Labour in South Africa.* David Philip, Cape Town, 1977.

WILSON, FRANCIS: 'Farming 1866–1966' in M. Wilson and L. Thompson (Eds.). *The Oxford History of South Africa, Vol. 11.* The Oxford Press, 1971.

WILSON, FRANCIS: *Labour on South African Gold Mines 1911–1969.* Cambridge University Press, 1972.

WILSON, FRANCIS; KOOY, ALIDE and HENDRIE, DELIA: *Farm Labour in South Africa.* David Philip, Cape Town, 1977.

WILSON, FRANCIS and WESTCOTT, GILL: *Economics of Health in South Africa, Vol. 1, Perspectives on the Health Service.* Ravan Press, Johannesburg, 1979.

WILSON, MONICA and THOMPSON, LEONARD: *The Oxford History of South Africa, Vol. 1.* Oxford University Press, 1969.

WILSON, MONICA and THOMPSON, LEONARD: *The Oxford History of South Africa, Vol. 2.* Oxford University Press, 1971.

WOLPE, HAROLD: Capitalism and Cheap Labour Power in South Africa, from Segregation to Apartheid. *Economy and Society,* Vol. 1, 1972, pp. 425–458. Routledge and Kegan Paul, London.

WORLD BANK: *World Bank Tables 1976.* John Hopkins Press, 1976.

WORLD BANK: *World Bank Development Report 1980.* Oxford University Press, 1980.

GOVERNMENT PUBLICATIONS

Official Year Books

Union Statistics for 50 Years. Bureau of Statistics, Government Printer, Pretoria, 1960.

South African Statistics 1964. Bureau of Statistics, Government Printer, Pretoria 1964.

Official Year Book 1974. Department of Information, Government Printer, Pretoria 1974.

South African Statistics 1974. Bureau of Statistics, Government Printer, Pretoria 1974.

South African Statistics 1976. Department of Statistics, Government Printer, Pretoria 1976.

South African Statistics 1978. Bureau of Statistics, Government Printer, Pretoria 1978.

Handbook of Agricultural Statistics 1904–1950. Department of Agriculture, Economics and Marketing, Government Printer, Pretoria, 1960.

Government Reports

U.G. 19/1916, *The Report of the Native Land Commission,* (Beaumont Commission), Government Printer, Pretoria, 1916.

U.G. 14/1926, *The Report of the Economic and Wage Commission 1925.* Government Printer Pretoria, 1926.

U.G. 22/1932, *The Report of the Native Economic Commission.* Government Printer, Pretoria, 1932.

U.G. 40/1941, *Third Interim Report of the Industrial and Agricultural Requirements Commission.* Government Printer, Pretoria, 1941.

U.G. 28/1948, *Report of Native Laws Commission of Inquiry,* (Fagan Commission). Government Printer, Pretoria, 1948.

U.G. 52/1948, *Social and Economic Planning Council Report No. 12, Central and Commercial Banking in South Africa.* Government Printer, Pretoria, 1948.

U.G. 61/1961, *Report of Commission for Socio-economic Development of the Bantu Areas within the Union of South Africa,* (Tomlinson Commission). Government Printer, Pretoria, 1961.

R.P. 24/1969 *The First Report of the Commission of Inquiry into Fiscal and Monetary Policy in South Africa,* (Franzen Commission). Government Printer, Pretoria, 1969.

R.P. 34/1970, *Report of the Commission of Inquiry into Water Matters.* Government Printer, Pretoria, 1970.

R.P. 84/1970, *The Second Report of the Commission of Inquiry into Agriculture,* (Marais/Du Plessis Commission). Government Printer, Pretoria, 1970.

R.P. 19/1972, *Third (Final) Report of Commission of Inquiry into Agriculture,* (Marais/Du Plessis Commission). Government Printer, Pretoria, 1972.

R.P. 69/1972, *Reports of the Commission of Inquiry into the Export Trade of the Republic of South Africa.* (Reynders Commission), Vol. 1 and 2. Government Printer, Pretoria, 1972.

R.P. 112/1978, *Interim Report of the Commission of Inquiry into the Monetary System and Monetary Policy in South Africa,* (De Kock Commission). Government Printer, Pretoria, 1978.

R.P. 28/1979, *Yearly Report of Division of Economics and Marketing for the Period 1.07.1977 to 30.06.1978.* Government Printer, Pretoria, 1979.

R.P. 32/1979, *Report of the Commission of Inquiry into Legislation Affecting the Utilisation of Manpower,* (Excluding the Legislation Administered by the Department of Labour and Mines), (Riekert Commission). Government Printer, Pretoria, 1979.

R.P. 47/1979, *Report of Commission of Inquiry into Labour Legislation, Part 1.* (Wiehahn Commission). Government Printer, Pretoria, 1979.

R.P. 85/1979, *Report of Auditor General for the Financial Year 1978–1979, Part 1.* Government Printer, Pretoria, 1979.

R.P. 94/1979, *Sixty-Ninth Report of the Public Debt Commissioners for the Year-end 31st March, 1979.* Government Printer, Pretoria, 1979.

Economic Development Programme, various issues. Office of the Prime Minister, Pretoria.

National Physical Development Plan 1975. Department of Planning and the Environment, Pretoria, 1975.

Transkei Publications

Republic of Transkei, *A Development Strategy for Transkei.* Transkei Government, Umtata, 1978.

Government Statistical Publications

Census of Agricultural and Pastoral Production in South Africa, various years, 1911–1976. Government Printer, Pretoria.

Census of Manufacturing Activity, various years, 1918–1976. Government Printer, Pretoria.

Census of Population, various years, 1911–1980. Government Printer, Pretoria.

Manpower Survey, various years, 1968–1977. Department of Labour, Pretoria.

National Accounts of the Bantu Homelands, various years, 1968–1976. Government Printer, Pretoria.

Gross Geographic Product by Magisterial District, various issues, 1968–1972. Government Printer, Pretoria.

Abstract of Agricultural Statistics, various issues, Division of Agricultural Economics and Marketing. Government Printer, Pretoria.

Report 09.16.03, *1975 Input Output Table,* Department of Statistics. Government Printer, Pretoria, 1977.

Short Term Economic Indicators, various issues, Department of Statistics, Pretoria.

Statistical News Releases, various issues, Department of Statistics, Pretoria.

Index